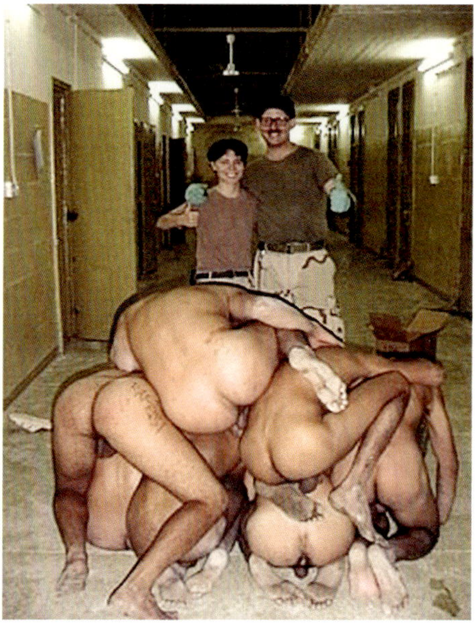

Abu Ghraib 11.51 pm Nov 7 2003. CPL GRANER and PFC ENGLAND posed for the picture, which was taken by SPC HARMAN.

From **Julian Stallabrass** 'The Power and Impotence of Images'

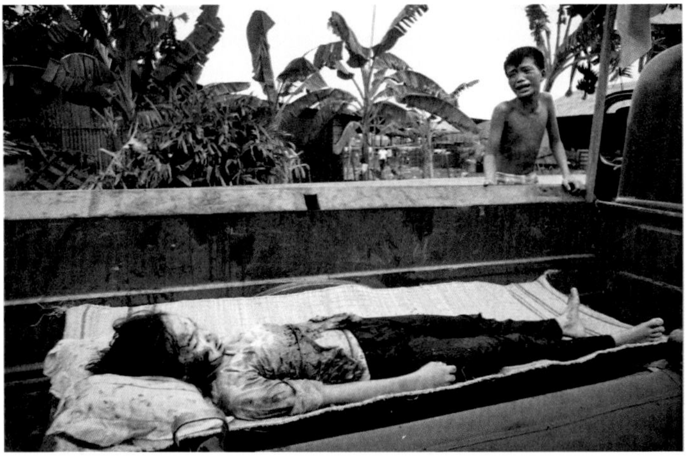

Philip Jones Griffiths The Saigon fire department had the job of collecting the dead from the streets during the Tet offensive. They had just placed this young girl, killed by US helicopter fire, in the back of their truck, where her distraught brother found her. When *The New York Times* published this photograph, it implied there was no proof that she was killed by American firepower, 1968

From **Philip Jones Griffiths** interviewed by Julian Stallabrass

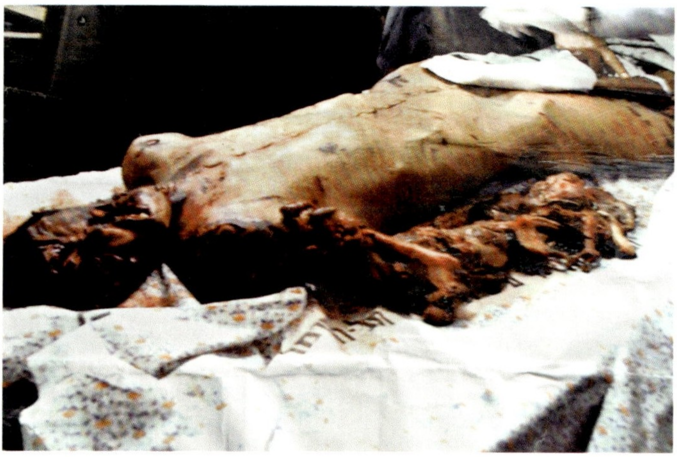

Thomas Hirschhorn *The Incommensurable Banner*, 2007, detail

From **Adam Broomberg and Oliver Chanarin** interviewed by Julian Stallabrass

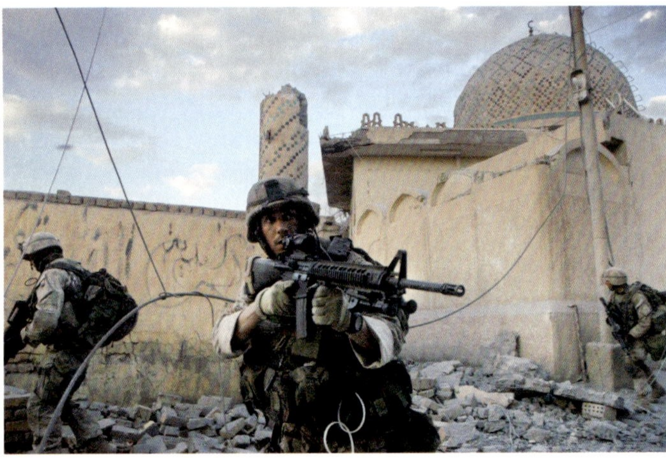

Ashley Gilbertson Fallujah, 2004. Marines run past a mosque that American jets destroyed after insurgents used it to attack them

From **Ashley Gilbertson** interviewed by Julian Stallabrass

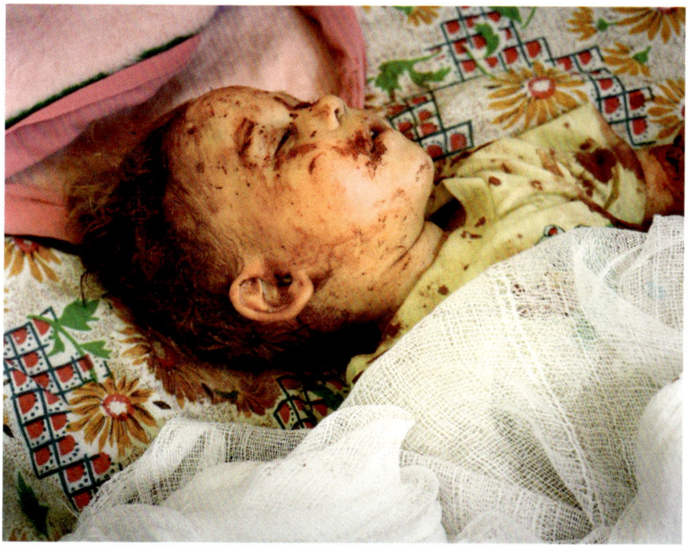

Simon Norfolk 18-month-old Zainab Tharmar, seriously wounded by an American-controlled explosion of Iraqi missiles. A FROG missile fell on her house and killed her mother and other members of her family. Many facts about this incident are disputed. Zafaraniah Hospital, Baghdad, 26 April 2003

From **Sarah James** 'Making an Ugly World Beautiful? Morality and Aesthetics in the Aftermath'

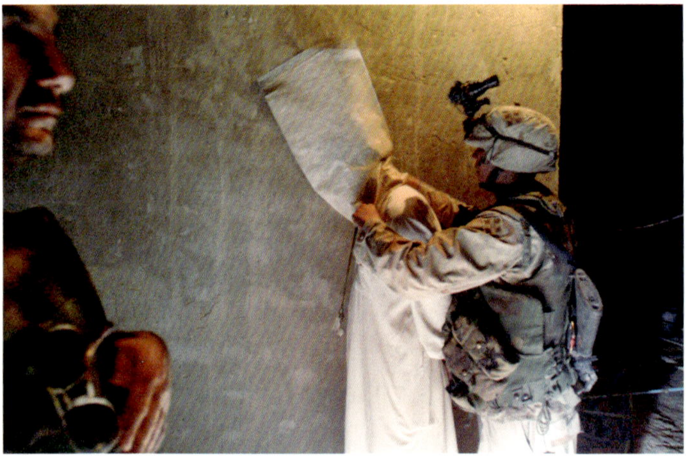

Rita Leistner American soldiers detain suspects in the Sunni Triangle, an insurgency hot spot during the early days after the fall of Baghdad. Balad, Iraq, 15 July 2003

From **Rita Leistner** 'Embedded With Murderers'

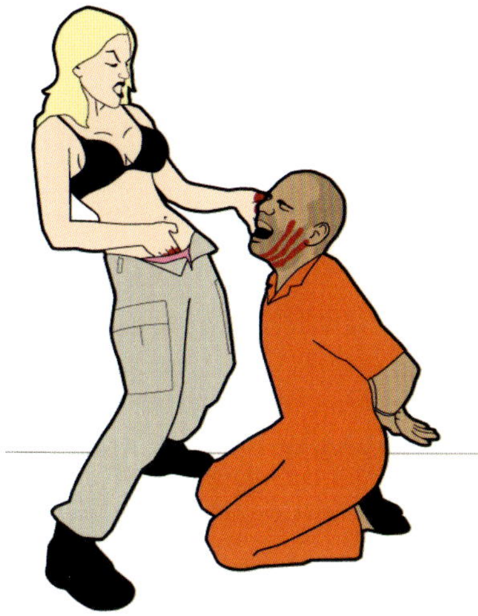

Coco Fusco 16. Fear Up Harsh. This tactic is so inflammatory that it should be reserved for only the most resistant sources. There is no way to resume a normal exchange after the severe emotional crisis that it is likely to generate

From **Coco Fusco** 'Now You See It, Now You Don't'

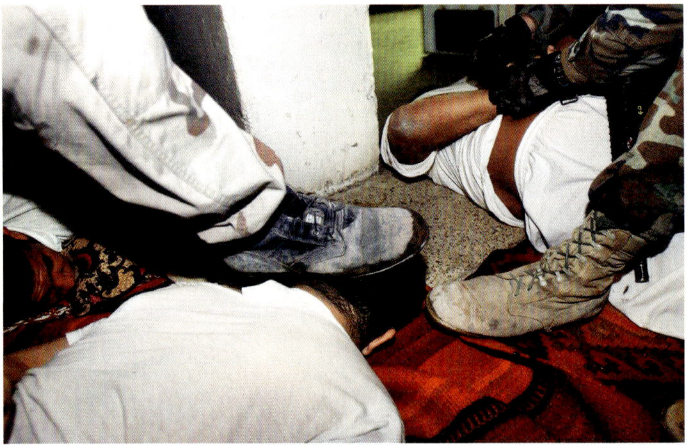

Geert van Kesteren Bravo Company 1/8 Infantry on a raid in search for insurgents, terrorists and weapons. These Iraqi men were arrested after soldiers found weapons in a nearby hotel. This is not the hotel but the house of the hotel-owner. All males were arrested: 'You never know, they can be insurgents', 2nd Lt Tumlinson said. The soldiers used their feet, on backs and heads, to handcuff the suspect. All Iraqis present were shivering in fear. Samarra, Iraq, 18 January 2004

From **Geert van Kesteren** interviewed by Brigitte Lardinois

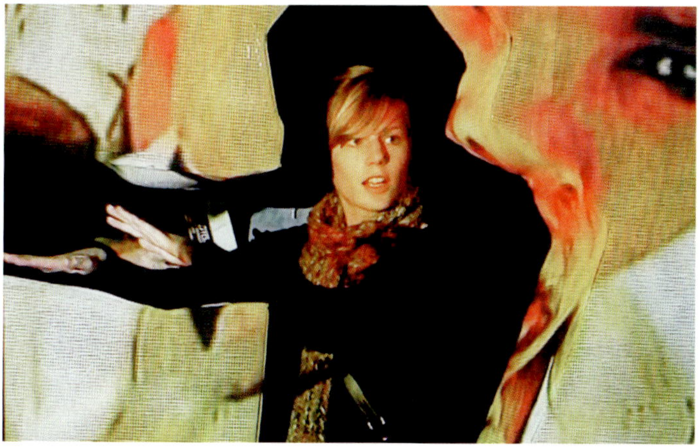

Stefaan Decostere *Warum 2.0*, installation view

From **Stefaan Decostere** 'Image, War, Impactology'

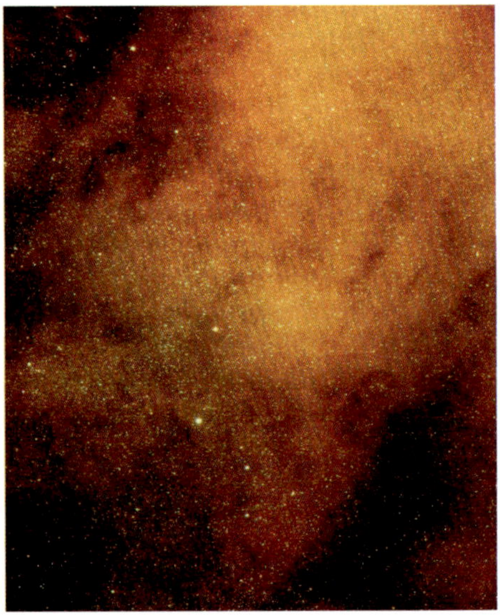

Trevor Paglen *Milstar 3 Sagittarius (Inactive Communication and Targeting Satellite; USA 143)*, 2008

From **Trevor Paglen** interviewed by Julian Stallabrass

Memory of Fire: Images of War and The War of Images

Edited by
Julian Stallabrass

photoworks

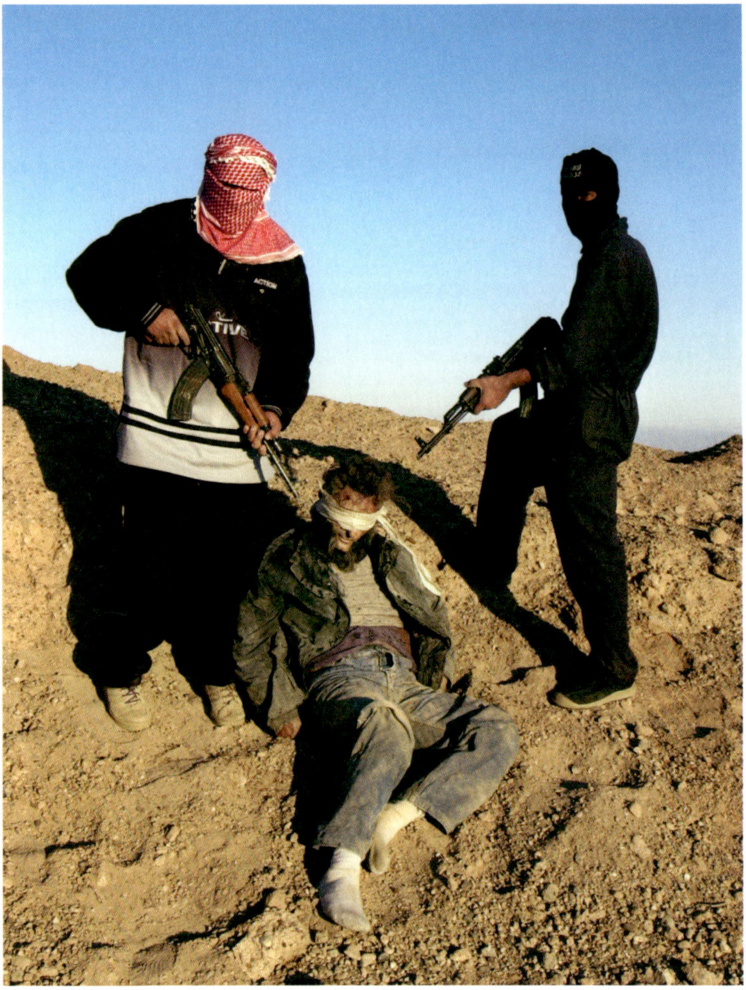

Bilal Hussein. A body which insurgents claim to be that of Italian national Salvatore Santoro, 52, in the desert outside Ramadi. Iraqi militants said they shot and killed an Italian citizen after he tried to break through a guerrilla roadblock on a highway outside the insurgent stronghold of Ramadi. 15 December 2004

Introduction
Julian Stallabrass

Memory of Fire: Images of War and the War of Images is a book that takes its title from the 2008 Brighton Photo Biennial which, in ten exhibitions and numerous events, explored the photographic depiction of war, and the ways in which images are used as agents of warfare. That series of events and exhibitions showed how war imagery had changed across a considerable time span, and how it took different forms in various places and over diverse genres. They covered a range of twentieth-century war photography from the Russian Civil War up to recent and current conflicts, particularly in Iraq and Afghanistan. It included work made by professional photojournalists, official military photographers, civilian and military amateurs, documentarians and artists. That diversity is reflected in the essays and illustrations in this book.

At the time, we planned to make a substantial catalogue to accompany the Biennial. Essays were commissioned and written, and image rights secured. The publication did not in the end appear due to lack of funds, but that material can now be found here. It is complemented by other elements that are connected with the Biennial theme, and bring the book up to date.

This book is comprised of essays and interviews by some of the most prominent theorists, artists and photographers working today. These cover the urgent issues of the depiction of war, the use of war images by the media, various forms of censorship, the military as a PR and image-producing machine, the circulation of unofficial images and the impact of the digital mediascape.

The book opens with a brief extract from Eduardo Galeano, from whom the title of the Biennial was borrowed. His *Memory of Fire* is an extraordinary history of 500 years of colonial oppression and resistance across Latin America, told in short narratives, one of which is reproduced here.[1] Galeano's book is structured as a long sequence of affecting snapshots, flashes of illumination in a history that remains obscure to those who confine themselves to conservative accounts which dwell on the powerful. It provided the model for a Biennial display of radical photography, *Photography & Revolution: Memory Trails Through the Latin American Left*, which I co-curated with Susie Medley at the Winchester Gallery.

There follow pairs of loosely associated essays and interviews. My essay explores the political, military and journalistic circumstances which informed the curation of the Biennial, and analyses some of the dilemmas of dealing with war imagery in gallery settings. The interview which follows is with one of the most celebrated British photojournalists of his generation, Philip Jones Griffiths. He talks particularly about his famous work in Vietnam, and also about the role of photojournalism in contemporary political and image culture.

---

1 Eduardo Galeano, *Memory of Fire*, trans. Cedric Belfrage, Quartet Books, London 1995.

One of the photographers we showed in an exhibition at the University of Brighton Gallery, *Iraq Through the Lens of Vietnam*, was an independent photojournalist, Rita Leistner. Her work was featured in the well-known book *Unembedded*, which examined the work of those photographers who choose not to travel with the military.[2] She had also done embedded work in Iraq, however, and here she writes an account of those circumstances, in particular her work with a US Army unit that became notorious for murdering civilians. In the interview, Ashley Gilbertson, who has made some of the most sustained and critical photography to emerge from within the embedding system in Iraq, writes of the opportunities and limits of such work, and the various dangers of prolonged proximity with troops.

In complete contrast, Sarah James writes about the genre of so-called 'aftermath' photography, made for gallery and museum walls, usually with large-format view cameras. This work, in its formality and in the distance it takes from its subjects, stands opposed to photojournalism with its focus on incidents and emotions. James unearths the moral and aesthetic dilemmas that lie behind such spectacular work. In their interview, Adam Broomberg and Oliver Chanarin, who have made large-scale photographs on the subject of conflict, talk about the range of their practice from their early documentary work in South Africa through to the series *The Day Nobody Died* in which they took a huge roll of unexposed photographic paper on an embed with the British military in Afghanistan.

The next pairing looks at makers of amateur images in war zones. Coco Fusco writes about the disturbing role that female soldiers played in the system of torture, sexual humiliation and photography established in many US detention centres, including Abu Ghraib. Under what perverted regime did their very gender come to be used as a weapon? From the other side of the divide between occupiers and occupied, Geert van Kesteren assembled an extraordinary collection of photographs taken by Iraqis on their camera phones. These were used to communicate with the millions of Iraqis forced into exile by the war and the ensuing sectarian conflict, and they show both the violence and degradation of life under the occupation, but also mundane scenes of family and friends, made to assure the recipients: 'we are alright'. In his interview with Brigitte Lardinois, Van Kesteren talks about the closing down of opportunities for photojournalists to work in Iraq, and of how as a response he came to curate phone imagery.

---

2 Ghaith Abdul-Ahad, Kael Alford, Thorne Anderson and Rita Leistner, *Unembedded: Four Independent Photojournalists on the War in Iraq*, Chelsea Green, White River Junction, VT, 2005.

In the Biennial we wanted to show new media work, but were unable to commission the pieces that we wanted. In the same year as the Biennial, Stefaan Decostere staged a remarkable interactive installation using video material taken in combat zones, *Warum 2.0*. In his essay, Decostere writes about how his ideas on media impact developed, in dialogue with Paul Virilio and other theorists, and how they came to be realised in the installation. Trevor Paglen has become well known for his extraordinary images of the secret elements of the US military–industrial complex, from covert bases and black sites to spy satellites. In his interview, Paglen talks about these works, the research that lies behind them, and their relationship to knowledge, art history and aesthetics.

In the years since 2008, the subject of war and its depiction in photography and video has (unfortunately) remained as relevant as ever, as old conflicts and occupations drag on, as the US continues to murder suspects and bystanders, as new wars are threatened, and as new technologies forever change the media landscape into which such conflicts are launched. I hope that the range of materials in this book—images as well as texts—will serve as a resource to reflect and act upon these issues.

Excerpt from *Memory of Fire*
Eduardo Galeano

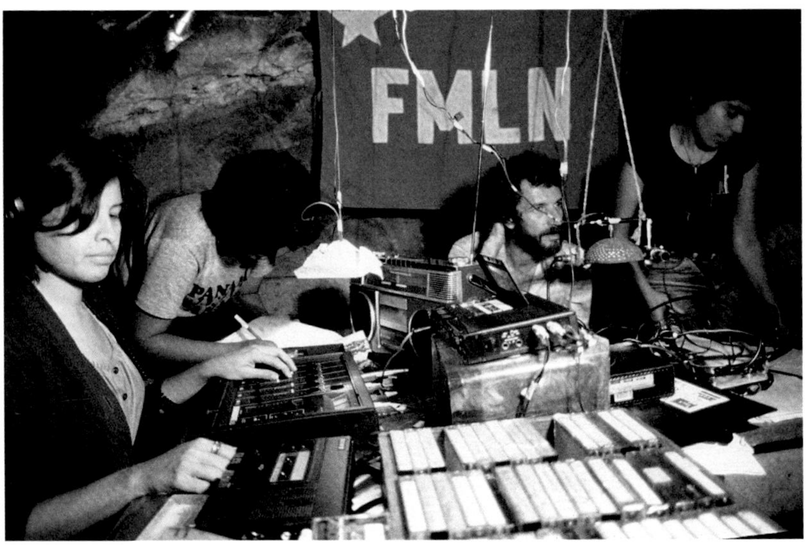

Anonymous photographer, Radio Venceremos.

1984: Rio de Janeiro
Mishaps of Collective Memory in Latin America

Public accountant João David dos Santos jumped for joy when he managed to collect his many overdue accounts. Only payment in kind, but something. For lack of funds, a social science research center paid him its whole library of nine thousand books and over five thousand magazines and pamphlets devoted to contemporary Brazilian history. It contained very valuable material on the peasant leagues of the Northeast and the Getulio Vargas administration, among other subjects.

The accountant dos Santos puts the library up for sale. He offered it to cultural organisations, historical institutes, and various ministries. No one had the money. He tried universities, state and private, one after another. No takers. He left the library on loan at one university for a few months, until they started demanding rent. Then he tried private citizens. No one showed the slightest interest. The nation's history is an enigma, a lie, or a yawn.

The unhappy accountant dos Santos feels great relief when he finally succeeds in selling his library to the Tijuca Paper Factory, which turns all these books, magazines and pamphlets into tinted toilet paper.

Overleaf Frank Hurley, An episode after the Battle of Zonnebeke, 1918

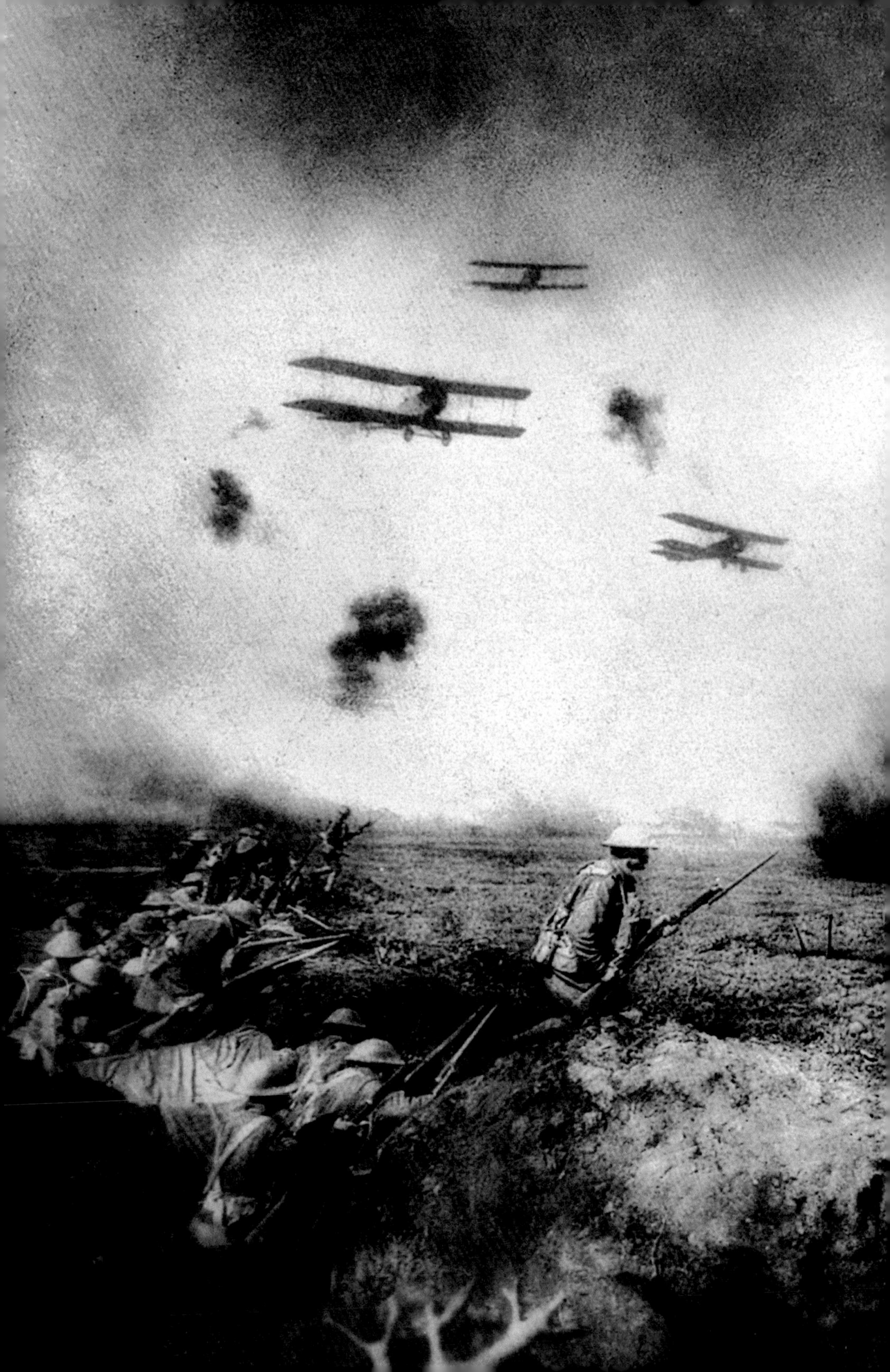

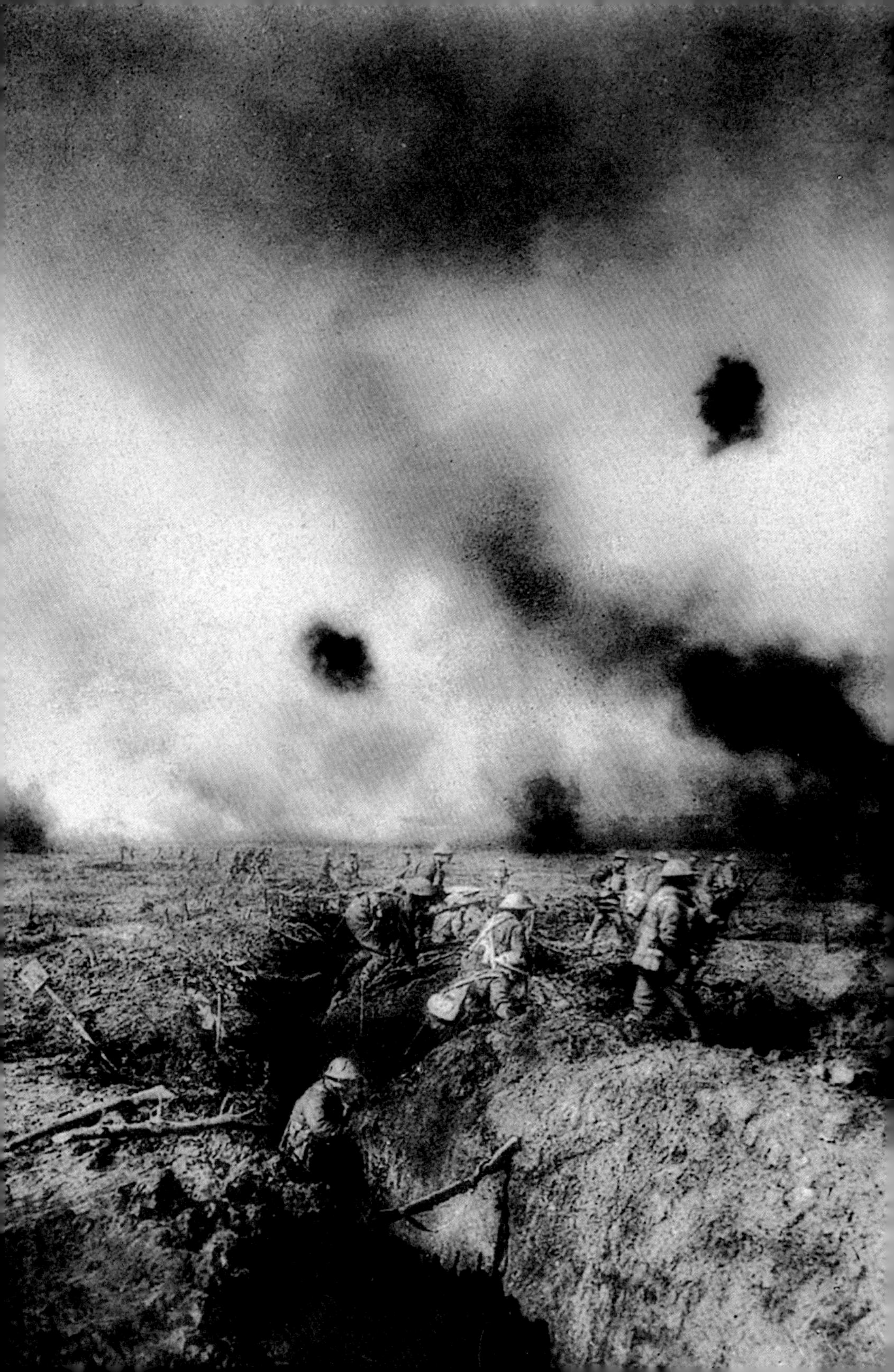

The Power and Impotence of Images
Julian Stallabrass

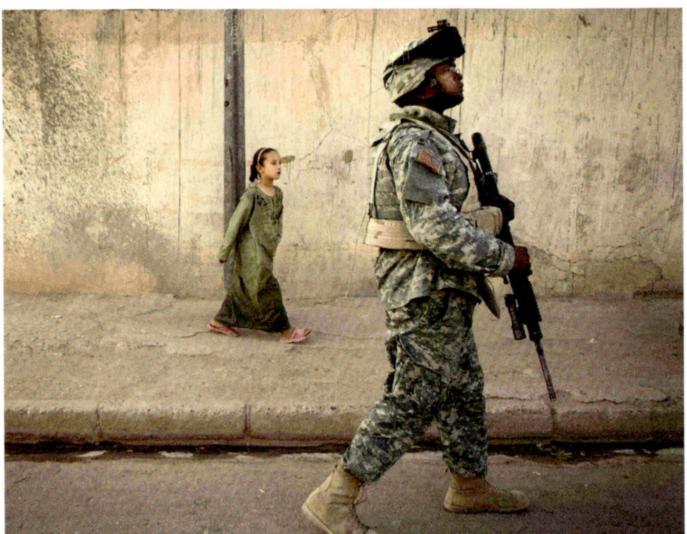

Air Force Staff Sgt Jacob Bailey, August 22, 2006: Spc Antoine Davis, from the 1st Brigade Combat Team, 1st Armored Division, patrols Tal Afar, as an Iraqi child walks alongside

In 1942, Vasily Grossman, a journalist with the Red Army, wrote in his notebook as the Soviet troops advanced south of Kharkov:

> *Severe frost. The snow is creaking. Icy air makes one catch one's breath. The insides of one's nostrils stick together, teeth ache from the cold. Germans, frozen to death, lie on the roads of our advance. Their bodies are absolutely intact. We didn't kill them, it was the cold. Practical jokers put the frozen Germans on their feet, or on their hands and knees, making intricate, fanciful sculptural groups. Frozen Germans stand with their fists raised, or with their fingers spread wide. Some of them look as if they are running, their heads pulled into their shoulders ... At night the fields of snow seem blue under the bright moon, and the dark bodies of frozen German soldiers stand in the blue snow, placed there by jokers.*[1]

As the curator of the 2008 Brighton Photo Biennial, which was devoted to the theme of images of war, I constantly had a dreadful sense that my task was comparable to that of Grossman's 'jokers'. It felt wrong to arrange photographs of corpses and the wounded in a way that made cogent sense, or to judge how they could be best placed to produce a coherent formal ensemble.

To have any chance of being curatorially adequate to the subject, three realms had to be brought together: the theoretical, the actual circumstances of the making of war imagery, and the aesthetic. What were the theoretical innovations that had been brought about by the renewal of documentary practice in the art world and the long war on terror? How had politics, warfare, the military, the media and the technologies of image-making changed? What were the aesthetic, perceptual and ideological effects of bringing images of war into the gallery? In this essay, I will consider each in turn.

As the Biennial was being planned from 2006 onwards, a strange and novel conjunction of events seemed to demand curatorial exploration: the invention of a new method of producing military propaganda; the foundering of illusions about the swift and clean efficacy of US military power in the wrecking of Iraq, and its descent into something close to civil war; the apparent failure of photojournalism to describe the new circumstances of war

---

1 Vasily Grossman, *A Writer at War: Vasily Grosssman with the Red Army 1941–1945*, ed./ trans. Antony Beevor and Luba Vinogradova, The Harvill Press, London 2005, p. 86. Grossman went on to write one of the most remarkable novels of the Soviet era, drawing on his experiences of the war: *Life and Fate*, trans. Robert Chandler, The Harvill Press, London 1985.

and occupation; and the rapidly evolving field of citizen journalism and other amateur imagery which offered an alternative view to the standardised fare of the mainstream media.

This new scenario of warfare, media and technology had a rapid and remarkable effect on the theoretical and historical writing about documentary photography and photojournalism. In the twilight of the liberal era, in which documentary served a humanist, ameliorative and reforming role, such photography had come in for harsh critique from those who highlighted its cruelty and bad faith, its concealment of the real causes of oppression, and its masking of dark ideologies under the cloak of a universal love for humanity.[2] Susan Sontag's views, in particular—of documentary photography as a drug for media addicts, dulling its users into political torpor—for a long time became the horizon of common sense. Of a Leica advert that reads: '... Prague ... Woodstock ... Vietnam ... Sapporo ... Londonderry ... LEICA', Sontag writes that sports, colonial wars and youth antics are all equalised in a 'chronic voyeuristic relation to the world which levels the meaning of all events.'[3] The reawakening of documentary theory was caused by the over-reach of neoliberal power in the long and continuing 'war on terror'. In launching controversial wars, starkly dividing the globe into allies and enemies, and violating democratic principles, photojournalism and documentary were thrust into renewed prominence in the news media and beyond. This stimulated a substantial wave of theoretical re-evaluation of documentary, given its new roles and its new social and political situation—by Ariella Azoulay, Judith Butler, Susie Linfield, Jacques Rancière and many others.[4]

Yet, in an apparent irony, while the power and the empowering character of the image was being brought to light, the photojournalism that galvanised the anti-war movement around the world at the time of Vietnam seemed to have lost its power. The images that emerged from Iraq did little to revive the anti-war

---

2 Respectively, Susan Sontag, *On Photography*, Penguin Books, London 1979; Martha Rosler, *Decoys and Disruptions: Selected Writings, 1975–2001*, MIT Press, Cambridge, MA, 2004, especially her celebrated essay 'In, Around, and Afterthoughts (On Documentary Photography)', 1981; Allan Sekula, 'The Traffic in Photographs', *Art Journal*, vol. 41, no. 1, Spring 1981, pp. 15-25. **3** Sontag, *On Photography*, p. 11. **4** For an indication of this considerable literature, see Ariella Azoulay, *Death's Showcase—The Power of Image in Contemporary Democracy*, MIT Press, Cambridge, MA, 2001, and *The Civil Contract of Photography*, Zone Books, New York 2008; Judith Butler, *Frames of War: When is Life Grievable?*, Verso, London 2009; Georges Didi-Huberman, *Images in Spite of All: Four Photographs from Auschwitz*, trans. Shane B. Lillis, University of Chicago Press, Chicago, IL, 2008; Robert Hariman and John Louis Lucaites, *No Caption Needed: Iconic Photographs, Public Culture, and Liberal Democracy*, University of Chicago Press, Chicago, IL, 2007; Susie Linfield, *The Cruel Radiance: Photography and Political Violence*, University of Chicago Press, Chicago, IL, 2010; Jacques Rancière, *The Emancipated Spectator*, trans. Gregory Elliott, Verso, London 2009.

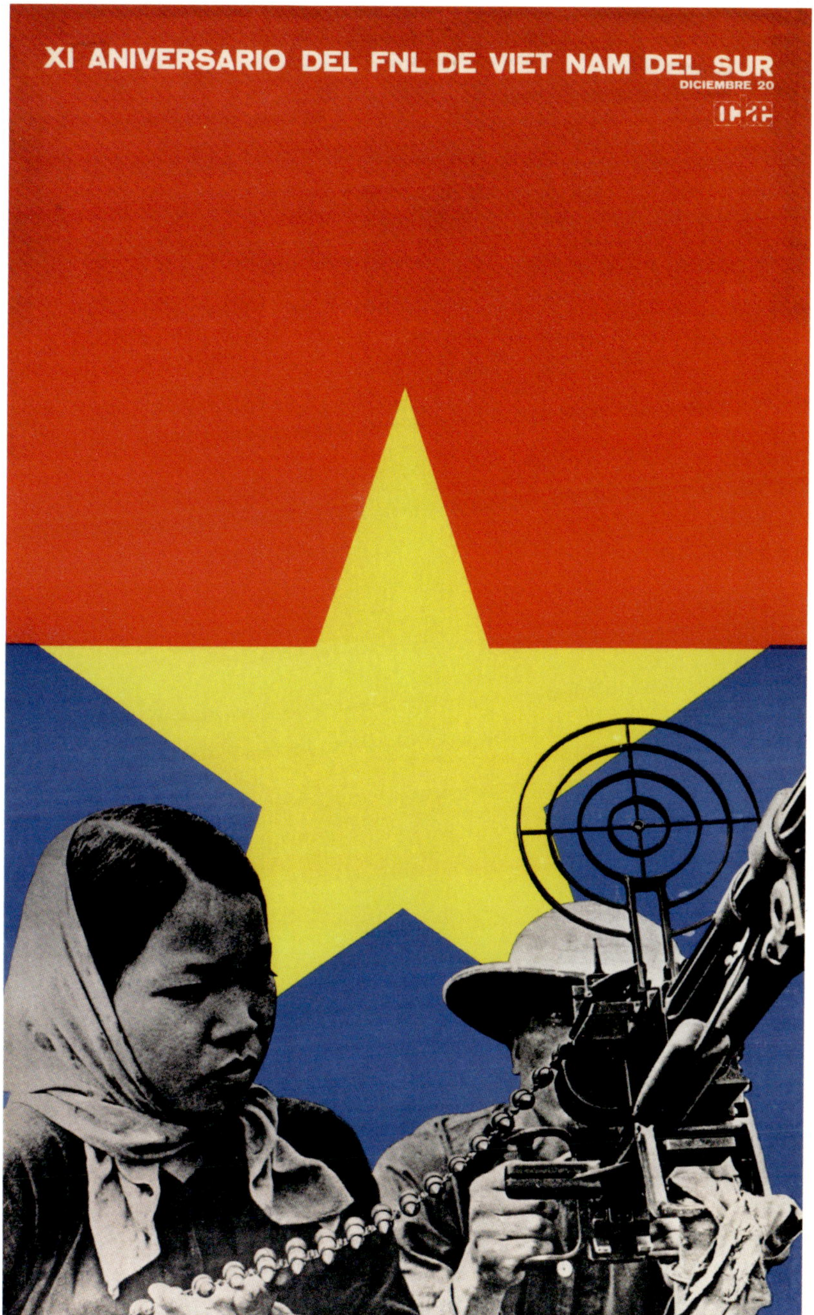

Poster published to mark the 11th anniversary of the National Front for the Liberation of South Vietnam (Vietcong) by the OCLAE (Latin American and Caribbean Students' Association). Designed by Félix Beltrán, 1971

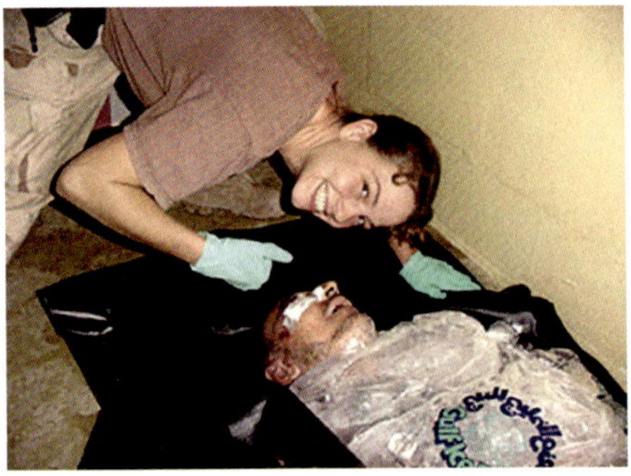

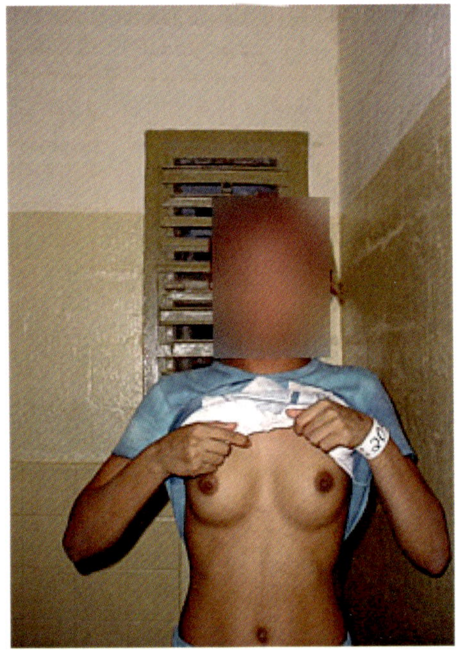

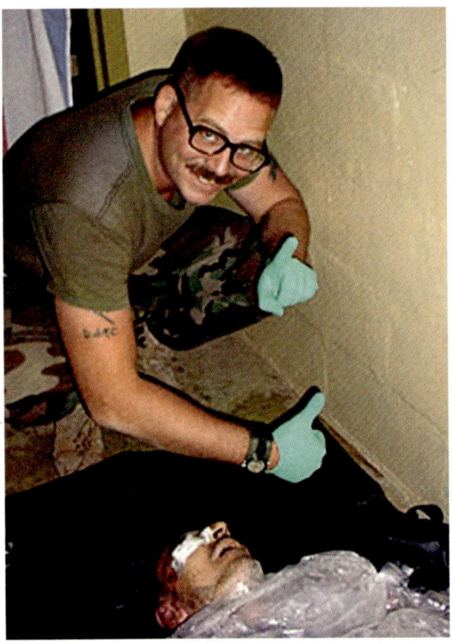

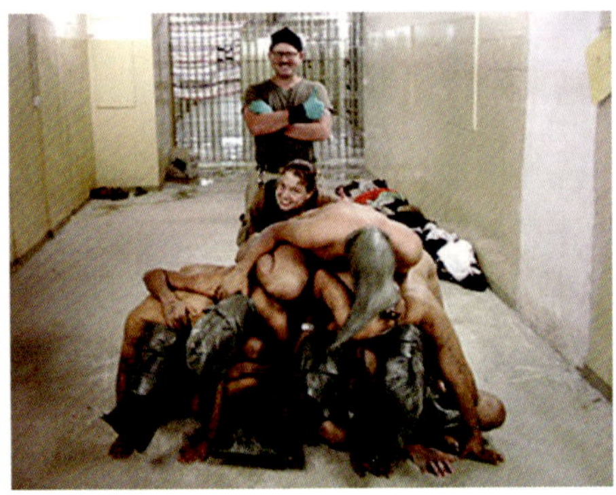

Clockwise from top left Abu Ghraib 11.35 pm Nov 4 2003. The body bag was opened so CPL GRANER and SPC HARMAN could take pictures of the detainee
3.44 am Oct. 29 2003. It was believed that CPL GRANER took this picture in the series to follow with the female in a number of poses
11.50 pm Nov 7 2003. CPL GRANER and SPC HARMAN pose for picture behind the nude detainees
11.38 pm Nov 4 2003

movement that had flourished so spectacularly before the invasion was launched. While in the Vietnam era, torture (small and large scale) was the secret of state policy, and was revealed in part through photography, in the wars in Afghanistan and Iraq, torture is the overt policy but its effects often remain unrepresented or, even when they are shown, they pass with insufficient comment or effect.

To begin with torture:

> *On the rare occasion that I forget to take my medicine, I usually have nightmares. When that guy was screaming in the shower, I hear that in the middle of the night. It'll wake me up, freak me out. It's always going to be there. The way he was screaming, it was just a death scream. He was screaming at the top of his lungs constantly. And you're right in the next room. It's like it's vibrating your whole body, it's so loud. I don't think I'll ever get that out of my head.*[5]

So one of Abu Ghraib's torturers reflects on how she is haunted by what she did. There are many things that cannot be photographed, and many more that for all kinds of reasons are not photographed. But Lynndie England's statement, in which the trauma of another is buttressed between a description of her own, points to the silence and stillness of those notorious images, to all that they do not show, but which they gesture towards.

Torture and its depiction have become central to the very image of the neoliberal system. In Naomi Klein's account of the system, *The Shock Doctrine*, torture is the keystone of the neoliberal edifice. This challenges head-on the right-wing association between democracy and free markets, which pretends that there is a perfect correlation between the two, so that communism and enslavement sit at one end of the spectrum, and the untrammelled free market and perfect personal freedom at the other. What Klein shows, remorselessly and in graphic detail, is a different association, long familiar in the 'developing' world: that the imposition of unrestrained markets is so unpopular and drives so many into penury that it can only be forced on people, and that its essential tools are torture and terror.[6]

This association is far from new, and has merely stepped out of hiding. Here is Noam Chomsky, writing many years ago about viewing a photograph of another war of occupation:

---

5 Lynndie England, as cited in Philip Gourevitch and Errol Morris, *Standard Operating Procedure: A War Story*, Picador, London 2008, p. 276. **6** Naomi Klein, *The Shock Doctrine: The Rise of Disaster Capitalism*, Allen Lane, London 2007.

> *The things we have seen and read during these horrible years surpass belief. I have in front of me now an Associated Press photo from the* New York Times *with this caption:*
>
> *HOMELESS CHILDREN: Girl holds her wounded baby sister as South Vietnamese rangers move through their hamlet. Children had been rescued from a bunker under their house, burnt down when US helicopters fired on the Vietcong. The scene is the Mekong Delta, south-west of Saigon.*
>
> *I cannot describe the pathos of this scene, or the expression on the face of the wounded child. How many hundreds of such pictures must we see before we begin to care and to act?*
>
> *I suppose this is the first time in history that a nation has so openly and publicly exhibited its own war crimes. Perhaps this shows how well our free institutions function. Or does it simply show how immune we have become to suffering?*[7]

Torture on a small scale, person-to-person in underground rooms, was writ large when applied to those nations or peoples that would not bow to the appropriate gods. The general destruction of the peasantry, land and environment of Vietnam was regulated by policy, and increased gradually as the US government strove to find the breaking point of those resisting the occupation. Daniel Ellsberg, in deciding to risk jail by leaking the Pentagon Papers about the prosecution of the war, gave some of the copied documents about the bombing policy to his wife, Patricia. She read such phrases as 'a need to reach their threshold of pain', 'one more turn of the screw', about the use of the water-drip technique of occasional raids that hit them with 'greater pain', 'squeezing them', 'painful surgical strikes', and so on. She recognised it as 'the language of torturers', and urged Ellsberg to expose the papers to the press.[8]

Ellsberg spent his savings to photocopy the massive number of documents that constituted the Pentagon Papers, and, in leaking them, revealed many secrets.[9] The leaders of the US, under Bush, were open about their use of kidnap and torture; under Obama they are open about murder. They proudly

---

7 Noam Chomsky, *American Power and the New Mandarins*, Penguin Books, Harmondsworth, 1969, p. 12. The AP photograph was published on 13 April 1967. 8 Daniel Ellsberg, *Secrets: A Memoir of Vietnam and the Pentagon Papers*, Penguin Books, New York 2002, p. 364. 9 Neil Sheehan, Hedrick Smith, E.W. Kenworthy and Fox Butterfield, *The Pentagon Papers as Published by* The New York Times, Routledge & Kegan Paul, London 1971.

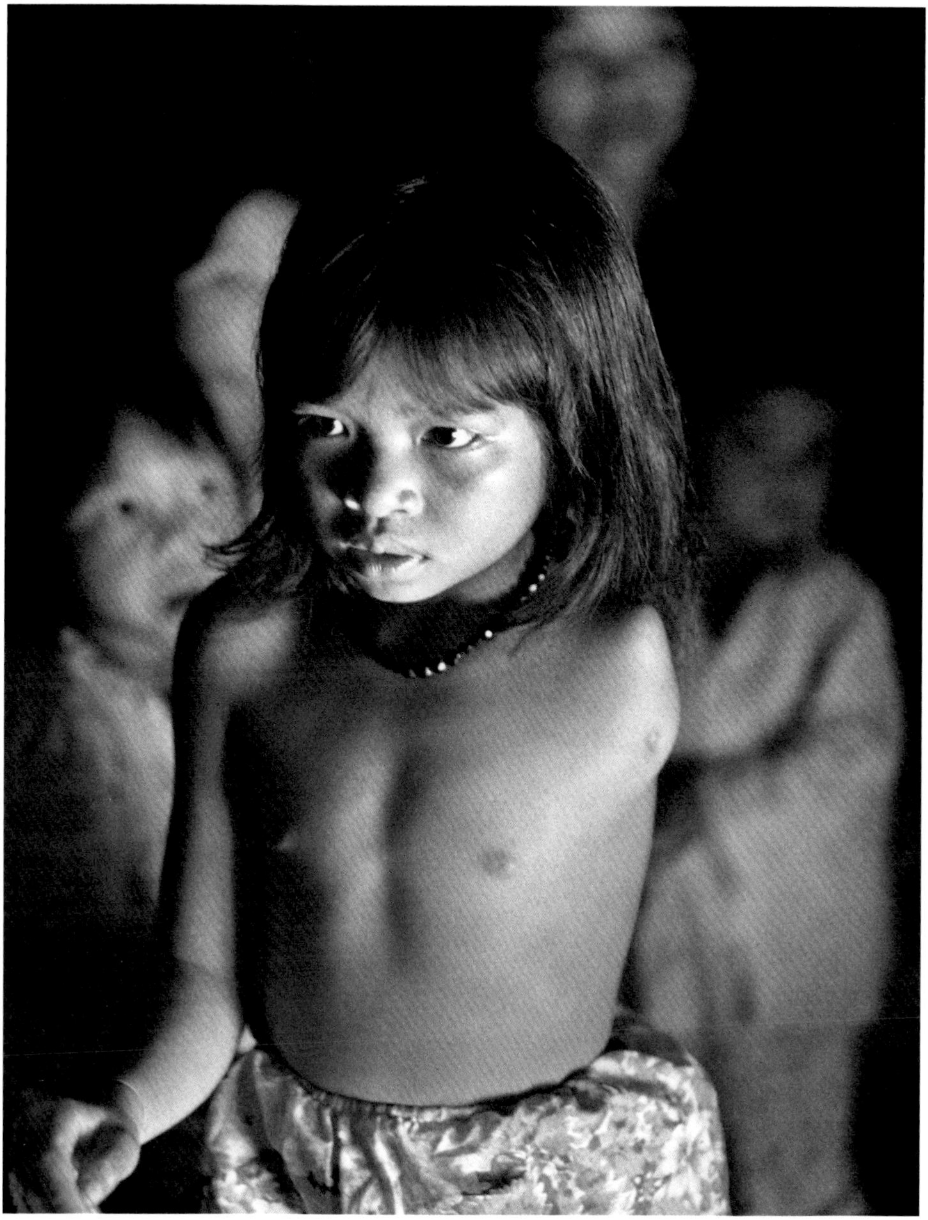

Philip Jones Griffiths, Quynh Lan, 11 years old, at her home in A Luoi, Vietnam. Her father was sprayed with Agent Orange many times

proclaim that they have assassinated some Taliban or Al-Qaeda suspect by bomb, missile or hit-squad (and too bad about the bystanders).

All this takes place within an image culture which is a dance of veiling and revealing, highly evolved by state and military media-managed bodies, and newly minted for an age of hyper-visibility. As the authors of *Afflicted Powers* asked: how is war waged in an age of spectacle?[10] In itself, media war is hardly new. The battlefields of the American Civil War were photographed after the fighting had finished for souvenir albums, and (as with Grossman's 'jokers') corpses were moved into pretty arrangements.[11] In the Mexican Revolution, Pancho Villa struck a deal with US film makers to document the struggle, and altered his battle plans to favour the cameras.[12] Nevertheless, the sheer scale of media engagement with war has changed profoundly. When in the First World War the British Army decided that they wanted to make official photographs to counter similar propaganda from the German side, they employed just two photographers, and freelancers were banned.[13] In Vietnam, by contrast, at the height of Western press interest, there were about 1000 journalists in the South, 700 of them with official accreditation.[14] For the Iraq War, there were over double this number, including 700 'slots' created for embedded journalists.[15] It would be the most intensively reported war in history.[16]

Yet it is curious that, out of such a plethora of reporting, a vast cascade of images that minute-by-minute filled television screens, websites and the pages of newspapers and magazines, few seemed to stick in the mind. Arguably, none of the professionally made images have come to define the war and the issues around it, as a number of photographs had done for the Vietnam War—notably, Eddie Adams's 1968 photograph of the summary execution of a guerrilla suspect, Ron Haeberle's hideous photographs of the massacre at My Lai, and Nick Ut's 1971 photograph of a girl in agony from napalm burns running down a road. Even Sontag acknowledged the power of the latter.[17]

The amateur images taken at Abu Ghraib did threaten for a time to become the signal images of the war, and they still stand as such (along with a vast

---

10 Retort (Iain Boal, T.J. Clark, Joseph Matthews and Michael Watts), *Afflicted Powers: Capital and Spectacle in a New Age of War*, Verso, London 2005. **11** Harold Evans, *War Stories: Reporting in the Time of Conflict from the Crimea to Iraq*, Bunker Hill, Charlestown, MA, 2003, p. 33. **12** Michael S. Sweeney, *From the Front: The Story of War*, National Geographic, Washington, DC, 2002, p. 123. **13** They were Ernest Brooks and Warwick Brooke. See Paul Wombell, *Battle Passchendale 1917—Evidence of War's Reality*, Travelling Light Photography, London 1981, p. 11. **14** Sweeney, *From the Front*, p. 253. **15** Philip Seib, *Beyond the Front Lines: How the News Media Cover a World Shaped by War*, Palgrave Macmillan, New York 2004, p. 51. **16** Christopher Paul and James J. Kim, *Reporters on the Battlefield: The Embedded Press System in Historical Context*, RAND Corporation, Santa Monica, CA, 2004, p. 55.

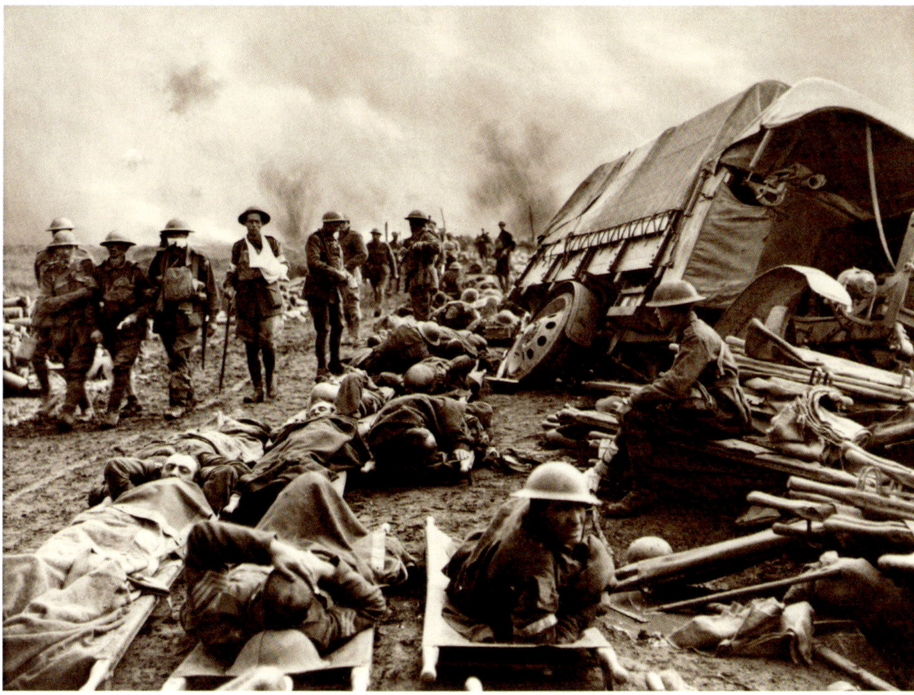

Frank Hurley, *The Battle of the Menin Road*, 1917/18

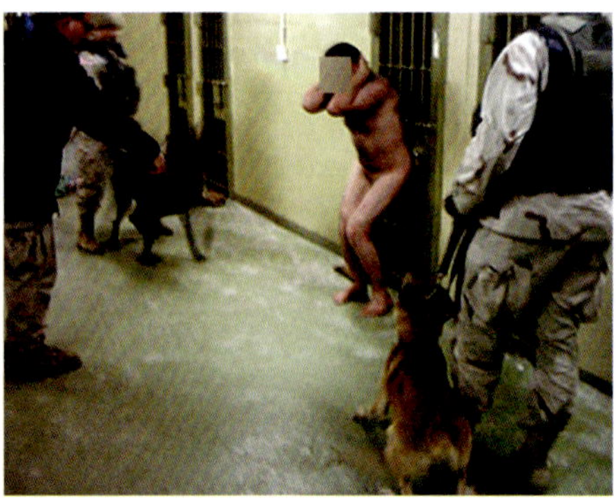

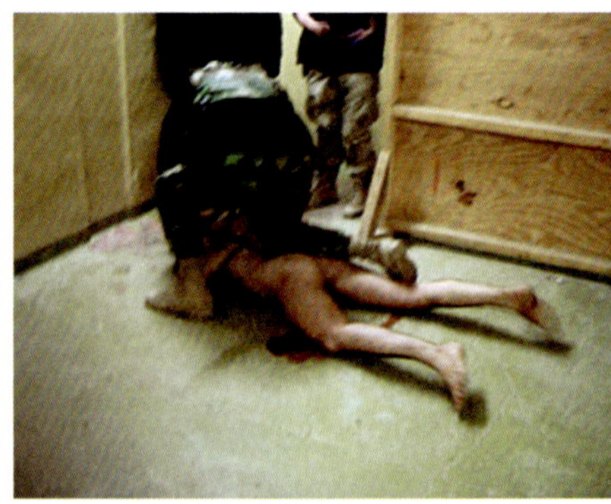

From left to right 10.47 pm Dec 12 2003. Two dog handlers have dogs watching detainee while GRANER orders detainee to floor
10.51 pm Dec 12 2003. Detainee after dog bite
10.55 pm Dec 12 2003. Detainee after dog bite
11.22 pm Dec 12 2003. SPC HARMAN and possible medic look at injured detainee

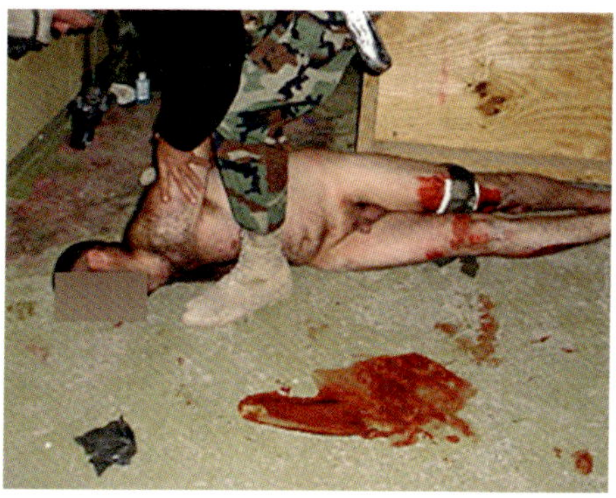

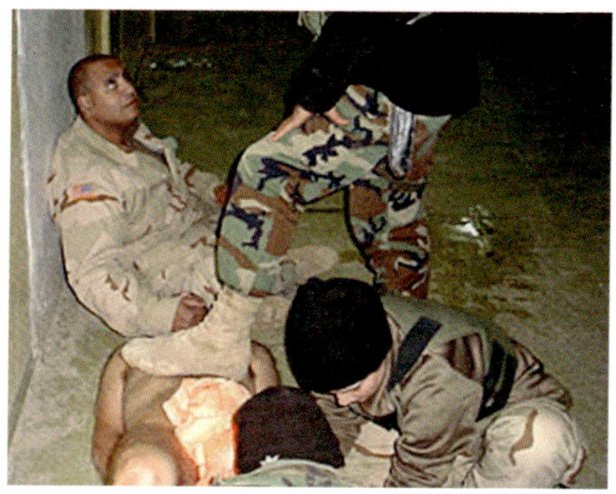

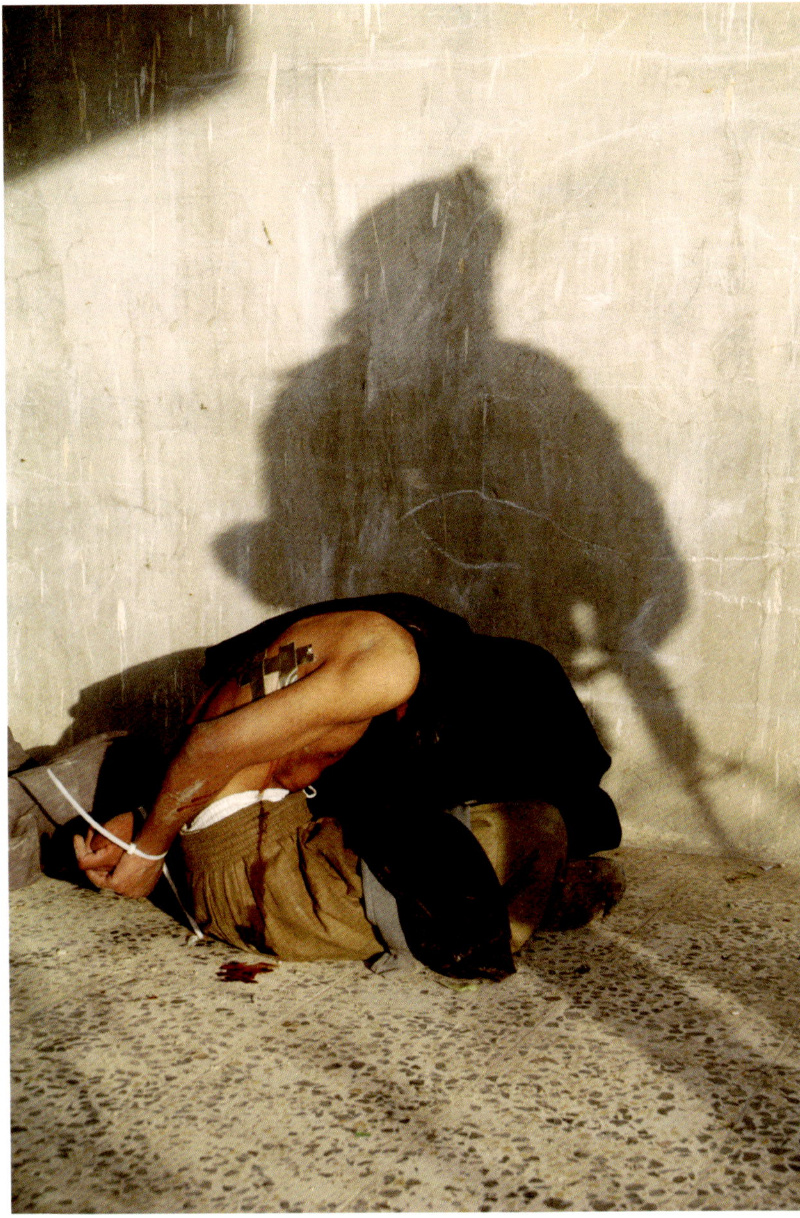

Ashley Gilbertson, The captured fighter claimed to be a student in Fallujah. The marines responded, 'Yeah, right, University of Jihad, motherfucker.' Iraq, 2004

number of other images of the routine destruction and humiliation that the occupying forces dispensed) in the Arabic media. They have no difficulty deciphering such images. Why do we?

The Military

The major military innovation of the Iraq War regarding the media was, of course, the embedding of journalists. Under this system, writers, TV crews and photographers gained relatively unrestricted access to the war at the price of being tied to a particular troop unit. One of the lessons that the US military drew from their defeat in Vietnam was to place very heavy restrictions on media coverage of combat. The embedding system was a response to dissatisfaction at the lack of access to US military adventures in Panama and Grenada from which the media had been excluded. Even in the Gulf War, while the press were invited, they were pooled, usually kept far from the battlefield, and closely censored and instructed about what they should show. CBS Cameraman Mario deCarvalho complained that it was like being with the Soviet Army.[18]

Embedding was the system devised to grant journalists largely uncensored access to military operations while strongly encouraging them to take a positive view of what they saw. Since many embedded journalists were placed in dangerous circumstances under the protection of the troops, and lived with them for extended periods, this usually fostered a strong identification with their new comrades. They were generally grateful for the access to spectacular stories, admiring of their protectors, and appreciative of the troops' various travails.[19] The Pentagon had come to see the media as an opportunity to exploit, and even as a weapon, rather than a dangerous hindrance to be kept at a distance.[20]

Yet many in the media were also aware of the disadvantages to this privileged view of the war, which tied them to particular troops units, and cut them off from information about the wider circumstances of the war. David Zucchino summarised his seven-week series of embeds for the *LA Times*, praising the access that the embed system had granted him, but continuing:

> *Yet that same access could be suffocating and blinding. Often I was too close or confined to comprehend the war's broad sweep. I could not interview survivors of Iraqi civilians killed by US soldiers or speak*

---

17 Sontag, *On Photography*, p. 18. 18 Bill Katovsky and Timothy Carlson, *Embedded: The Media War in Iraq*, Lyons Press, Guilford, CT, 2003, p. 382. 19 Many accounts of the war by embedded journalists are gathered in the interviews in Katovsky and Carlson, *Embedded*. 20 See Paul and Kim, *Reporters on the Battlefield*, pp. 23, 25.

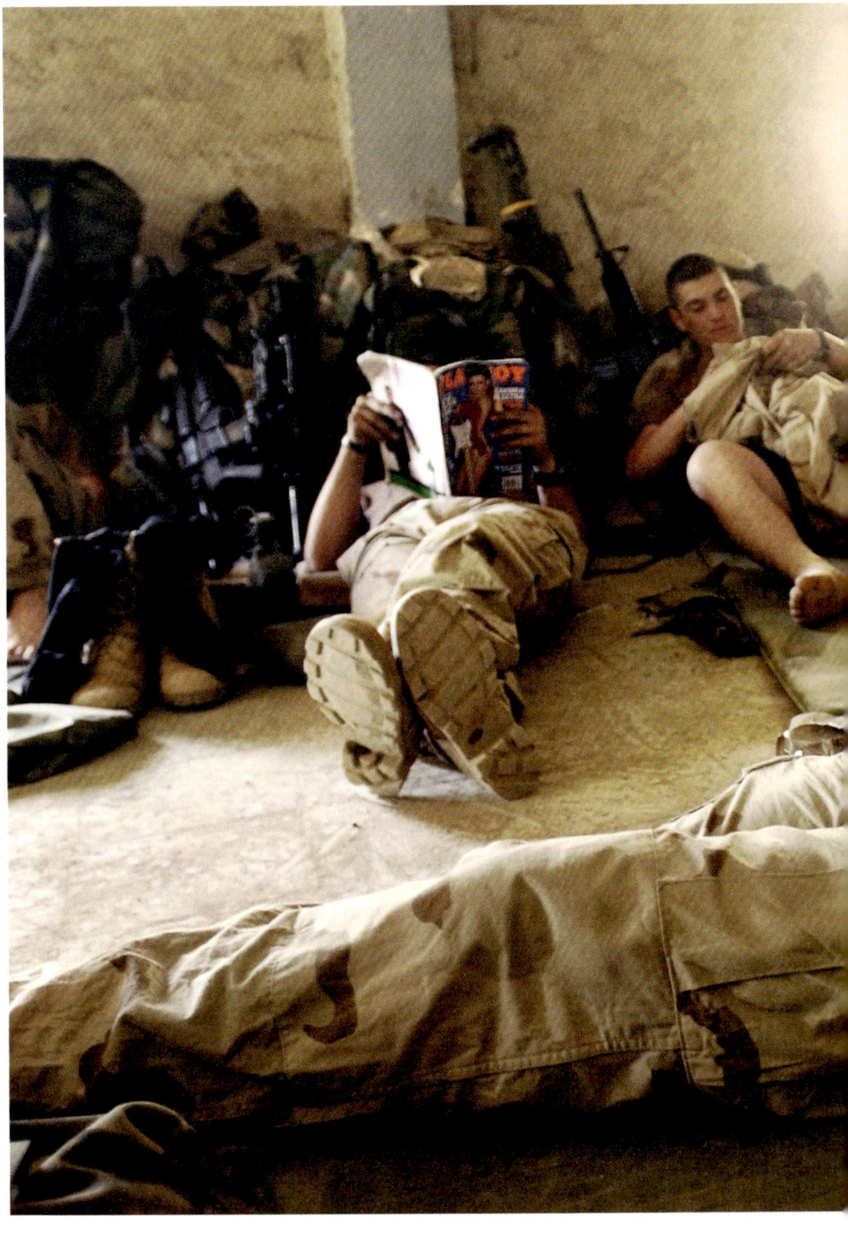

Benjamin Lowy, Iraq, 4 May 2003, Soldiers with the 3rd Battalion of the 1st Brigade of the 101st Airborne Assault Division puruse some gentlemen's entertainment while at their makeshift barracks in Al Kufa, a suburb of An Najaf

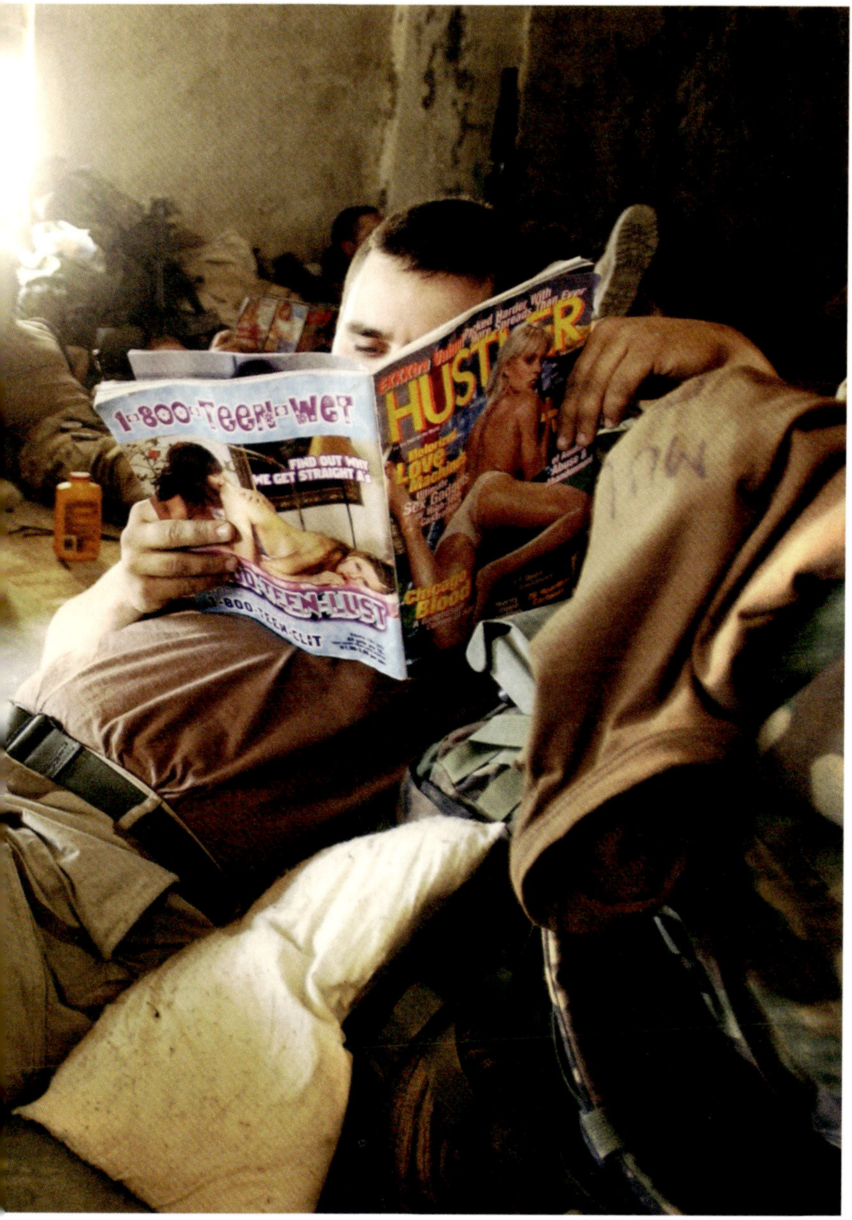
1-800-TEEN-WET
FIND OUT WHY
Love
Chicago Blood
1-800-TEEN-CLIT

> *to Iraqi fighters trying to kill Americans. I was not present when Americans died at the hands of fellow soldiers in what the military calls 'frat', for fratricide. I had no idea what ordinary Iraqis were experiencing. I was ignorant of Iraqi government decisions and US command strategy.*[21]

It was a common complaint. A survey of the system by the Project for Excellence in Journalism concluded:

> *The embedded coverage … is largely anecdotal. It's both exciting and dull, combat focused, and mostly live and unedited. Much of it lacks context but it is usually rich in detail. It has all the virtues and vices of reporting only what you can see.*[22]

Embedding produced a narrow view of the war, then, and one focused on the experiences of Coalition troops. This was a part of the story, but a very limited one. Despite frequent laments about its deficiencies, it continued to dominate coverage of the Iraq conflict, and still does so in Afghanistan. This was in part, as we shall see, because of the attitude of the Iraqis and other forces resisting the occupation, but also because it fitted the demands of the news organisations in the US and the UK, for spectacular, live or at least up-to-the-minute reports, high on emotion and low on analysis, and likely to stiffen patriotic sentiment.

The embedded journalists' coverage was at first largely uncensored—they were understandably not allowed to report troop locations and other sensitive information that might have been of use to the Iraqi armed forces, and they were not allowed to show US casualties until their families had been informed.[23] As the system developed, however, it turned out that soldiers at various levels evolved their own set of rules, which, in concert with the sensibilities of the mass media, produced a censored and sanitised view of the war. This can be seen clearly in the contrast between the work of the embedded photojournalists and those working independently among the Iraqis. In the latter, unsurprisingly, the experience of Iraqi civilians and resistance fighters is reflected, and the picture of the war is darker, bloodier and more desperate. In their work, something can be glimpsed of the systematic destruction of a society already deeply damaged by sanctions. The US armed

---

21 *LA Times*, 2 May, 2003, cited in Katovsky and Carlson, *Embedded*, p. 142. **22** Project for Excellence in Journalism, *Embedded Reporters*, p. 1; cited in Paul and Kim, *Reporters on the Battlefield*, p. 87.
23 The rules for embedding are reproduced in Katovsky and Carlson, *Embedded*, pp. 401–17.

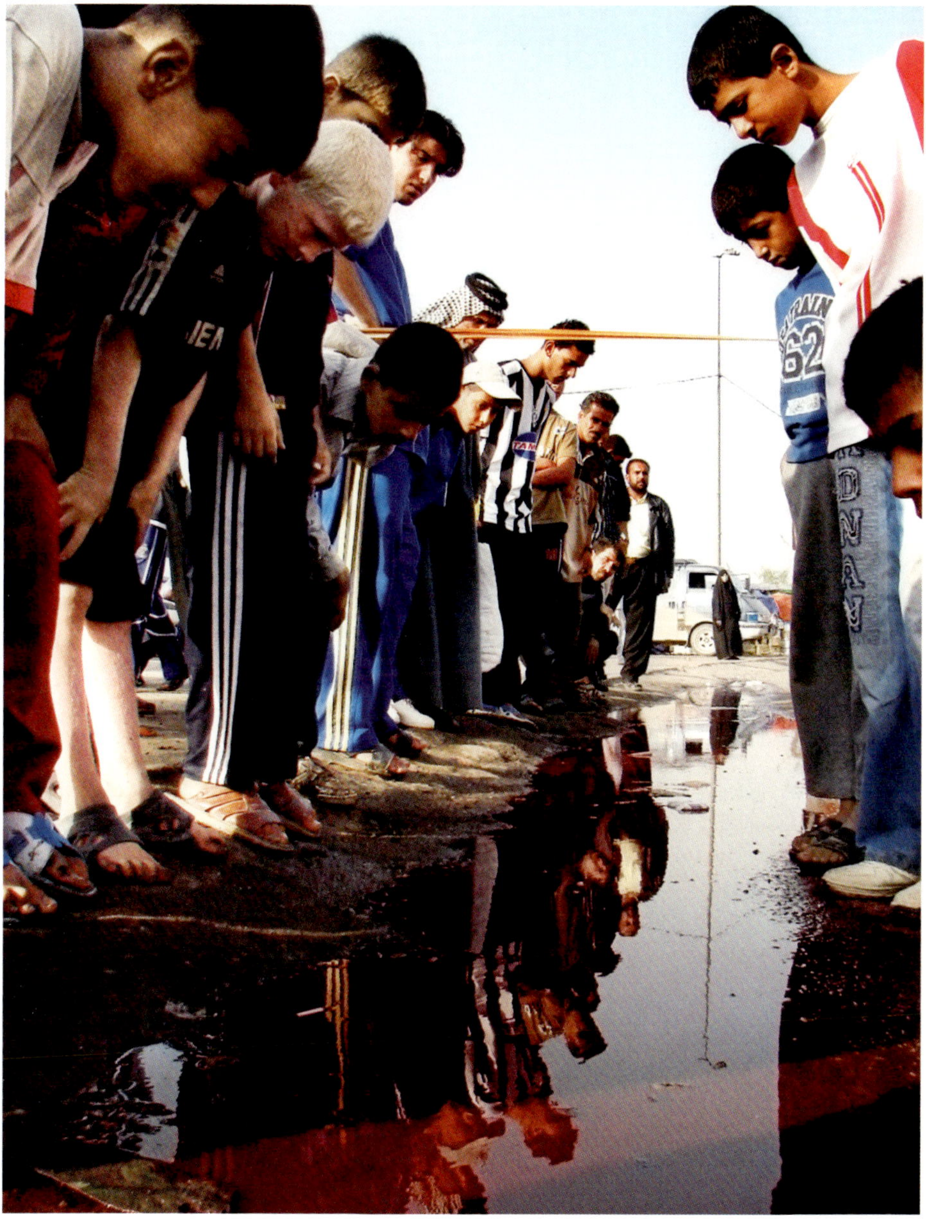

Wissam Al-Okaili, Baghdad: Iraqi youth gather around a pool of blood left behind following a bomb blast in the Shiite neighbourhood of Sadr City, 30 October 2006. A deadly bomb attack had ripped through a crowd of Shiite labourers in Sadr City, scattering 29 bodies through the restive Baghdad suburb, one day after unidentified gunmen slaughtered 17 police instructors

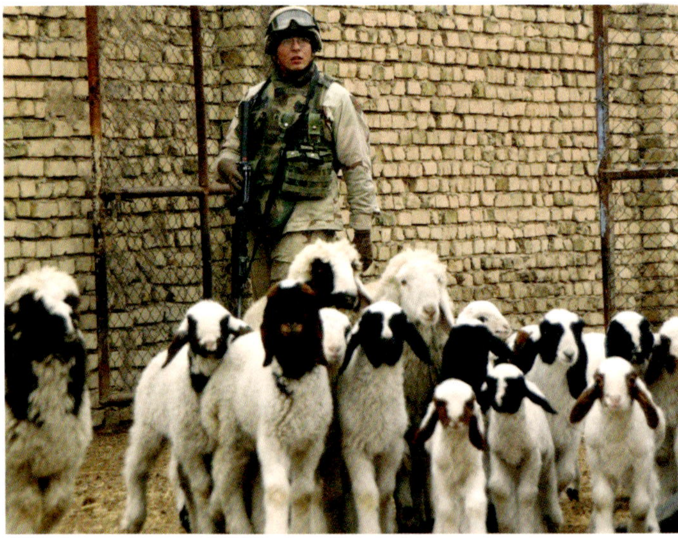

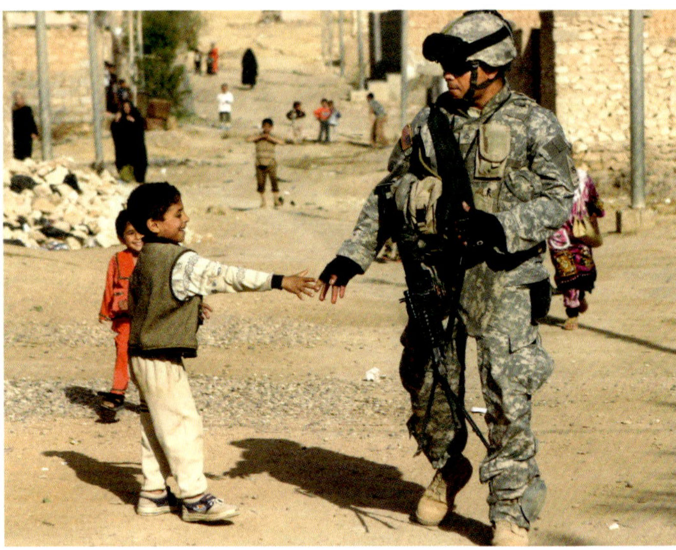

Top Cpl Sam Kilpatrick, Sgt Robert Hufford of Charlie Company, 82nd Engineer Battalion at FOB (Forward Operating Base) Gabe, conducts a cordon search for suspects after an IED (improvised explosive device) attack on his convoy during a patrol in the Diyala province of Baquba, Iraq, 3 January 2005
Bottom Cpl Brian M. Henner, Pfc Joel H. Timarong from Moreno Valley, California, with Alpha Company 1st Battalion, 36 Infantry, greets a local Iraqi child while on patrol through the city of Hit, Iraq, 17 March 2006

forces were not fond of these 'unilaterals'. Troops often stopped independent journalists from reporting and were sometimes responsible for their deaths: Terry Lloyd of ITN was assassinated by them, and the Baghdad office of Al-Jazeera was attacked by missiles in April 2003, killing Tareq Ayyoub, its correspondent in the city.[24]

As the occupation continued, photography became more and more constrained, partly because Iraq became extremely dangerous for anyone thought to have any link to the occupation, or even anyone thought to have any money or professional status, and partly because of an evolving system of censorship. In an audio blog, photojournalist Michael Kamber described the situation:

> *Today in Iraq there's so many things we can't photograph any more. Car bombings and suicide bombings are now off limits, it's actually illegal to photograph those scenes. We can't photograph wounded soldiers without their consent. We can't photograph dead soldiers, coffins of dead soldiers. A few years ago the Army used to invite us to photograph the memorials. Every time a soldier was killed, there'd be a memorial ... Now those are off limits ... We can't photograph battle-damaged vehicles, we can't photograph hospitals, morgues are off limits now. So pretty much everything that gives evidence that there's a war going on is almost impossible to photograph.*[25]

There was in any case little desire among the US public (at least as it was imagined by the mainstream media organisations) to see such things, little motive for the media to show them (since they are poison to advertisers), and so the photographic view of the war became bloodless and anodyne.

One consequence of this debility of the press was that the Coalition's opponents were easily and casually characterised as unthinking religious fanatics, with whom Western readers and viewers can have little sympathy or understanding. Some of them, particularly the foreign Al-Qaeda fighters, were that, and have amply proved that they have as little regard for the lives of Iraqis as they have for those of the invaders. Their actions were viewed with horror by many in the Arab world, and weakened the movement in all those places where people had experience of their brutalities.[26] Most of the resistance,

24 Terry Lloyd was shot in the head by US forces in Basra in 2003; in October 2006, an Oxfordshire coroner's court ruled that he had been unlawfully killed. **25** Podcast on Battlespace project: http://www.daylightmagazine.org/podcast/june2008 See also: http://www.battlespaceonline.org/ (accessed 10 August 2008).

as Jonathan Steele argues, were far from unthinking, and their opposition came out of a deep historical awareness of the imperial roles that the US and the UK have long played in the region, along with a natural reaction to the savagery of the invasion and the occupation.[27]

Of course, this was not how the resistance was generally seen in the Western media. Sectarianism, which had been fostered by Saddam Hussein as a method of control, and was similarly seized on by the Coalition in a typical imperial divide-and-rule policy, was presented as though it was a deep, ancient hatred, dyed into the very identity of what it meant to be Iraqi.[28] As Ahdaf Soueif puts it:

> *The old language of colonialism surfaces once again. Politicians and pundits insist on describing Iraqis in ethnic and religious terms, although Iraqis describe themselves (in the Arabic media) in political and economic terms.*[29]

When the war could be used to tell a clean and straightforward story of noble Western troops overthrowing a foul dictator and bringing democracy to the Arab world, this was easy to illustrate, especially since the US military laid on many photo-ops. The complex struggle that followed, that the campaign did not go as planned, and that Iraq was pitched into anarchy, with violent struggles between those battling for political position and the control of resources, was uncongenial—except when it was turned to reinforce the view of the Arab as fundamentally irrational, violent and cruel. Western media interest in the conflict swiftly declined, not least because, after the drama of the invasion, the heavily censored war was no longer photogenic. IEDs and car bombs do not lend themselves to the heroic scenes that play well with the media.

Finally, and perhaps most importantly in terms of the military management of photojournalism, much of the war was staged for the cameras. It opened with the infamous 'shock and awe' assault on the Iraqi infrastructure in Baghdad, a bloody firework display intended to terrify the Iraqi Army into surrender, and as a demonstration over the global media of overwhelming US military power. Reporters, photographers and TV crews in the Palestine Hotel had a ringside view of the bombardment taking place across the river. In this, and in similar staged photo-ops, the media were co-opted as part of the military force:

---

26 This is one of the main themes of Jason Burke, *The 9/11 Wars*, Allen Lane, London 2011. **27** Jonathan Steele, *Defeat: Why They Lost Iraq*, I.B. Tauris, London 2008, ch. II. **28** On this issue, see Ibid., ch. VIII. **29** Adhaf Soueif, 'Mezzaterra', in Joe Sacco et al., *War With No End*, Verso, London 2007, p. 113.

> *one of the objectives of Operation Iraqi Freedom was to scare the enemy into submission. What better way to achieve this objective than to give Iraqis a televised view (courtesy of ABC) of the lines of 3rd Infantry Division tanks stretching beyond the horizon as they crossed into Iraq?*[30]

The 'shock and awe' display was only the most obvious example of a military action designed for lenses. The combination of censorship, both military and civilian, of embedding and military photo-ops led to a predominant view of the war that was about the experiences, courage, resilience, technological prowess and competence of the troops. The appalling consequences that the invasion and occupation caused for ordinary Iraqis—the collapse in basic services (power, clean water, medicine), the destruction of the environment and above all the encouragement of sectarian violence that brought death, abduction, rape and torture to almost every family in the country—all that, the greater story, went under-reported and under-represented.

The Media

Looking at the technology alone, this should be the golden age of photojournalism. Pictures of photojournalists in Vietnam show them festooned with cameras, each equipped with different lenses and film (zooms were then clumsy, heavy and of poor optical quality). Digital cameras today can automatically adjust the film speed setting to the available light, are much better than film in very low light, have rapid autofocus, and can be used with zooms that give good optical quality across a wide range. With a laptop and a satellite phone, pictures can be adjusted and sent to the publisher in minutes.

Yet the profession has been in long decline since the fall of the great illustrated magazines such as *Vu*, *Time* and *Picture Post* that had made their best photographers stars, and had lavished resources upon them. While the decline is old, and was caused by the rise of TV news, it has been exacerbated by other, newer features, not least the extraordinarily wide ownership of digital cameras (often integrated into phones), and the ease of sending such photographs which produced the rise of usually unpaid 'citizen-journalists'. Economically pressed news organisations often prefer to provide cameras (but little training) to willing locals rather than fly out professionals to a scene of conflict. Rates paid for the publication of newspaper photographs have been in steep decline. Foreign news—and indeed all hard news—has been

---

30 Paul and Kim, *Reporters on the Battlefield*, p. 54.

squeezed for resources and space by cheaper and more advertising-friendly features on lifestyle, products and celebrities.

The news media have long been conservative. Towards the end of the Vietnam War they faithfully reflected the split in elite opinion about the conduct and utility of the war, permitting, at least in print (much less on TV), limited dissent and the publication of brutal scenes of warfare. The appearance of such images would be quite unimaginable now. Following the neoliberal turn, the media have become much more conservative as they became concentrated in gigantic conglomerates, which look to their media arms to reinforce their commercial interests through cross-branding exercises.[31]

In his book *Flat Earth News*, Nick Davies argues that the news industries, and particularly the newspapers, have been remade as purely commercial concerns.[32] While the old press barons ran them for their influence over public opinion and state policy, and so took the quality of news seriously, profit is now the prime motive. As a result, stories are covered with remarkable rapidity and there is little time or money to check or research. Papers tend to relay the material handed down from the international press agencies (which are themselves subject to the same pressures) and PR agencies, including of course the military. The extension of the news media into the online realm and into 24-hour news intensifies these pressures. As a result, aside from the sheer quantity of PR fabrication that sails into publication, received opinions are the quickest and easiest to convey, and cliché reigns. These pressures affect the context in which photojournalism is seen, its captions and accompanying stories. The photographs take their place in a press that has become degraded in public opinion as unreliable, gullible and venal—not so much a guardian as a polluter of public life.

Davies rightly argues that the fate of the news media under this set of priorities is disastrous for readers and for society itself.[33] Once again, this is an area in which the operation of unrestrained capitalism works against democracy. With our current wars, it allows the exercise of brutal and totalitarian methods against those unfortunate enough to live in areas of strategic importance under inconvenient dictators. The US has engaged in the kidnapping, torture and murder of those it has chosen as its opponents. Gulags, secret and in the public eye, have been set up across the globe. Children have been seized and

---

31 This is the main argument of Robert W. McChesney, *Rich Media, Poor Democracy: Communication Politics in Dubious Times*, The New Press, New York 2000. **32** Nick Davies, *Flat Earth News*, Chatto & Windus, London 2008. **33** Davies, *Flat Earth News*, pp. 396–7.

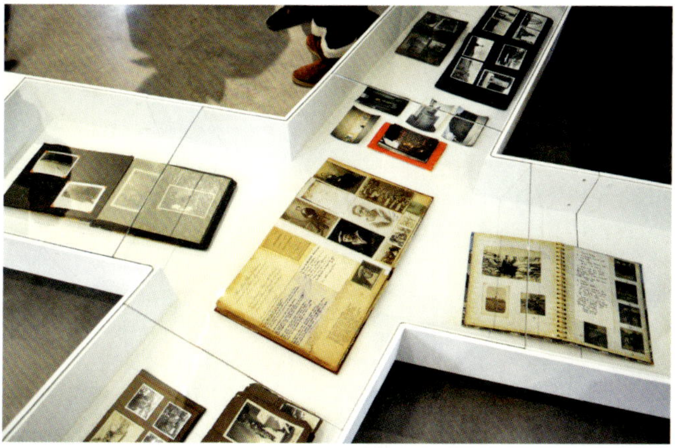

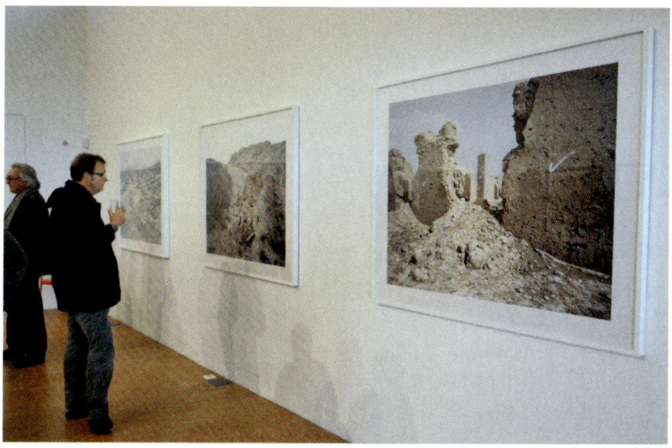

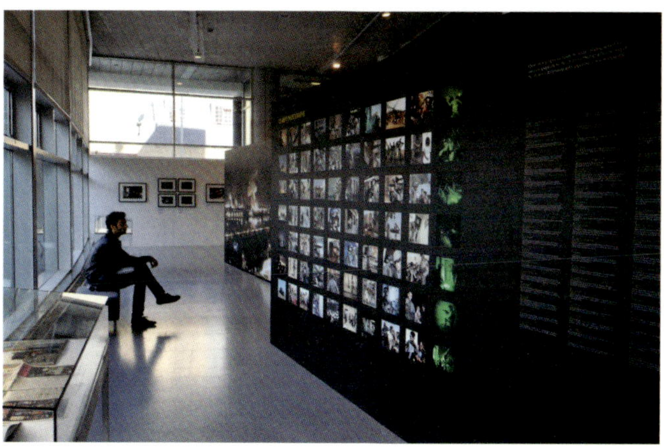

Top Brighton Photo Biennial 2008: Julian Germain, *War Memorial*, Aspex Gallery, Portsmouth
Middle Paul Seawright's work as shown at *The Sublime Image of Destruction*, De La Warr Pavilion, Bexhill-on-Sea
Bottom *Iraq Through the Lens of Vietnam*, University of Brighton Gallery. All photos by Julian Stallabrass

held to extort information from their parents.[34] These are tactics worthy of the Nazis, yet they pass with little comment through the democratic press, at least in the nations of the combatants, and (as we have seen) with little published photographic representation.

Against this scenario of the failing power of critical images within the mainstream media, the image world is being changed by the increasing circulation of amateur photographs and video. The camera has long been a weapon of war in the hands of amateurs. It has been used to make propaganda, take trophies and humiliate enemies. Here is one episode from Eduardo Galeano's *Memory of Fire*, his 500-year account of colonial oppression and resistance in Latin America:

> 1923: Buenos Aires
> Snapshot of a Worker Hunter
> *He peruses the firearms catalogues lasciviously, as if they were pornography. For him the uniform of the Argentine army is as beautiful as the smoothest of human skin. He likes skinning alive the foxes that fall into his traps, but prefers making target practice of fleeing workers, the more so if they are reds, and more yet if they are foreign reds.*
>
> *Jorge Ernesto Pérez Millán Temperley enlisted as a volunteer in the troop of Lieutenant Colonel Varela, and last year marched to Patagonia for the sport of liquidating any strikers who came within range. Later, when the German anarchist Kurt Wilckens threw the bomb that blew up Lieutenant Colonel Varela, this hunter of workers swore loudly to avenge his superior.*
>
> *And avenge him he does. In the name of the Argentine Patriotic League, Jorge Ernesto Pérez Millán Temperley fires a Mauser bullet into the chest of Wilckens as he sleeps in his cell, then has himself immediately photographed for posterity, gun in hand, striking a martial pose of duty done.*[35]

Many of the troops in Vietnam (exterminating a people they often termed 'Indians'), carried cameras and regularly took photographs of the atrocities that they had committed. A US nurse recounts wounded GIs regularly showing her pictures:

---

34 Philip Morris and Errol Gourevitch, *Standard Operating Procedure*, Pan Macmillan, London 2009, p. 115. **35** Eduardo Galeano, *Memory of Fire*, trans. Cedric Belfrage, Quartet Books, London 1995, p. 674.

> *This usually happened at night, because then everybody was asleep or at least quiet. I'd go over and sit at the side of some guy's bed and he'd pull out a cardboard box full of pictures. I knew from the start that we would get around to the atrocity photos. It happened every time. They took pictures of the things they did.*[36]

These pictures were a form of souvenir taking, alongside looting and the collecting of body parts. The soldiers' albums all seemed to contain the same shots, wrote Michael Herr, the 'obligatory Zippo lighter shot' of Marines burning homes, the severed head shot, or lines of heads in a row with a burning cigarette in each of the mouths, the NLF suspect being tortured, the very young dead with weapons in hands, Marines holding ears, dead women with pyjamas stripped off and 'legs raised stiffly in the air'. 'Half the combat troops in Vietnam had these things in their packs'.[37]

Those photographs, physical prints, stayed in their packs, and were passed around between trusted comrades, secret and eventually secreted or destroyed. When the same habits were pursued with digital media, most notoriously at the jail at Abu Ghraib, control over the circulation of this imagery was lost. Torture was unveiled, alongside photography as torture.

The Field of Images

This was the field into which the Biennial was launched, and its main aim was to offer through a series of diverse exhibitions a view of the differentiated scope of war photography, both historically and in its current diversity. Historically, the Biennial took in the First World War photographs of Frank Hurley, including his controversial montages, which sought to convey the simultaneity of events on the battlefield that were beyond the capabilities of the camera and film technology of his day. Julian Germain, working in Portsmouth with military families, showed a display of photographs taken by soldiers and other military personnel that spanned the British intervention in the Russian Civil War, through the various world and colonial wars of the twentieth century and beyond. Amateur imagery, including the Abu Ghraib images and photographs relayed by the Iraqi resistance, featured in the exhibition that compared the image wars of Vietnam and Iraq. Geert van Kesteren selected and presented photographs that Iraqis took on phone cameras. Photojournalism was shown against museum photography and artists' installations. Campaigning

---

36 As quoted in Mark Baker, *Nam*, London 1982, p. 151. **37** Michael Herr, *Dispatches*, Picador, London 1978, p. 161.

humanist documentary (Philip Jones Griffiths' *Agent Orange* series and Harriet Logan's work on women in Afghanistan) was seen against the work of committed Latin American revolutionaries and Cuban poster-makers. Above all, causal links between these contrasts were suggested: that the images made out of the embedding system in Iraq were the product of a military effort to make a war and an abiding set of pictures that would forever banish the memory of Vietnam and the restraints it set on the exercise of US power; that museum photographs took on structurally opposed characteristics to those usually found in photojournalism; that amateur images, similarly, had a force and a distinct aesthetic that reverberated in and affected the image world as a whole.

Contemporary photojournalism exceeded, as it always has, the bounds of the main outlines of its publication in the mass media, and some photographers (including some of those embedded) evolved sensitive and intelligent responses to the terrible situation in Iraq. We may get some sense of its place in the current variety of war photography by comparing photojournalism with these other types; against the stately, reserved, severely composed 'aftermath' images that dominate the depiction of war in the museum, photojournalism embodies speed and intimacy, both of which are written into its style as well as its content. In photojournalism, the focus falls above all on the face, and on readable emotion. Against citizen journalism and the ghastly amateur productions of the troops, photojournalism embodies professional values; while its aesthetic often encompasses the apparently casual, its bears the sheen of photographic competence, and the visual quality of high-definition digital cameras or fine film and sharp lenses. As against official military photography (which shares the same production values) it has too great a variety to be dismissed as mere propaganda, and does not so readily fall into generic categories. When on occasion an openly propagandistic image is made by a photojournalist (as with Luis Sinco's famous portrait of a Marine smoking in Fallujah), it is the subject of controversy as well as celebration. As against the photographs of atrocity, of the bloodied corpses of those blasted by modern weaponry that circulate in certain magazines and websites, published photojournalism is tempered and restrained, standing on its dignity.

If there is a governing aesthetic here, it is modelled on the notorious work of James Nachtwey, and is the shallow assemblage of visually striking elements into arresting combinations before the lens, and the sublime spectacle of the remarkable ability to do this under very dangerous conditions. It is clear from the presentation of Nachtwey's photographs in exhibitions and in his book *Inferno* that the pictures are considered to be first Nachtwey's and only secondarily images of the specific events that they depict.[38] When photojournalism goes beyond this play with form and shadow, it is because the photographer has matched a deeper political intelligence about the subject with an evolving aesthetic, and this hard-won synthesis, perhaps because of the pressure to produce daily spectacle, is relatively rare.

It is unsurprising, then, that widespread suspicion surrounds such products. News management by the state and the military has made people sceptical of the manufactured images that they see in newspapers and on TV. The ease and speed with which digital photography can be altered (along with a few well-publicised examples of photojournalists doing just that), and increased awareness of the extent to which meaning can be manipulated by selective framing, produces deep scepticism about war photography. In blogs, the meanings of imagery are debated passionately and often furiously, with political partisans of all persuasions finding reasons to dismiss any photographic evidence laid before them which challenges their views. Here, at least, photojournalism is thought to matter.

The most fundamental divide separating our Western media world from that of the Vietnam era is the lack of a strong opposition with a cogent world view that could assemble the evidence, words, pictures and video (of which there are a multitude) into a condemnation of the war that could not be ignored, that would gnaw at us and torture us as it did Chomsky and so many others. The war in Iraq has not so much ended as been privatised, with troops being replaced by mercenaries, and the nation is still bloodied by sectarian violence; in Afghanistan a deeply corrupt and unpopular regime is propped up by foreign troops with predictably dire consequences. Yet the sheer intensity of commercial competition in a symbiosis with war imagery (from celebrity culture to YouTube to the fictional renderings of the 'war on terror' such as *24* and *Zero Dark Thirty*), the speed of gossip and self-fashioning through trivia, makes it too easy to forget that bloody subterranean murmur which should stain our whole experience.

So it seemed necessary to rearrange corpses. Such acts violate the implicit edicts against curatorial tinkering with images of trauma (aesthetic tinkering is permitted, and indeed encouraged, if you bear the label 'artist'); and also against displaying in galleries images which may be complicit with violence, or were made as a part of dealing out violence.

The point of those objections can be grasped in the many unattractive statements made by journalists, crowing over some scoop that had involved

---

38 James Nachtwey, *Inferno*, Phaidon, London 1999.

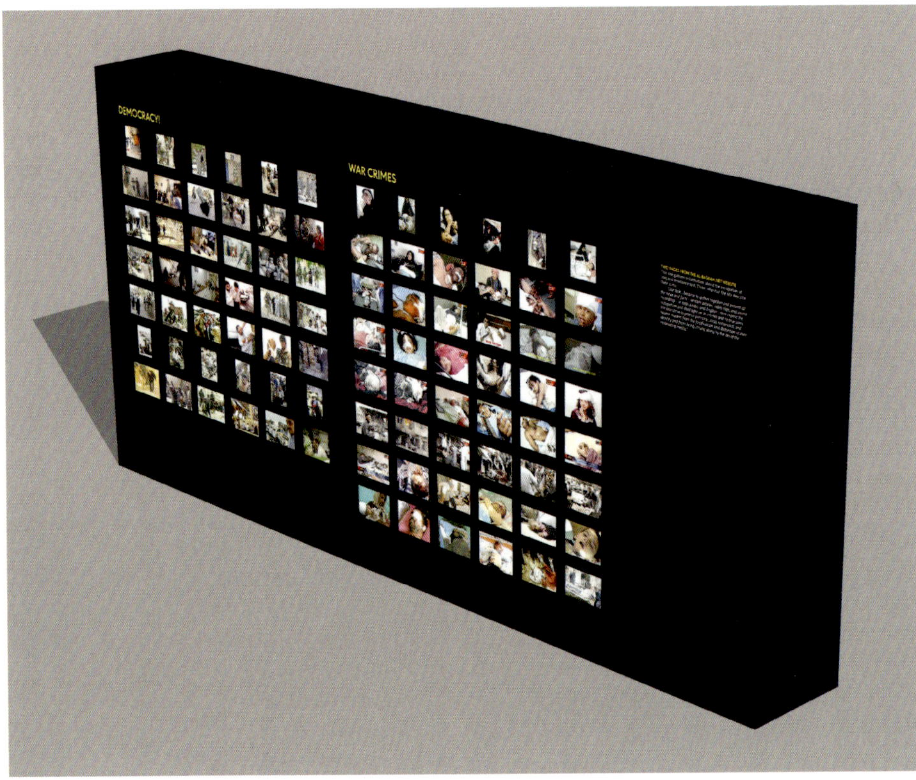

Design for the wall of images showing two pages from the Al-Basrah.Net website. This site gathers information about the occupation of Iraq and resistance to it. As shown at *Iraq Through the Lens of Vietnam*, University of Brighton Gallery, Brighton Photo Biennial, 2008

tragedy for its subjects. To take a single example, Evan Wright of *Rolling Stone* magazine was embedded with the US Marines, and had witnessed a young, trigger-happy troop-member firing at civilians. He later came across the bloodied victims:

> *Again, being a reporter, I'm thinking in the back of my mind, 'This is gruesome. This is awesome. This is perfect. I've got everything now. This is the honest truth. I was there when the shooting happened, and everyone knew that Trombley was the one who shot them'.*[39]

The 'gruesome'/ 'awesome' combination is telling about the journalist's yearning for blood, but is it right to judge the 'awesome' as merely the voice of journalistic ambition? After all, Wright's delight at getting the story was a feeling that comes from fitting events together to establish cause and effect, as well as to seize upon a narrative that has the force of recognisability: the consequences of putting young men, raised on bloodthirsty war movies and games, brutalised by Marine training and the very ethos of the Corps, into a battleground which is the home of civilians. So while the triumphalism of Wright's statement may be ugly, there is something about his activity which is valuable: making sense of a situation which goes beyond the immediate, one-thing-after-another accounts that characterised much embedded reporting.

So there is, first, the 'rearrangement of corpses' to makes sense of their deaths—and to do so politically, militarily, socially and ideologically. This is surely an essential task of any curation that dares to broach such topics. But what of aesthetic ordering? What does it mean to make such images look good, either individually or when seen alongside others? One model of a response is seen clearly in the work of Thomas Hirschhorn, not least in *The Incommensurable Banner* (see pp. 140–1), which was exhibited at Fabrica in Brighton. This is a protestor's banner writ large, which (like Brian Haw's display in Parliament Square, before its destruction by the police) contains a collage of corpses torn apart by modern weaponry. Such weaponry has been developed not merely to kill, but to destroy the body, and the horrific remains are left as a lesson for those tempted to resist further. The underground circulation of these images, online and in disreputable magazines, has a similar function to the placement of torture chambers by the Latin American dictatorships in the centre of cities: that the consequences of opposition should be known by all without being officially broadcast.

---

39 Katovsky and Carlson, eds., *Embedded*, p. 336.

The roughness of Hirschhorn's work—its lack of finish, its overtly cheap materials and spatchcocked construction, which always reveals its own methods—would seem to blunt the aesthetic. These elements set his work and its politics apart from the carefully made and polished art objects that are sold out of galleries flanked by other shops purveying jewellery, antique furniture, tailored clothes and other domestic accoutrements of the rich. With Hirschhorn's exploration of the worst images of warfare, this rough and open method of working matches the vulgarity of its photographic sources, which in many other pieces are juxtaposed with commercial imagery, including pornography. Whether these pieces are exactly composed is open to question: Hirschhorn has said that he wants to 'give form' but not to 'make forms', a formulation that implies a privileging of meaning over beauty, and is backed up by the artist's frequent references to protest culture.[40]

Yet the aesthetic cannot be banished quite so easily. As the first photographic formalists discovered, there is a large overlap between photographic qualities which may be taken as aesthetic and the functional characteristics of the medium. The strictures of the Group f/64 manifesto, for example, produced a particular aesthetic result, but also one—in the insistence on contact printing, sharp focus, maximum depth of field and full tonal range—that yielded a level of descriptive detail never before seen. In attempting to fix on the essential characteristics of photography, these avant-gardists could not but make finer-grained descriptions of the world. Fine printing for the gallery prints shown in the Biennial aided the clarity and visibility of the subjects depicted, while simultaneously ensnaring an aesthetic outlook with its own history and ideology. There was a danger that some of the objects on show in the gallery setting would be taken as works of art, recommended by some intellectual and aesthetic authority. So the aesthetic is both unavoidable and perilous, and it is best to be conscious of it, to highlight it and declare it openly.

There is, however, a deeper objection to any rearrangement, and it is particularly pertinent to photography: these images are not merely generic products of the war machine but are also depictions of particular people suffering a particular act of violence or humiliation. A photograph of a boot stamping on a head is not just an invocation of Orwell but shows a perpetrator with a name, a victim with a name, and a specific time, place and circumstance, from which a portion of light has reflected into a lens. Is it right to handle

---

40 From an interview with Hirschhorn by Craig Garrett, 'Thomas Hirschhorn: Philosophical Battery', *Flash Art*, no. 238, October 2004.

these representations for instrumental purposes, rather than present them as what they are in themselves, and with as full an elaboration of their particular details as possible? In a less bloody and dramatic key, this problem infects the whole of curating, for are not art works themselves (on one view) delicate and particular emanations of a unique sensibility, best set down tenderly and at a distance from contamination by other works or interference by extraneous thoughts?

The model on which this Biennial was based is in explicit opposition to that view: as against art events which dare not throw a cage of cogency about their contents, this Biennial set out to be about something, and to have something definite to say. Its title ('Memory of Fire: Images of War and the War of Images') is plainly descriptive, as against those many curatorial 'concepts' that have only the virtue that they do not exclude anything (a couple of recent examples: 'Think with the Senses, Feel with the Mind' and 'Tales of Time and Space').[41] The corollary of this position, to take a standpoint, is that viewers had the opportunity to respond publicly to what they saw—on the Biennial website and in comments books—and many did so.

I am also not convinced of the need to treat all objects with equal consideration and gentleness. Alongside museum photography, the Biennial showed photojournalism that has achieved some status in the art world (by figures such as Larry Burrows and Don McCullin), along with current photojournalism that has not, and some that perhaps never will; photographs taken by members of the armed forces, both those serving as professional photographers and the many amateurs, including the Abu Ghraib pictures; and photographs built into many contexts in magazines, newspapers and on the Web. Obviously, not all of this material is recommended aesthetically or otherwise, except to say that it is worthy of critical attention. Much of the material is overtly generic—this becomes apparent, for example, in a trawl through the thousands of images of the Iraq War on the US Army site, in which a definite series of genres emerges, from ball games played with Iraqi children to the heroic soldier shot from below, to displays of military competence, to technophile lingering over high-tech equipment, to soldiers silhouetted against the setting sun. A large number of these images were printed in a grid to highlight their generic character, so that they would be seen as particular

---

41 These were the titles respectively of the Venice Biennale of 2007 and the Folkestone Triennial of 2008. Two recent books about curating offer principled defences of the events and exhibitions that resist cogent concepts: Paul O'Neill, *The Culture of Curating and the Curating of Culture(s)*, MIT Press, Cambridge, MA, 2012; Terry Smith, *Thinking Contemporary Curating*, Independent Curators International, New York 2012.

examples of a type, and not (as the art work is habitually, if wrongly, seen) as unclassifiably unique.

In displaying such a variety of images, I hoped that an interplay of particularity and generality would emerge. Some of the difficulties of doing this were raised in discussions about the inclusion in an exhibition, 'The Sublime Image of Destruction', of an image of a wounded child by Simon Norfolk (see p. 5). Both Norfolk and I wanted to show the image because it frankly described the consequences of the war. Norfolk had been encouraged to take the picture by Iraqis at the scene, doubtless for similar reasons. Nevertheless, the proposed enlargement of the image to museum photography scale, and that it should be displayed under the concept of the sublime troubled the artist and the curators at the De La Warr Pavilion. How did the image, with its focus on the face of an individual, fit with the more general scenes of ruination in the exhibition? What did the inflation of size do to its meaning as the depiction of an individual? Had the child survived (viewers would surely want to know)? We eventually decided not to include the print. But our uncertainty about this image raised the difficulty of keeping both particularity and generality in the mind: that the cruelties depicted are typical, and that they happen to individuals—to this child, who should not be reduced to an icon of the general.

So the question was how to balance this interplay curatorially, and whether doing so necessarily involves aesthetics. Clarity of depiction is an aid to grasping particularity, and also unavoidably an aesthetic quality. Photojournalism, which was at the heart of the Biennial, has its own strongly generic characteristics, for example in its fixation on the event, the gesture and especially the expressive face. Again, this is a descriptive and aesthetic matter. Through juxtaposition across exhibitions and the website, the Biennial attempted to bring into view a larger structural picture, one which allowed comparison and contrast, and encouraged critical examination of different generic forms of image production.

A biennial of a few exhibitions and events was, of course, powerless to alter the large forces it described and analysed. It set out to provide some resources for thinking about the range of war imagery, and the role that photojournalism plays in the media and democratic politics. For if, through the actions of our troops and allies abroad, we act like Nazis, and if that cannot be grasped conceptually or in pictures, and if it does not cause a fundamental questioning of our political system, then something somewhere about our democracy is broken.

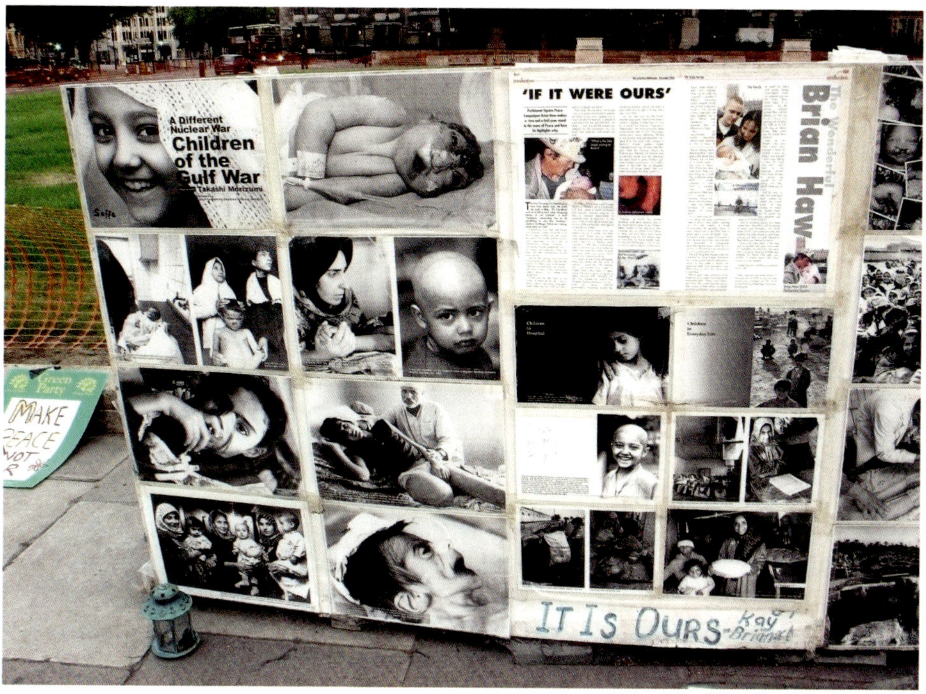

Anonymous photograph, Part of Brian Haw's protest installation, Parliament Square, London, 2001–6

Interview with **Philip Jones Griffiths**

Geert van Kesteren/Brigitte Lardinois/Julian Stallabrass

Philip Jones Griffiths was one of the foremost documentary photographers of his generation. His landmark book, *Vietnam Inc.*, was the most systematic and politically acute book of photography about the war, and still serves as a model for the possibilities of engaged and radical documentary. His recent books, *Agent Orange* and *Viet-nam at Peace*, chart the continuing and dire environmental effects of the war, and conditions in the newly business-friendly nation. The republication of *Vietnam Inc.* has made it available to a new generation of anti-war activists in a period of intense ideological struggle over the production and circulation of images. This interview took place at Magnum's London offices in 2007.

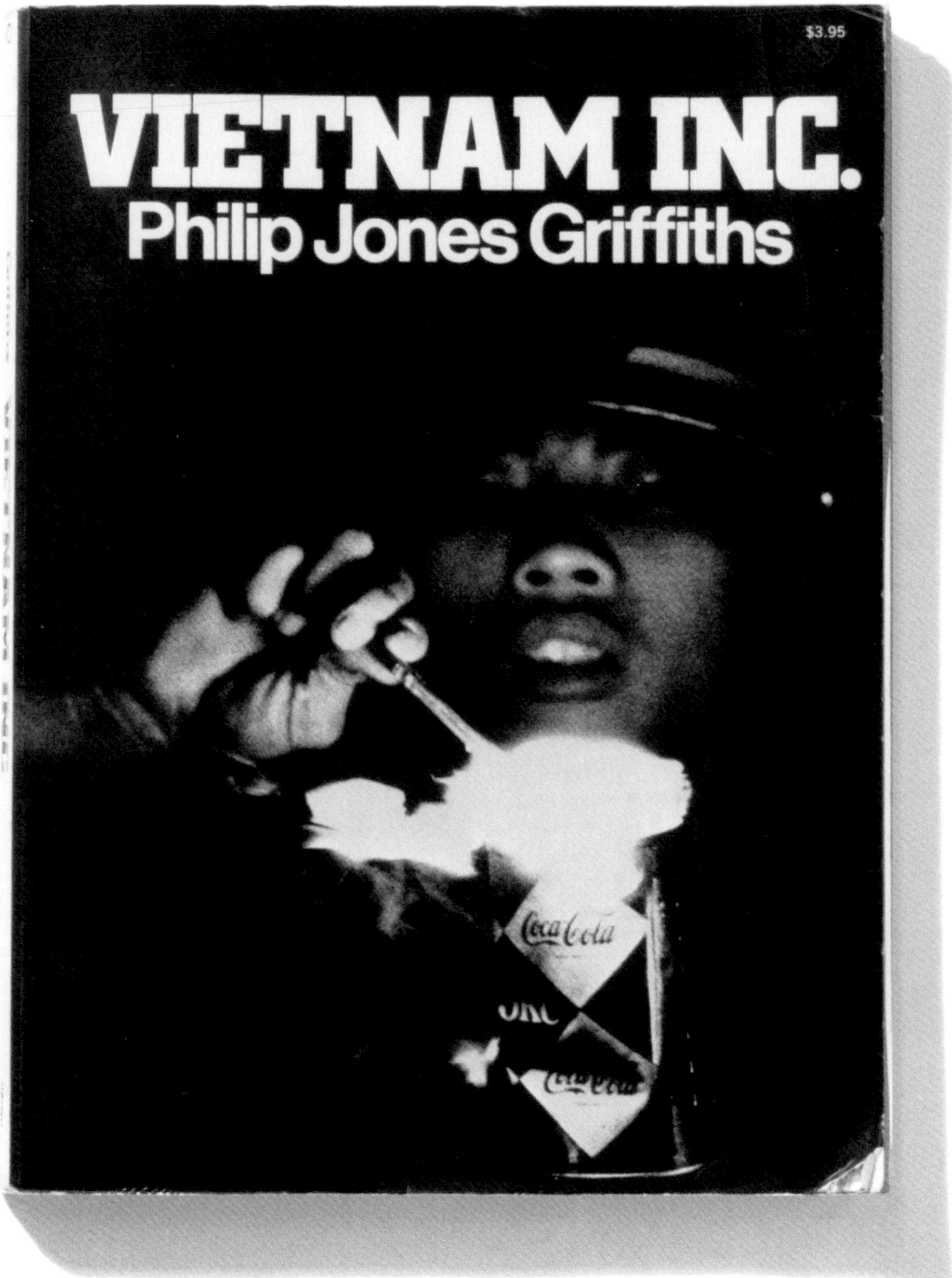
$3.95
VIETNAM INC.
Philip Jones Griffiths
Coca-Cola

Julian Stallabrass One of the extraordinary things about both books, *Vietnam Inc.* and *Agent Orange*, is their political intelligence. I find it hard to think of other photojournalists who have such a developed view of the world that is reflected in each picture and the way it is used.

Philip Jones Griffiths On Fleet Street, I was told to go after 'who, what, why, where and when', and it didn't take it long for me to work out that 'why' was the only important one. Also, when I was about eight or nine years old, I had my first lesson in political awareness. American jeeps arrived in our little school in Wales, all these huge soldiers emerged, the first black people I had ever seen. They made us all stand in a line and gave us a Mars bar each, and I wondered: what's going on, what are they trying to do? Who would have thought that all those years later I would be photographing them doing exactly the same thing in Vietnam? And without it being rammed down our throats in any way, we were always conscious in Wales that there were two societies. There were us, the Welsh, who were being quickly overtaken by the English coming over the border, especially the holidaymakers during the summer. So I grew up with a keen appreciation of the ills of hegemony.

JS In terms of what you were reading during the war, was the position in *Vietnam Inc.* something that you just worked out for yourself while taking the pictures? Did you have links with the anti-war movement?

PJG No, none whatsoever. I distrusted them in a way because I grew up in the ban-the-bomb period in Britain, and one became suspicious of those weekend, armchair communists. One often felt that the people who were most vociferously anti-war were not those who had resolved their own problems first. I approached Vietnam rather like chemist analysing an unknown substance in a pharmaceutical exam. When I arrived I methodically travelled the whole country to try and work out what was going on. Looking back on it, I tried to approach it very logically so that when I would see a group of refugees being forced at gunpoint from their homes, and the officer would turn to me and say, 'Oh, it's great to see these people voting with their feet', I would start laughing. Marched off to camps surrounded by barbed wire and with a big sign over the gates saying 'Welcome to Freedom' was, apart from anything else, amazingly funny, and it didn't make sense, it didn't add up. It was pretty obvious that all Vietnamese hated the Americans.

Bridgitte Lardonois *All* Vietnamese?

PJG Yes. Of course, there were pockets of people who were less anti-American, the Catholics, for instance, in the South, but even they, when you really got to know them, would become very critical. So why weren't the Vietnamese blowing up the Americans all the time, why weren't they carrying out acts of violence? It would have been so easy to do so—all the bars, all the cafes were open and it would have been so easy to just toss a grenade in, as they did in the Algerian war. But nobody did. So why didn't they? The whole thing had to be directed in some way, there

had to be some mechanism at work, and my obsession became to try to understand what it was.

In my third year there, I did something that came about because a young American gave me a story that ended up on the front page of *The New York Times*. An American senior district advisor, as they were called, was using villagers to clear mine fields: 'they planted the things, they should know where they are' was his attitude. He was forcing the villagers to walk in front of the troops, with the result that they had more legless people there than anywhere else. The young American had helped me get the pictures, and we got Gloria Emerson to do the text. The guy who gave me the story was immediately fired and was pretty penniless so I hired him as my assistant. I told him that I wanted to go on a trip from one end of Vietnam to the other but the only condition was that he could not speak one word of Vietnamese (for he was fluent), all he was to do was listen. It was absolutely amazing to discover what people were actually saying. It was such a confirmation of what I had assumed all along. It was a great affirmation that I had worked it out correctly; that almost everything the Americans said, all the positive things they claimed about their effect in Vietnam, were simply not true. I felt that somehow I had passed an exam and was therefore qualified to write my book.

JS One of the most striking things about *Vietnam Inc.* was the use of text in the book, both the extended captions to the pictures and the longer texts on various subjects with which you punctuate the picture sequences.[1] At that time in the late 1960s and early 1970s and even earlier, at least implicitly in the work of photographers like Robert Frank, there was a critique of photojournalism and documentary of the classic type, of the broad and unspecific humanism of Henri Cartier-Bresson and Dorothea Lange, and part of that critique was about the detachment of photographs from framing texts. How aware were you of that critique?

PJG Well, I was aware of it because I absorbed everything that I could find. I was familiar with Ed van der Elsken's photographic novel, *Love on the Left Bank*.[2] There was a lot of text in it, except I couldn't read it because it was in French or Dutch. One was also aware that Frank was putting out images that were simply there as images, that had no text and no signposts whatsoever. But at the same time, Eugene Smith was practically writing poems instead of captions.[3] I had absorbed all of that, I suppose. What I tried to do in *Vietnam Inc.* was the old 'one-two': what I never do in the text is describe what's in the picture. It would be nonsensical to do that. And there are pictures in the book for which there are no captions—Magnum will complain about that. In the text pages, there are little pictures, and some of those have

---

1 Philip Jones Griffiths, *Vietnam Inc.*, Collier Books, New York 1971. **2** Ed van der Elsken, *Love on the Left Bank* André Deutsch, London, n.d. The book was first published in 1954 and there were editions in French and Dutch. **3** See, for example, W. Eugene Smith, *W. Eugene Smith: His Photographs and Notes*, Aperture, New York 1969.

Overleaf Philip Jones Griffiths, *Vietnam Inc.*, 1971: Government poster attached to the barbed wire fence of a 'refugee' camp that serves as a constant reminder of the hazards of rural life. No village would be foolhardy enough to fly the Vietcong flag, and no pilot was ever deterred from dropping his bombs by not seeing one

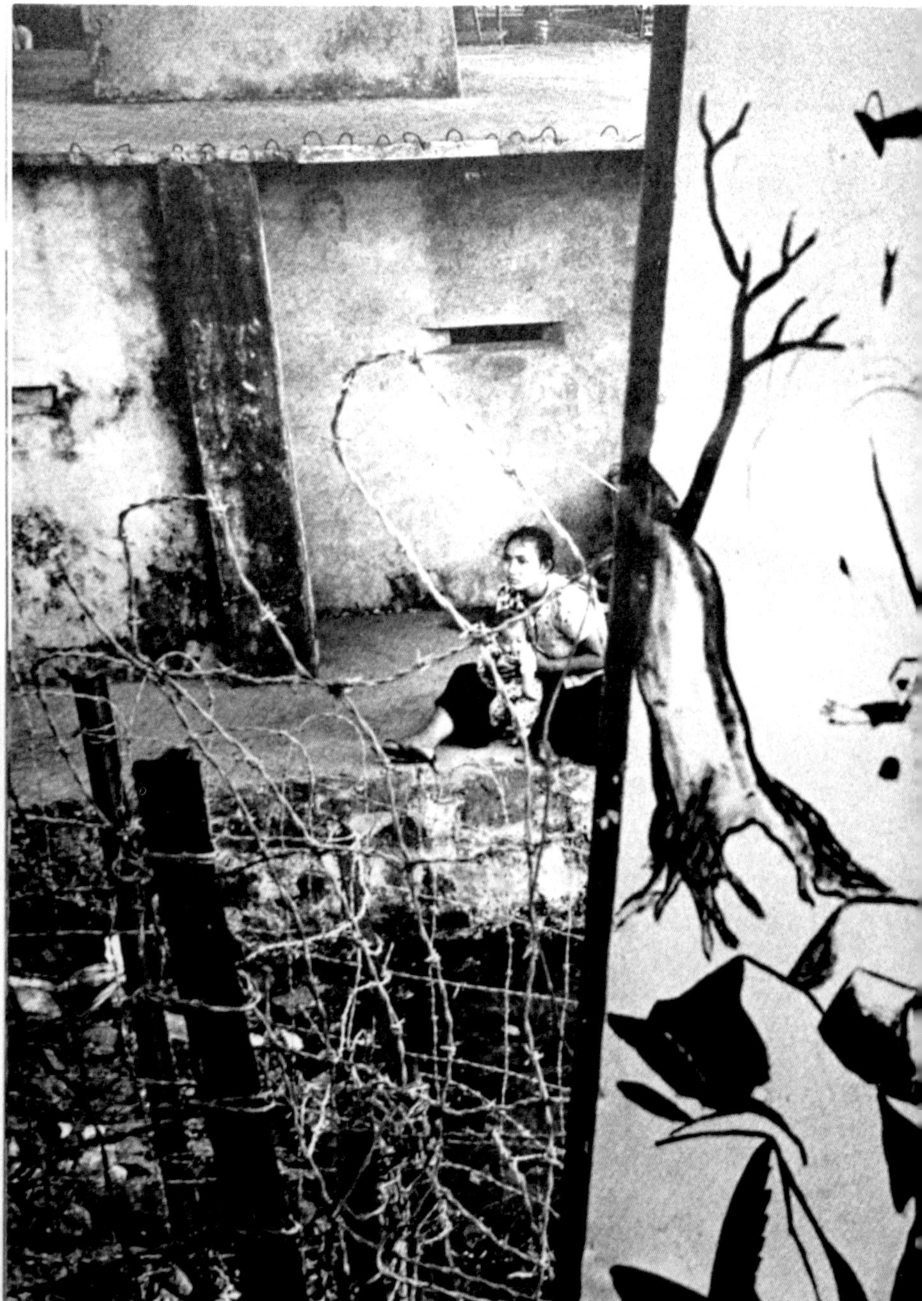

GOVERNMENT POSTER attached to the barbed wire fence of a "refugee" camp that serves as a constant reminder of the hazards o

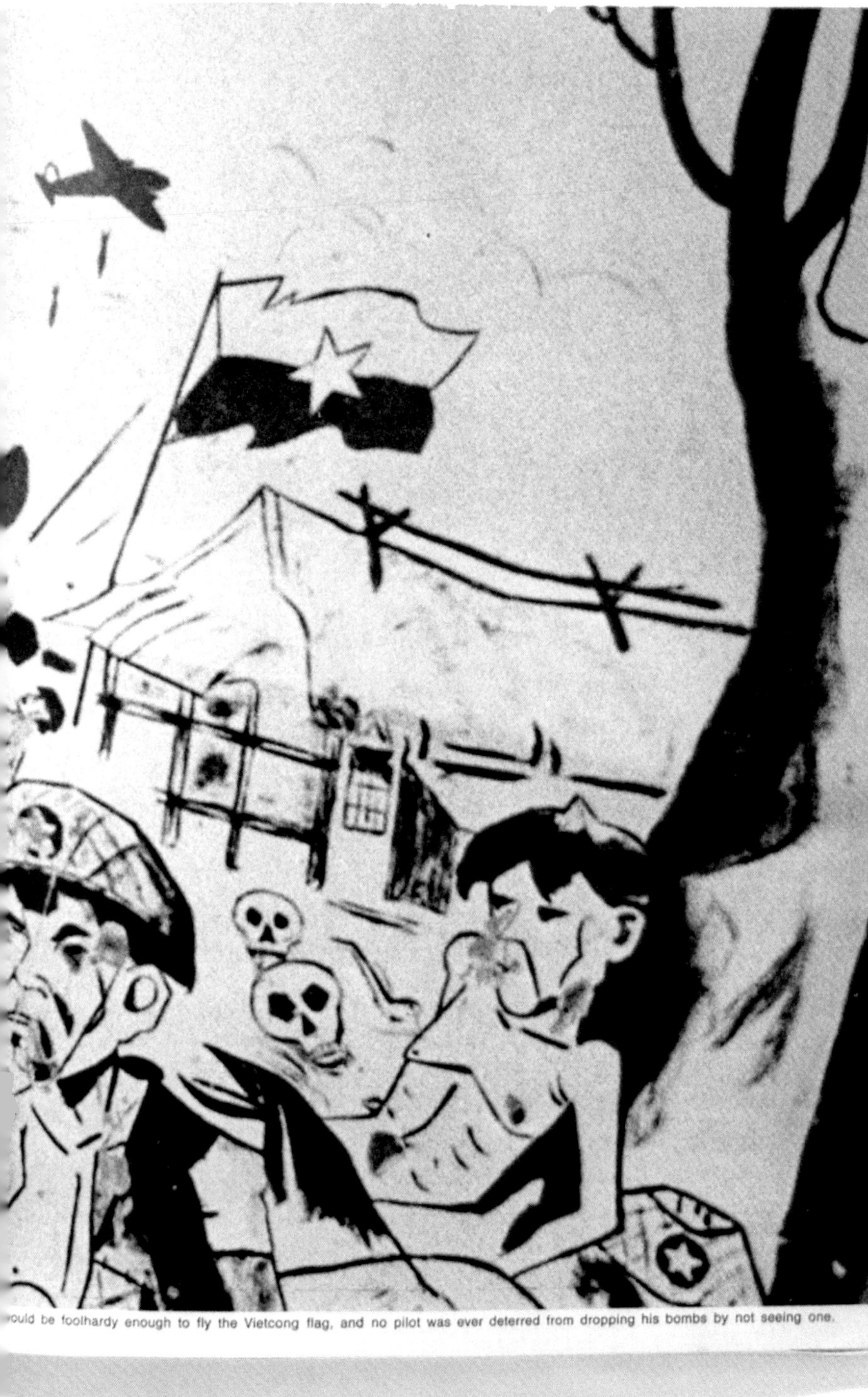

would be foolhardy enough to fly the Vietcong flag, and no pilot was ever deterred from dropping his bombs by not seeing one.

no captions—they are meant to be self-explanatory. For me, there was a greater possibility for putting over a message using words as well as photos. I wasn't setting out to turn the clock back, to say 'let's go back to long captions'.

JS The text is highly organised and very specific about its subjects. It is at the opposite end from the conventional caption that would just say 'Vietnam, 1968'. In this way, it prefigures other practices from photographers of the Left, such as Allan Sekula, who have built their photographs into extensive textual accounts of their subjects, such as *Fish Story* about global maritime trade.[4]

PJG I was always aware that captions channel communication. At *Look* magazine, they had a machine that would film people looking at the pages. They saw that people would glance at the pictures in a particular way—it had an S sweep or a Z sweep to it—and then they would read the caption and that was what they desperately wanted to see. In a sense, because they wanted to make sure that their perception of the picture was correct, so that the caption rewarded them for getting it right, exactly as in a quiz show. Captions still count. With *Vietnam Inc.* you can simply glance at the pictures, or you can go through it a second time and read the captions and a third time to read the text. It was specifically designed like that. What I wanted to avoid was huge blocks of text that no one would respond to.

BL You did the whole concept of the book and the entire layout. How did that work?

PJG It was very easy. The publishers gave me a designer and I took a box of prints to show him, and as we went through them, he said, 'Cor, she's got big tits!', so I went back to Collier Macmillan, saying I would very much like to design this book myself. They said: let's see what you can do. So I just did it.

JS The design does have a functional, sparse feel to it that suits its subject matter.

PJG There was a lot of criticism at the time about the number of pictures on a page, with people at Magnum saying, why don't you just publish your contact sheets? At the time a company had said to its sales people that if they sold a certain amount of goods, they could have their picture in *The New York Times*. About 5,000 did, so you opened *The New York Times* and it gave you an instant headache because they had printed all those tiny pictures on a huge spread. I woke up one morning and Burk Uzzle had pinned it up above my bed saying 'this could be the layout for your book'.[5] The general feeling then was that there were far too many pictures. Looking back on it now, I just don't agree.

JS I don't know if you have seen any of those websites about the Iraq War put up by the resistance and the anti-war movement; they often look like the spread you suggested with hundreds of pictures in a grid...

---

4 Allan Sekula, *Fish Story*, Richter Verlag, Düsseldorf 1995. **5** Burk Uzzle was a photographer with Magnum and president of the organisation 1979–80.

PJG I have seen these, yes...

JS And as you click on each, it brings up an enlarged version of the image. Their power is in their sheer repetition, of so many separate acts of oppression—US boots on Iraqi heads, for example—and of wounding and death.

PJG *Life* did a book on 9-11 where the cover is like that, all the faces of the victims, the size of each hardly bigger than dots, making up an image of the Stars and Stripes.[6]

BL It is hard for you to say, perhaps, but what is your view of the effect of *Vietnam Inc.*, did the book really shift the opinion of people at the time it appeared?

PJG 'The book that stopped the war' and all that...

BL That was the Magnum story at the time.

PJG But seriously, I think that it had a big effect. They did a huge print run and it sold out in a couple of weeks. There was a great appetite for the book. Collier Macmillan was—and still is—a very right-wing publishing house, and the people who ran it were all very pro-war, but there was this one guy who was the Vice-President whose son had been killed in Vietnam, and he said 'let's do the book'. The downside of that was that there was no support from anyone, and the antagonism I got from the production department was horrendous.

BL They saw you as a traitor?

PJG Yes, to give you an idea, if you have time, compare the text in the original version with the reprint.[7] The whole book was put together in upper New York State; Burk Uzzle had a farm up there. I had finished correcting the proofs and put them on the bus to New York. I phoned Collier Macmillan to tell them, and they said 'Oh, don't bother, we printed the book yesterday'. That was an example of how cavalier they were about the whole project. So in the original version there were many grammatical mistakes that I corrected for the new edition, though I didn't change the meaning of anything.

JS You hadn't been published before in the States, is that right?

PJG No, nothing.

BL Did the press immediately pick up on the book?

PJG Oh yes, it was reviewed in *The Times*, *The New York Times*, *Newsweek* and many other publications... The review in *Time* was pretty positive; the one in *Newsweek* was outrageous, saying I was obviously some kind of lunatic. It said: how dare he suggest that these brave ARVN soldiers are off to loot and rape in Cambodia?[8] That's exactly what they did—I know because I was there. And then they talked about a picture of a man who was about to be tortured and killed; and again, how could I write such dreadful things?

6 Editors of Life Magazine, *One Nation: America Remembers September 11, 2001*, Little, Brown, New York 2001. 7 *Vietnam Inc.* 8 Ibid., pp. 38–9.

JS You talk in one interview about how during Tet you photographed a man who was showing you his wounded child as you walked in step over a bridge.[9] Were there other times when your subjects, whether US or ARVN troops or civilians, actively contributed to the pictures? Were their times when they stopped you taking pictures?

PJG The only time I can remember being stopped was in an officer's mess when a young female dancer hired to entertain the men started feeding them pretzels in a rather original way.

The man crossing the bridge is also the only occasion I can recall of anyone contributing to a picture. Most of the time the Vietnamese acted the fool in front of the camera. I remember after a month 'in country' I wrote to a friend that I could publish a book on palmistry—children automatically lifted their hands in front of the lens whenever I put the camera to my eye. However, when people were scared, they tended to ignore the camera.

JS I know that you were not facing formal censorship but in general did you find restrictions about how many images you were able to publish and what rules did people lay down as you photographed them?

PJG There were no rules. Anything went, there was nobody telling me what I could and couldn't do. Once I had my little card that said I was a journalist, I could get on and off helicopters, people would feed me when I was in the field. I was very lucky because just by pure chance I met a guy who worked for the CIA. What happened was that in the 'Continental Shelf' as we used to call it, the place where everyone went for drinks after the daily briefing, I saw him trying to get a Nikon motor-drive to work. The Nikon motor drive was destined to make you believe in a higher power because it was almost impossible to get them to work. But I knew how to fix them. I fixed his, and he was very grateful. He explained that he was in charge of communications at the CIA and his job was to Xerox field reports that came in and send them off to the various departments. So I would meet him most weeks and he would hand me any reports that the CIA had written about me, and it was wonderful stuff: 'This correspondent is of the astonishing opinion that we generate refugees—keep an eye on him!'

So although I was never conscious of being followed or watched, obviously I was. But the main problem was not so much what I did but what got published. They had a very efficient system; the organisation was called JUSPAO (Joint United States Public Affairs Office) that got copies of every newspaper and magazine published in America shipped to Saigon. So they would check up whether a correspondent had a 'positive attitude' to the war or not. In my case, after a few months, they started to get suspicious because I wasn't publishing anything, and they started to ask whom I was working for. I had to send telegrams to Magnum saying that I had to get

9 *Vietnam Inc.*, p. 150; see Susan D. Moeller, *Shooting War: Photography and the American Experience of Combat*, Basic Books, New York 1989, pp. 355–6.

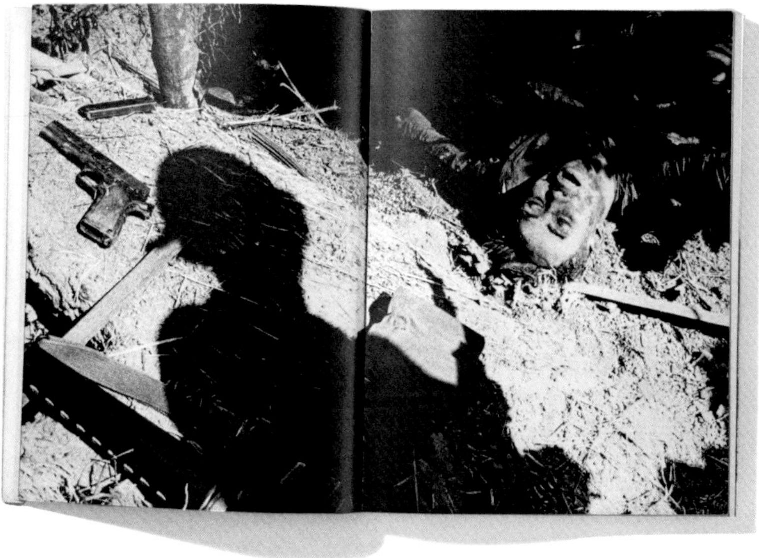

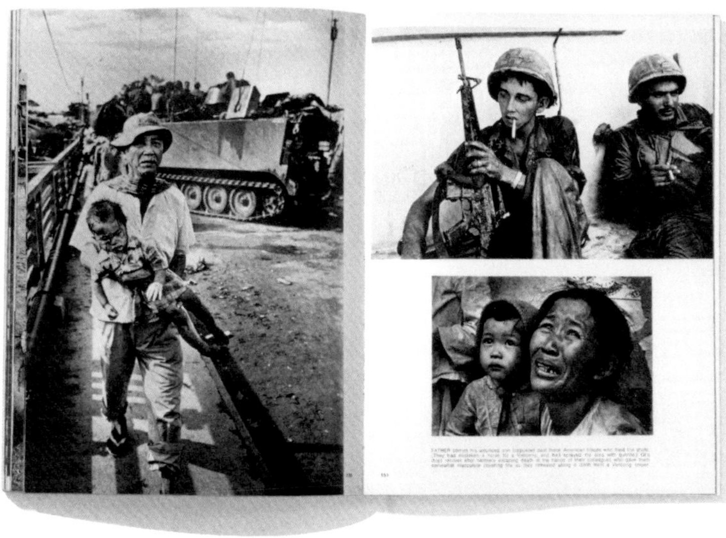

Top Philip Jones Griffiths, *Vietnam Inc.*, 1971: Quang Ngai, 1967. This guerrilla fighter had just thrown a grenade, killing one member of the platoon and wounding two others. In the resulting fracas, he too was killed. The incident occurred in what had once been a quiet hamlet in central Vietnam, probably in the very field in front of his home where he'd spent his youth tilling the soil
Bottom Philip Jones Griffiths, *Vietnam Inc.*, 1971: A father carries his wounded son past those American troops who had fired the shots. (They had mistaken a horse for a Vietcong and sprayed the area with gunfire)

something published to allay their suspicions. So Magnum did in fact get me two assignments and, once those pictures were published, I was no longer considered suspect. Those stories were relatively positive, in a sense.

JS They put your pictures into a pro-war frame?

PJG It was mutual I would say. One story was about Marines looking after refugees, which was obviously pro-war on one level, though they were not particularly nice to the refugees and the story did produce some critical pictures. The other was about a mobile inflatable hospital that could be shipped to a battle scene, very similar to those huge inflatable structures you see in New York a lot nowadays, where they play tennis. I did that story for *Look* magazine. It legitimised me, so I wasn't looked on as some MI6 plant.

JS As the war went on and you continued to publish work, did that change?

PJG No, because hardly any of the work was published. In those days, Magnum was two fiefdoms, Paris and New York. Paris was run by Marc Riboud who thought that I as a foreigner had no right whatsoever to be poking my nose into legitimate French foreign affairs. New York was run by Burt Glinn, who was a very interesting man insofar as his parents were solid communists of the John Reed era, so Burt went exactly the opposite way. He was convinced I was just some kind of commie, and it was very easy for him to get the office to push the work of some photographers and neglect others.

JS So when the book appeared, it was a bombshell.

PJG Absolutely, for everyone, including the people in Vietnam. I remember a wonderful Welshman called John Morgan who used to write for the *New Statesman*. He wrote, 'I was in Vietnam, I hung out with Philip quite a bit and never once saw him take a picture!' Though generally, I didn't hang out with the press. I lived with a Vietnamese family for much of the time.

JS Was this a usual thing for a photojournalist to do? Who were they and did they add to your understanding of the country?

PJG Most photojournalists rented apartments or lived in hotels. In my case the reason was primarily economic. The husband was a professor and the family were staunchly anti-communist, so I got to hear the latest gossip about the war from the side of the bourgeoisie.

I tried to be as low key as possible. In fact, on one occasion, I had become a non-person. I'd met this extraordinary journalist who had a fool-proof conspiracy theory about what was really happening in Vietnam. He told me that the following morning there would be a demonstration, the police would drag a young student into a building and then her body, covered in blood, would be handed back, resulting in the students going on the rampage. Anyway, it was highly structured; the girl they were going to throw out was not the same girl but a corpse they had found the day before.

Sceptical as always, I went along and everything happened exactly as he said, it was almost as if he'd organised the thing himself. So I found myself in the middle of this melee, in which everybody, including the foreign press, was getting the shit beaten out of them—all except me. An AP photographer, who was rather wisely standing down at the end of the street with a long lens, captured the moment and he got an amazing scene of everyone being kicked and punched and me in the middle with a 28[mm lens] shooting away untouched. Afterwards, when somebody saw the photograph, they were on their way to the American Embassy with a print to complain that the CIA was being far too obvious. At the last minute someone said: 'That's Phil! He's Welsh, he couldn't be in MI-anything'. Even to this day I don't know why I was unharmed. The Dutch *Life* photographer, Co Rentmeester, ran up as I was going into a school building to photograph some students. A policeman stopped him, while I was allowed in. He complained, 'I'm *Life* magazine and if he can go in, why can't I?' The policemen grabbed Co's camera and smashed off his 200mm lens with his truncheon. It was one of those strange, strange things that happened; but the point of telling the story is that no one knew my identity. I was unfamiliar enough not only to Americans who were going to report me to the Embassy for being CIA but to the Vietnamese who were equally confused. So keeping a low profile had really paid off.

JS Were journalists often attacked?

PJG Not by the NLF. There was a time in Hue, during the Tet Offensive, when I was in an alleyway with a US Marine. We were waiting to move quietly shortly after dark to a new position so that the NLF soldiers would not know where we were. The Marine was a large man wearing a flak jacket with a raised collar that protected his neck, so only a small part of his face showed above the jacket and beneath his helmet. He lifted his arm to wipe his brow and suddenly the contents of his chest were spilling over me. Because of his size, there was a gap at the side of his flak jacket and the sniper had put a bullet in there. He could have shot me at any time, but I had long hair, no weapons and was carrying cameras, so he didn't waste the bullet.

JS The NLF used their spies to find out where journalists were going and went out of their way not to harm them?[10]

PJG I don't know about that, but it's true that they would not deliberately target journalists.

BL Why was that? Because they knew they were against the war?

PJG No, I would say that 89 per cent of the journalists there were completely in favour of the war; another 10 per cent approved, but disagreed with US tactics; and a tiny number (Catherine Leroy and myself, really) were totally opposed

---

10 Tim Page, *Another Vietnam: Pictures of the War from the Other Side*, ed. Doug Niven and Chris Riley, National Geographic, Washington, DC, 2002, p. 46.

to it.[11] The authorities on the other side knew that it was in their interest to have the circumstances of the war exposed, even with those odds.

BL But you were barely published?

PJG True, but lots of others were. I think, looking back on it all, as Ho Chi Minh would say, from every disadvantage something positive emerges. I think if Magnum had been enthusiastically promoting the pictures I shipped and getting them published it's possible that the authorities in Saigon would have made life difficult for me. And perhaps I would never have got the pictures I finally ended up with. I didn't get one single picture published in any French newspaper or magazine during the whole war. And the best spread was in, of all places, the *Weekend Telegraph* magazine, and that only happened because John Ansty, the editor and the art editor were away and some student laid out the whole story. So little happened to alert the authorities.

Geert van Kesteren Did you make the book out of frustration that you couldn't get published?

PJG Not really, no. The single biggest mistake that a photographer can make is to believe in the profession, to believe in magazines and newspapers. When that happens, you have already failed. One must work first and foremost to satisfy oneself. And in my case I always knew my goal was a book on the war. I know so many colleagues who, now that the business has contracted, are learning Photoshop, scanning for other people or going into interior decorating, because they believed in *Life* magazine. What's *Life* magazine now? Four pages slipped into a newspaper somewhere in America—it's a disgrace. So the secret is to have a passion, stick to that passion and ignore the rest.

JS Can I ask you about the style of the pictures? A lot of them seem to be taken with quite wide-angle lenses; you mentioned a 28mm lens earlier, did you have anything wider than that and were you playing with those distortions, or was it rather a matter of necessity?

PJG The vast majority of the pictures were taken with a 35. I could probably tell you what lens each picture was taken with. There are certainly some pictures there taken with a 200 and a lot with a 105. I used to carry a very tiny bag; a couple of Leicas, one with a 28 and one with a 35. A Nikon with a 105 and one with a 200; and I had a spare 28 for the Nikon and a 21 for the Leica. Very few pictures were shot on the 21. In general, my feeling is that when you look at a picture, you should never really be conscious of what lens it was taken with. I don't have the genius of Cartier-Bresson who did it all on a 50. With something like that [US Marines tending a wounded troop member][12] I would have shot on a 105, partly because, with moments like

11 Catherine Leroy was a French photojournalist who worked in Vietnam from 1966. She edited *Under Fire: Great Photographers and Writers in Vietnam*, Random House, New York 2005. 12 *Vietnam Inc.*, p. 127.

that, you don't want to be on top of them with a 28, you want to give them a little distance.

There are virtually no cropped pictures —one or two. The picture of the people roped around the neck is cropped, not so much because of my ineptitude but because the horizon is at an angle.[13] The early picture of the woman with a sickle is also cropped a bit to get rid of a light area in the background.[14] But in general they are all full frame.

BL And in principle, you don't allow other people to crop your pictures.

PJG No, no. And in America one can be prosecuted for such deeds.

JS In terms of printing them, did you do a lot of work, dodging and burning...

PJG Yes, indeed. Though not in any way to distort the reality. But certainly in Vietnam one of the big problems is that people wear those big hats for a reason, and that is to keep off the sun, and the difference between the top and the underneath of the hat is something like five stops. In my darkroom you will find lots of sheets of black paper with different sized triangles cut out, trying to burn some detail in those hats!

JS The photographs are printed in a quite contrasty way; I suppose I am trying to get at the aesthetic choices you are making as well as the political ones and how you see them match up, if you think that they do.

PJG I have always tried to print in a fairly dramatic way if it fits the subject matter. I have printed pretty consistently and have not got darker or lighter as I've got older.

JS In terms of photographers who you looked to at the time you were working, who were the ones who meant most to you?

PJG It's boring to say, but obviously Cartier-Bresson is always the photographer one thinks of in terms of those big influences. I suppose some of that drama, that amazing drama, that one gets with Eugene Smith's printing techniques rubbed off along the way. What is interesting about *Vietnam Inc.* is that between a quarter and a third of the pictures were originally in colour.

JS Really! I was going to ask if colour ever tempted you...

PJG They were converted into black and white.

BL Why?

PJG Very early on there was an operation that took place—the pictures are in the book—of something called Cedar Falls in an area known as the Iron Triangle, and I photographed it, I think, very well.[15] *Life* laid it out over eight pages, so suddenly I was going to be rich. Then Magnum cabled me with the disastrous news that the magazine had some colour advertising and asking if I shot any colour. I said no, so they ran three pages

---

13 This volume, pp. 80–1; *Vietnam Inc.*, pp. 52–3. **14** *Vietnam Inc.*, pp. 6–7. **15** *Vietnam Inc.*, pp. 84–91.

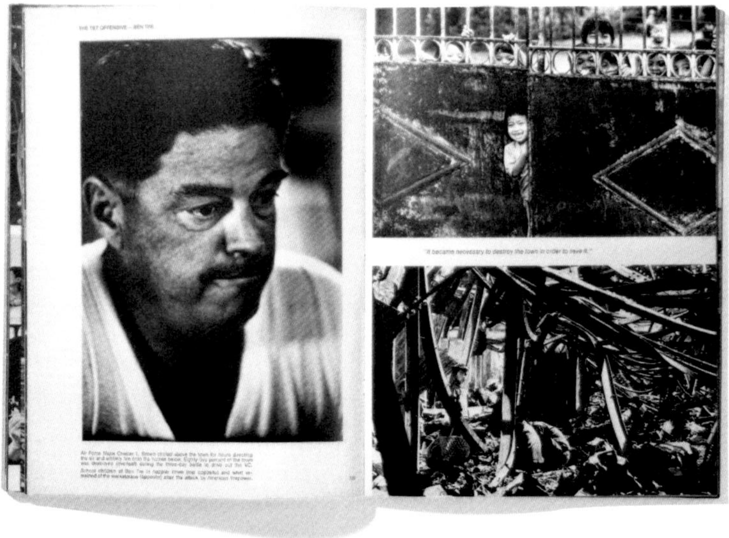

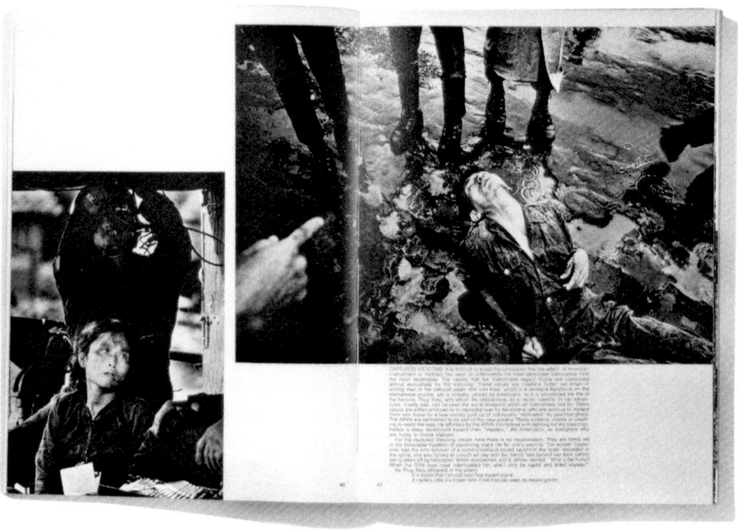

Top Philip Jones Griffiths, *Vietnam Inc.*, 1971: Ben Tre: 'It became necessary to destroy the town in order to save it.' Air Force Major Chester L. Brown circled above the town for hours, directing the air and artillery fire onto the homes below. Eighty-five per cent of the town was destroyed during the three-day battle to drive out the Vietcong
Bottom Philip Jones Griffiths, *Vietnam Inc.*, 1971: Wounded Vietcong, Cambodia, 1970

in colour by a stringer, but none of mine. That's in colour [picture of dead girl shot from a US helicopter].[16]

JS Tim Page was there shooting the same scene in colour and of course published it in colour.[17]

PJG I actually did print it in colour for the first time about a month ago for the *Sunday Times* exhibition.

BL Is this when Ian Berry also did a lot of colour to black-and-white conversion, for he has many famous pictures that are known in black and white though shot in colour?[18]

PJG I think that's right. We used to hang out together in the old days. You see, my pharmaceutical training was useful. When I used to run Magnum, I made sure we made black-and-white copies of all the colour work that came in, and those copies were usually good enough to make press prints and even sometimes exhibition prints. Generally for exhibitions you need to go to the original slide and make a 4x5 negative from it. I did something that few people would do, which was to use a lot of filters to change the relationship between the tones. Also I used to get a Beutler two-part developer from Germany so that if I had a very contrasty image I could develop it with essentially two different developers to reduce the contrast. A lot of my big exhibition prints were made from those 4x5 negatives.

JS You were never tempted to publish in colour?

PJG Though I started shooting a lot of colour after that incident, the only time they were published was in *Zoom* magazine in Paris, a large-format photo magazine, which wanted images of Vietnam in colour.

JS You were not inclined to use colour for *Agent Orange*, which you worked on for so many years?[19]

PJG No, it was tempting at times because many of the earlier images were in colour, and they were good colour in as much as they were well-lit Kodachromes. Using a slow film meant carrying those big heavy flashguns, powerful enough to bounce off ceilings so that the light doesn't look like flash. They converted well to black and white so, in the end, it seemed more consistent to do the whole book in monochrome.

JS Did you use flash a lot?

PJG Only when I was using colour. In fact, in *Vietnam Inc.* there is only one solitary picture taken with flash. When I went back to Vietnam in 1980, I had to shoot colour, and that was all done on Kodachrome. Ceilings are usually

---

16 *Vietnam Inc.*, pp. 118–19. **17** 'Twelve-year-old girl mini-gunned by US choppers in the abattoir near Y-Bridge, mini-Tet, Saigon, '68' in Tim Page, *Tim Page's Nam*, Thames and Hudson, London 1983, p. 105. **18** Ian Berry is a Magnum photojournalist, best known for his work in South Africa. Among his books is *Living Apart: South Africa Under Apartheid*, Phaidon, London 1996. **19** Philip Jones Griffiths, *Agent Orange: 'Collateral Damage' in Viet Nam*, Trolley, London 2003.

very black in Vietnam, so to be able to bounce the light I had to use fairly large, heavy flashguns, especially as I wanted to shoot quickly in bursts of three. You know, Kodak scratches the first one, Magnum loses the second and the third you keep. Photographers have it easy nowadays because digital cameras deal so well with low ambient light.

The early wartime colour pictures are almost all on Ektachrome 64, which I used to process in Saigon, but when it comes to getting ultimate quality, Kodachrome wins every time. And when I scan Kodachromes I can always make them look like Ektachrome.

GvK An important question for me is that, when I spent time in Iraq, for a long time many people didn't want to compare the situation in Iraq to that in Vietnam. Being there, I found out that the most astonishing thing was that there was nothing for the Americans to relate to in Iraq, there was a different culture—there are not even bars. When it came to it, the essence of my stay was the attitude: forget winning hearts and minds, the Iraqis will never like you, they may as well fear you. Does that compare with what you found in Vietnam?

PJG There are obvious similarities with Vietnam, although they are never identical. There are more parallels, paradoxically, with the Algerian war where the FLN discovered very quickly that there was no way to beat the French army but they could create a civil war with huge numbers of deaths so that people related all their problems to the invaders. I think that there are many complex layers; the main difference is that Vietnam, despite what the Americans said, was a united country. Modern Iraq is of course a British invention.

JS In your text in *Unembedded*, you have some hard things to say about photojournalists who through the embedding system have to live and work with single army units.[20] What do you think are the prospects for photojournalism in this kind of war when, compared with Vietnam, there is both a good deal more control for those journalists who are embedded and also far more danger for those who are not?

PJG It's obvious that the US forces killed the TV journalist Terry Lloyd because he was not embedded.[21] I was very impressed when I heard Michael Weisskopf talk last night—he was the journalist who was in a Humvee with [James] Nachtwey when a grenade was thrown into the vehicle; he picked it up to throw it out but not before it took his hand off. He has written a book that is essentially a condemnation of being embedded, saying that the amount of control of journalists in Iraq has been the greatest of any conflict.[22] On the psychological level, control through

20 Ghaith Abdul-Ahad, Kael Alford, Thorne Anderson and Rita Leistner, *Unembedded: Four Independent Photojournalists on the War in Iraq*, Chelsea Green, White River Junction, Vermont, VT, 2005. **21** Terry Lloyd, an ITN journalist, was killed in Basra in 2003; in October 2006, an Oxfordshire coroner's court ruled that he had been unlawfully killed. **22** Michael Weisskopf, *Blood Brothers: Among the Soldiers of Ward 57*, Henry Holt, New York 2006.

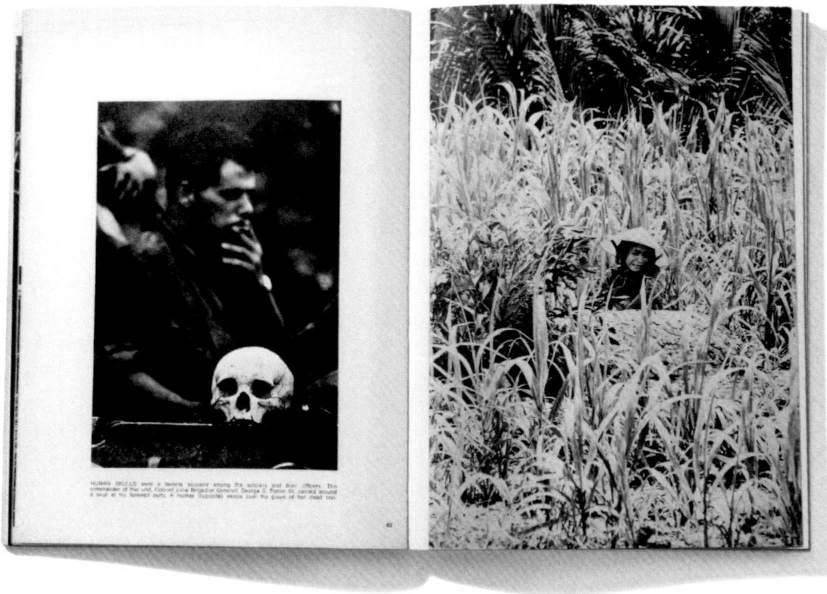

the embedding system worked amazingly well for America, and he explains how: when you do everything with a small group, you go along with them, there is a friendship that builds up; and in his case, he was the first and only journalist to be treated at the Walter Reed Medical Centre; he was treated as a combatant, not as a journalist. He felt that he may have won but journalism lost. (And after the recent revelations about treatment at Walter Reed his achievement may have been Pyrrhic victory!)

BL The Abu Ghraib pictures were taken by soldiers themselves, and even in Vietnam, a lot of soldiers took photographs—of atrocities—and these are still around, though they were never published.

PJG I remember once this guy coming to me, elbows in the mud, bullets flying overhead, saying to me, 'I'm going to Hong Kong on my R&R, I want to buy the new Nikon...' I said: 'I can't persuade you not to buy it as long as you also promise to also buy a Konica C35, which is a little tiny film camera, and carry it with you at all times and photograph everything that you see.'[23] That's what your grandchildren will want to see. If you are going to buy for $1,000 (which was a lot of money in those days) a complete SLR system, you are never going to take it into the field with you. I've never seen atrocity

23 The Konica C35 was an inexpensive but well-made compact 35mm rangefinder camera, first manufactured in 1968.

Philip Jones Griffiths, *Vietnam Inc.*, 1971: Human skulls were a favourite souvenir among the soldiers and their officers. The commander of the unit, Colonel George S. Patton III, carried around a skull at his farewell party. A mother weeps over the grave of her dead child

pictures taken by soldiers. I have seen severed heads pictures and other things like that, but they were taken by photojournalists with units. The truth is that people take far more pictures now than they did 35 years ago.

JS The many Vietnam veterans' sites carry lots of innocuous pictures taken by soldiers. Michael Herr and various others claim in their memoirs that the taking of atrocity photographs by the soldiers was pretty systematic, rather in the way that trophy hunting was carried out.[24]

PJG The skull on the tank, that was quite common. But 'systematic' I very much doubt. So few soldiers had cameras, and in those days there was no tradition of snapping away. I think Michael was wrong. I worked on him for a long time and I take credit for the end of *Full-Metal Jacket*, for which Michael wrote the script. You see, Michael came to Vietnam convinced he was going to be the Ernie Pyle of the Vietnam War, and write wonderful stories about brave soldiers doing wonderful things.[25] So I realised I had a lot of work ahead of me. The thing that really got through to him: I kept saying how brilliant the Vietnamese were on a psychological level, and they always tried to make sure that whenever Marc Riboud went to North Vietnam to photograph the anti-aircraft guns, it was always women who were firing them. Whenever they released pictures of captured American pilots, it was always a woman leading them away. There's one famous picture of a huge American and a tiny little woman behind him with a rifle. Hanoi always understood the stuff about the Marines marching up and down, gun in one hand the other holding their balls, singing 'this is my weapon, this is my gun, this one's for shooting, this one's for fun'. The Vietnamese understood that so well, to have the Americans' testosterone-driven finest shot down and captured by women. And in *Full Metal Jacket*, the Marines find that their deadly opponent is a woman.

JS The very last part of the film is also close to your book, because the Marines are marching through the devastated landscape, singing about Mickey Mouse, and the central message of *Vietnam Inc.* is that all this was done to make the world safe for consumerism.

PJG Indeed.

JS Could we talk about *Agent Orange*?

BL ...and your commitment to go back to Vietnam year after year.

PJG As Gilles Peress said, 'He's obviously not a war photographer. They don't go back 25 times after the war's ended.' There were all these rumours about babies being born with no eyes, and I thought it would make an amazing image. But whenever I went to Catholic orphanages, because they would always keep such babies alive, I was never

24 Michael Herr, *Dispatches*, Pan, London 1978, p. 161. 25 Ernie Pyle was a Pulitzer Prize-winning Second World War correspondent, known for this empathy with US troops, who was killed in 1945 on the island of Ie Shima near Okinawa.

allowed in, so I became convinced that an order had gone out that these kids should not be photographed. After the war, I went back and found them. It is one of the most disgraceful episodes in American history. Today all of us have dioxin in our bodies and it's killing us—it does not respect borders and there's no such thing as a permissible dose. One would therefore think that America would seize the opportunity afforded by Vietnam to do some basic research in the hope of finding a cure. Vietnam is the perfect place to look because it has ethnically identical people who were separated by a line drawn on a map. The South was sprayed, the North was not, so there is a built-in control group. There are a lot of Agent Orange kids in the North but every single one of them comes from a parent who fought in the South or drove a truck along the Ho Chi Minh trail. There is still no definitive answer to how many generations these deformities will continue or by what mechanism they are transmitted. The situation is confused by the fact that people are still ingesting large quantities of dioxin because there are hotspots all over South Vietnam contaminating the ecosystem. Of course, the Americans won't touch the problem on the grounds that they could be considered liable.

JS Though they compensated their own servicemen.

PJG If you are an American, you will get money, few questions asked. The widow of my friend Greg Davis, who died three years ago, out of curiosity, wrote to the Veterans' Administration, who promptly paid her compensation.

BL Is there any chance that your own cancer is related to this?

PJG I've always said no. But there is a picture in the book where I was obviously in the middle of a cloud of spray, so I am sure I have a lot of dioxin in my system. Also, when I lived with a Vietnamese family it was in downtown Saigon, there were no trees there because the military used discarded 44 gallon Agent Orange drums, which always had a few litres left in the bottom, for storing gasoline. When their vehicles burned that mixture, the dioxin was released, killing the trees, and we breathed it all the time.

JS Are there people in the US pushing for compensation for the Vietnamese?

PJG Absolutely there are, and there is a big court case proceeding. We lost the first round; someone said because the judge was so pissed off at getting so many copies of my book! The second round is supposed to happen towards the end of the year or the beginning of the next.

JS Do you have a sense that the book gave impetus to the campaign?

PJG Oh, absolutely. The interesting thing about the book is that there was a spike in sales when it was first published, and then it sank into oblivion. But over the last couple of years, sales have been ticking up and up, and each month is ten

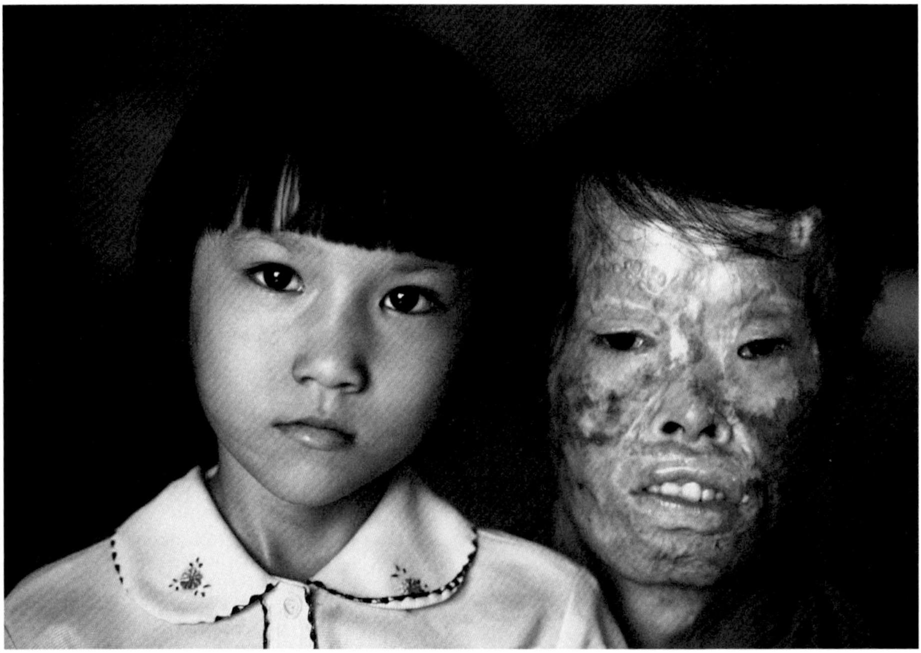

Vietnam, 1981. This woman, badly disfigured during a napalm strike, adopted this girl as a baby. The child was orphaned when her family died in an American attack

per cent better than the one before, which means it is being driven by word of mouth.

JS In a way, it seems like a companion volume to *Vietnam Inc.*, the use of text is similar...

PJG What do you think of *Viet-nam at Peace*?[26] It isn't doing very well though it is moving slowly but consistently. It is not as stark an issue as *Agent Orange*.

JS In *Vietnam Inc.*, you were able to say something that sounded simplistic but also somehow carried a ring of truth: that the war seemed to be a way to divide the virtuous from the corrupt Vietnamese. But now such judgements can't hold.

PJG I think that what has encouraged me is that in the toning down of the excesses that happened after the war, if they are able to do that so effectively, there is no reason why they cannot move on from what we see now, which is a period of transition, to something much better. I didn't write much about it because I am not privy to it, but obviously there is a lot of corruption and the usual panoply of social ills. It does boggle the mind that all those people who sacrificed so much have been pushed to one side by the nouveaux riches, who behave as they do everywhere.

JS You wrote in *Agent Orange* that during the war you rarely saw acts of kindness between Vietnamese but that since the war you had seen some repair of the social structures that had been torn up by the conflict, in the care taken of the damaged children, for instance.

PJG I think that I was struck throughout the 1980s by the way the Vietnamese cared for one another and were kind to each other in a way that I never saw during the war years, when everybody was just out for number one. But unfortunately, as consumer capitalism charges forward, you do see examples of people trampling over each other to get to the top. It's just the nature of the economic system. However, the traditional ways of earning status in Vietnamese society have not been eradicated completely, in fact on occasions they are coming back, as cultural activities are being encouraged. At other times, though, it's hard to tell the difference between Orange County and Ho Chi Minh City.

BL You are going back to Cambodia next week. What are you going to do there?

PJG The first thing is a workshop—I'm going to teach young Cambodians how to take pictures. A third of the time playing with my godchildren; a third of the time doing research; a third of the time taking pictures. This will be my third trip this year.

Cambodia is also going through a transition to become a consumer society. It's happening everywhere. The Murdoch media facilitate it. The thrall that it has over villages in India is immense. They buy a generator, a satellite dish, a little black-and-white

26 Philip Jones Griffiths, *Viet-nam at Peace*, Trolley Books, London 2005.

TV set and the whole village sits there every night watching Sky. No one gets up in the morning to feed the animals. There are a lot of ads. And, simply put, their message is: 'leave your village and go to the city'. That man is guilty of 'culturecide', if you only consider what he has done to China...

JS Do you see any hopeful elements in this general picture of the laying waste of indigenous cultures by the mechanisms of capital?

PJG The answer is that it looks pretty hopeless. I don't know where to look; I don't see anyone who is stemming the tide. The horrible truth is that the only societies doing anything about the problem are those intent on blowing us up. And their motivation for condemning us is nothing to do with the destruction of cultures; indeed, the Taliban were quite capable of doing it themselves. They have the effect of holding Western consumer capitalism at bay, though not for the right reasons.

JS Noam Chomsky in his introduction to the new edition of *Vietnam Inc.* says that the US anti-war movement was unprecedented: that you had a large portion of the population actually marching against their own nation and in support of its 'enemy'. About the current Iraq war, he has also pointed out that never have so many people demonstrated against a war before it took place. I wonder whether out of that process that you deplore comes a sense of connection between different people, who increasingly communicate, travel, migrate and share common experiences. Perhaps that may work against racism and the Westmoreland view that certain peoples don't have the same view of life and death, that they don't feel grief as deeply as we do, that finally it's OK to kill them?

PJG Maintaining one's cultural identity does not rely on isolation. All societies have benefited from interaction and have grown accordingly. However, such enlightenment should happen in an organic way, not be imposed. America is determined to compel the rest of the world to accept its version of consumer capitalism, not by kindly osmosis but by a tsunami backed by force if necessary.

Certainly the opposition to a war that had not been declared was unprecedented in the history of the world. I think that what happened once the war started was that essentially the means of persuasion that America has at its disposal were honed and put into top gear. As a result you had large numbers of people wanting to put Bush back in power.

JS The problem there was that the Democratic opposition was not anti-war and not even anti-torture. People had nowhere to go.

PJG True, and Nader's numbers didn't go up appreciably. What has happened is that the opposition to the war has taken a long time to build up. It takes time for people to discover for themselves how they have been hoodwinked.

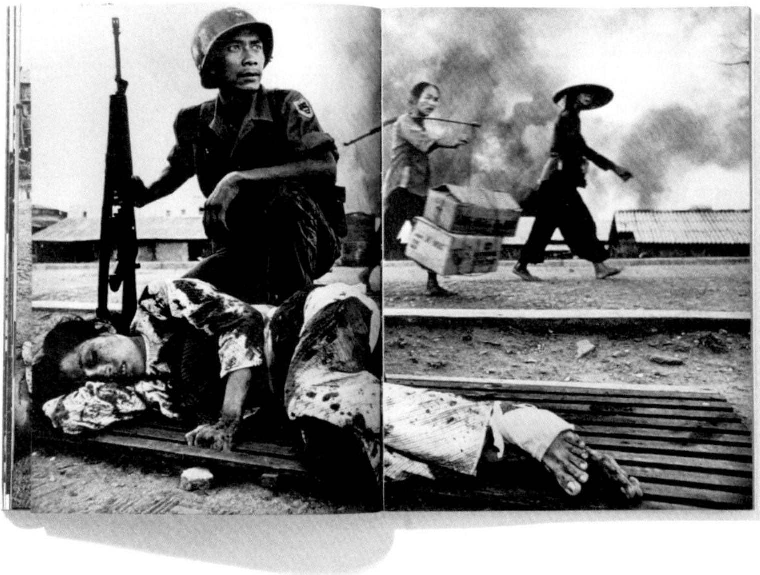

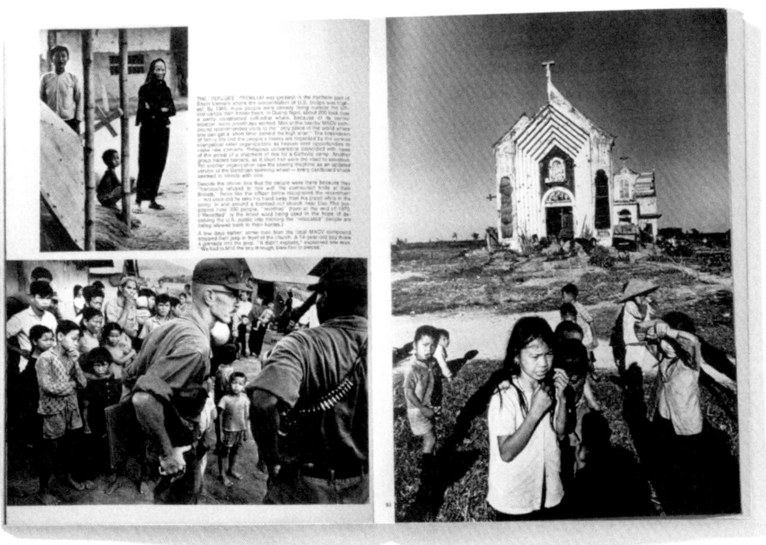

Top Philip Jones Griffiths, *Vietnam Inc.*, 1971: The battle for Saigon, 1968
Bottom Philip Jones Griffiths, *Vietnam Inc.*, 1971: Resettlement camp near Duc Pho, 1970. 'Resettled' is the latest word being used in the hope of deceiving the US public into thinking the 'relocated' people are being allowed back to their homes
Overleaf South Vietnam, Quin Hon. US soldiers with a group of captured Vietcong suspects, 1967

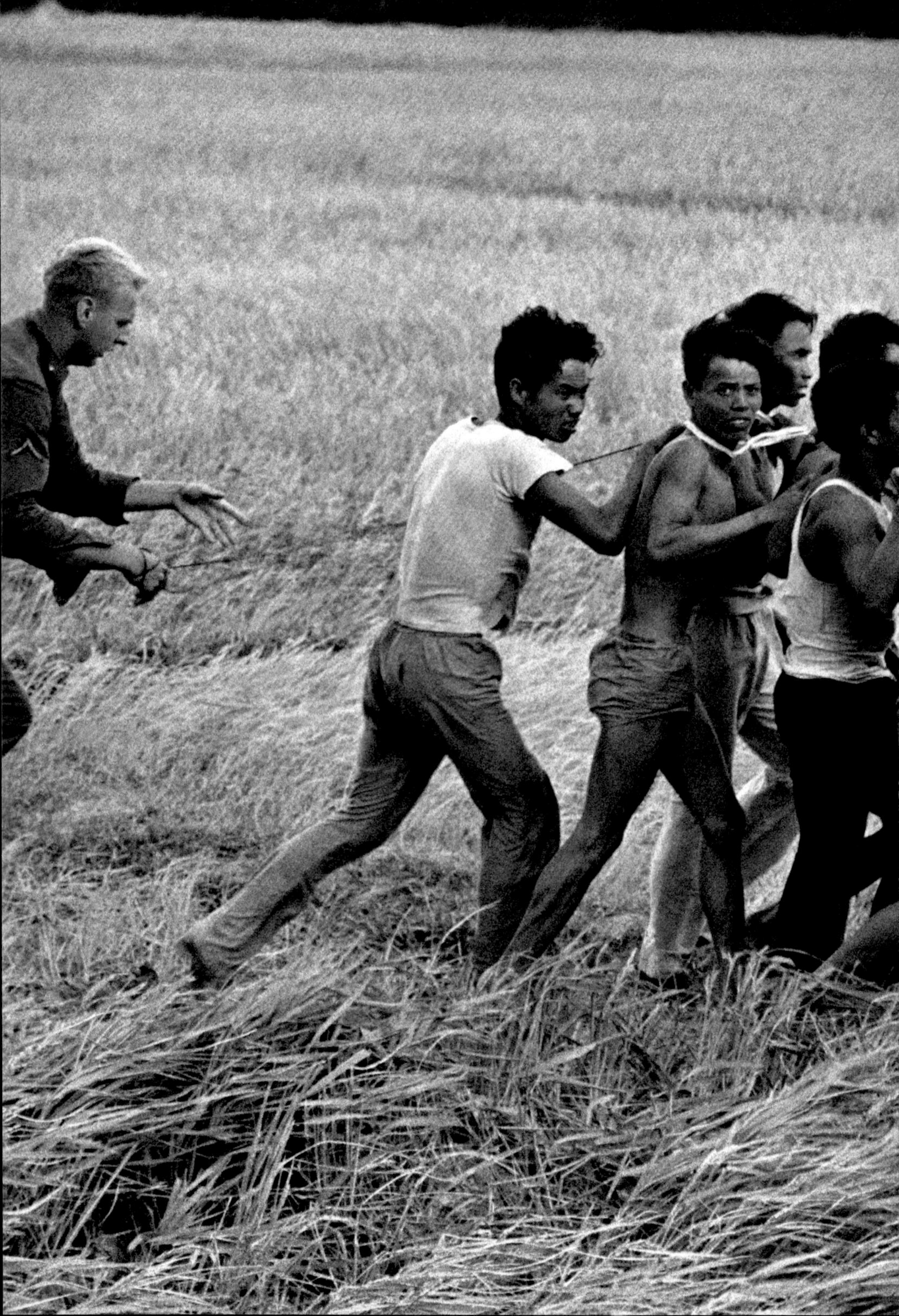

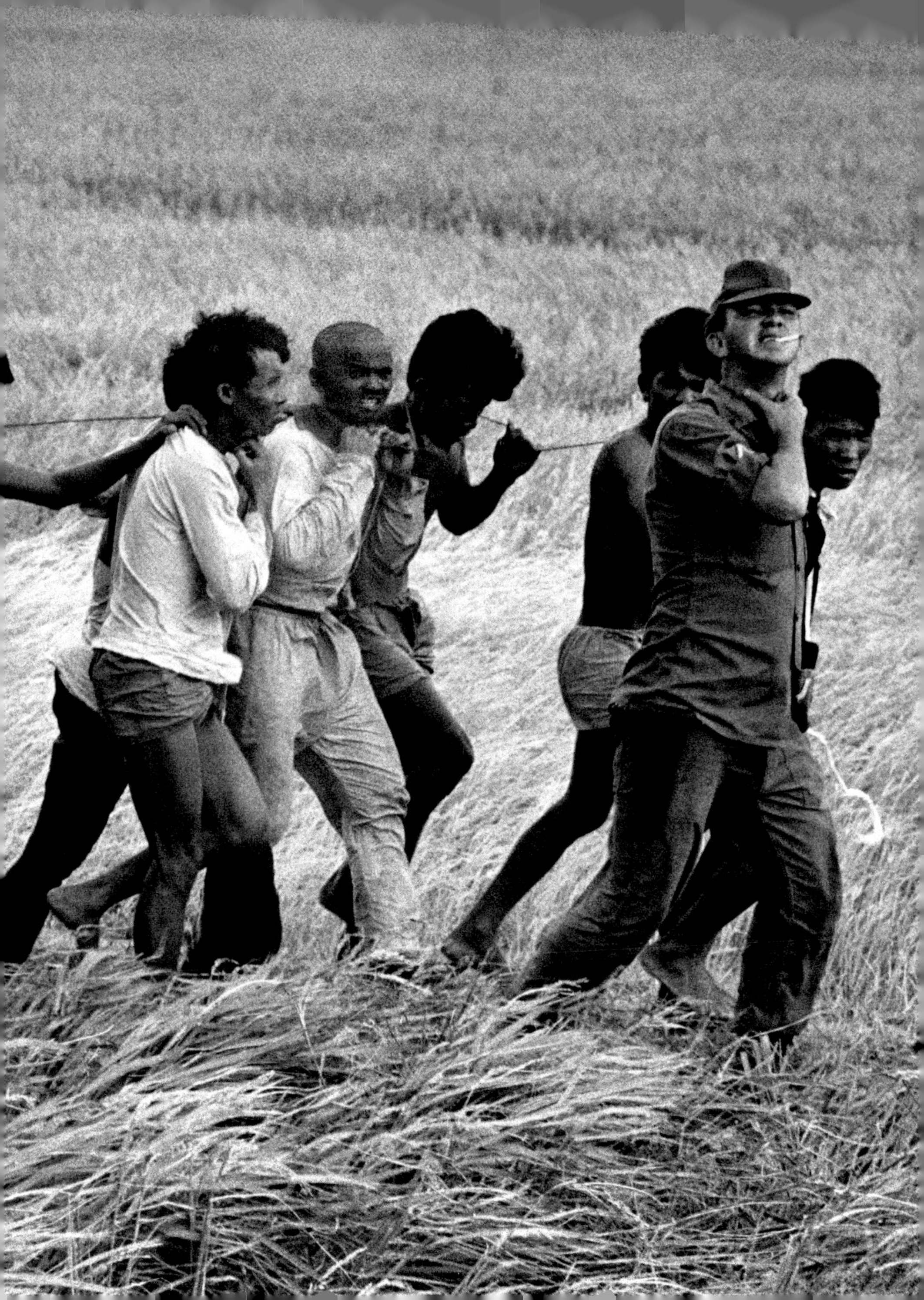

Embedded with Murderers: Balad, Iraq, July 15th, 2003

Rita Leistner

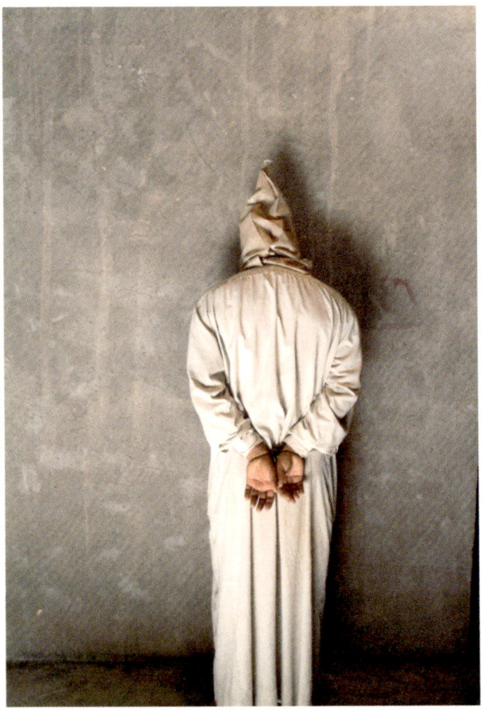

Detainee photograph—15 July 2003. Crossing paths with Alpha Company, 1-8 Infantry Battalion, 3rd Brigade Combat Team, of the Fourth Infantry Division

If I am known for anything, I think it is mostly for my co-authorship of *Unembedded: Four Independent Photojournalists on the War in Iraq.*[1] We took a little bit of flack for that title, because of course we were not the only journalists to work unilaterally in Iraq. Some photographers have been surprised when they heard that I did one of the longest embeds of the war, as if it were ironic or hypocritical. They saw *Unembedded* as a criticism of journalists who embedded, and I think found it doubly objectionable because we were independents. But that is to miss the bigger picture.

The point was not to criticise embeds as much as it was to emphasise that there are different ways of covering conflict. The book wasn't meant for other journalists, it was meant for people who had never been to war, and didn't know about how much the military embed system in Iraq created coverage that was heavily weighted towards embedded material. This was something that worked out very well, at least at first, for the US military and government. They created censorship by controlling access.

Yet I did do a lot of embedded work, and what follows is an account of the circumstances, limits and opportunities that the system allowed, and also of my time with a unit of the US Army that went on to murder Iraqi civilians in one of the best-documented atrocities of the war.

Unembedded into Iraq

I first went to Iraq on my own, 'unilaterally', or 'unembedded', mostly because I didn't have the means, knowhow, or contacts to get an embed with the US Military. Everyone knew that embedding was the easiest, safest, surest way to get into Iraq (on the shirt-tails of the invading forces). In the end, it probably worked out for the best, as I ended up with a different story than most. This is what independent journalists should do, after all: fill in the spaces where journalists on tighter deadlines and with more specific mandates (a cover photo for the story of the day, for example) can't get. So I started in eastern Turkey along with some 2,000 other journalists (who were also working unilaterally) who'd registered with the Press Office there during the month leading up to the invasion. When Turkey decided against opening the border to US troops (the 4th Infantry Division had initially been given the role of invading Iraq from the north), most of the journalists went home or flew to other points of possible entry into Iraq. I had no job to go home to, and a very small budget for the trip, so I stuck it out near the border, watching the war go by on television

---

1 Ghaith Abdul-Ahad, Kael Alford, Thorne Anderson and Rita Leistner, *Unembedded: Four Independent Photojournalists on the War in Iraq*, Chelsea Green, White River Junction, VT, 2005.

(which was of course very frustrating and demoralising). Then on April 10th, my friend and fellow Canadian photojournalist Steve Morrison met a guy at a taxi stand in Cizre who offered to smuggle us into Iraq for $1,200 a piece (a few weeks earlier, it would have cost at least five times that). The trip was considered extremely dangerous, because the Turkish border patrol had shoot-to-kill orders. In fact, a British private security forces guy (who went only by the name of 'Blue') threatened to report us to the Turks if we decided to go, 'for our own safety'. So we lied to him and everyone we knew, except a few of our closest friends, and set off the next day before dawn.

Circumstances were against us. The full moon illuminated the landscape and changes had been made in the border patrol routes, so what was meant to be a half-day hike turned into a gruelling three-day journey. We were continually fearful of being apprehended by Turkish border guards who had zero tolerance of illegal border crossing. Things were made far more difficult by the mountainous terrain, which was often so steep that we were three-point climbing with no safety ropes, and several hundred-foot drops below us. I have some climbing experience, and have spent years tree-planting in Canada, including in the Coat Mountains, but these were some of the most challenging climbs I'd ever done. We were also carrying a lot of gear (I had a 40-pound pack on my back). On top of that, time was a factor. We were moving at a fast pace, and rarely stopped to rest. We also walked at night when it was easiest to go unseen, which all seemed part of the complex strategy to avoid being apprehended. The first night I slipped on a steep cliff, badly twisting my knee. Had I fallen, it would have been to my death. Three hours later, we were at the base of the Tigris River, drinking tea in a cave, but my knee was in agony. By the time I woke up, it was badly swollen and I couldn't bend my leg. Fortunately, I had painkillers with me, and with the help of a stick and our smugglers, I was able carry on. We didn't share a language with our Kurdish guides, and we never knew how much further we had to go. We'd planned to use Steve's satellite phone for translation with a contact back in Diyirbakir, but we never managed to get through. The guides kept repeating the only words they seemed to know in English, 'two more hours', which we joked about for a long time afterwards. Back in Cizre, we'd been told it would be a half day's hike, but two days in, we were still deep in the mountains. Sometimes at night you could see the lights of the Turkish border-patrol towers on the snow-capped mountain crests. The patrols had obviously been ramped up, something even our experienced smugglers hadn't predicted. In the mountains, it was the three of them plus the two of us, but there had been a lot of middlemen at the front end of the trip, and would be more before we got to Iraq. I'd never met more experienced climbers. Even though they wore old plastic shoes, they were as agile as the mountain goats that they would occasionally stop to study on the surrounding rock faces. One time we ascended through waist-deep snow under the light of the full moon, too exposed to view for anyone's comfort. It was unusual to see fear showing in our smugglers' demeanours. We ascended as fast as we could. I dug my stick with all my might into the snow and pulled myself up the steep incline. My knee was in agony. When we got to the top, we all collapsed in exhaustion, snow-soaked, sweating and cold at the same time. As we looked over the crest, all we could see were miles of rocky snow-capped mountain ranges extending into the night. There was little time to rest, and no sooner had we caught our breath than we were on the move again. With only the snow and the moon to light our way, we leapt blindly downward, stumbling, running. I would have gone back home right then, if it were possible (it wouldn't be the last time I'd have regrets at a moment of danger). When we finally stopped to rest, I sat down and wept.

A day later, on April 14th, 2003, three weeks after the US first crossed the Line of Departure into Iraq from Kuwait, Steve and I were in northern Iraq, watching the fall of Tikrit—and the end of the first phase of the war—on an old TV set in a hotel room in Dohuk, in Iraqi Kurdistan. When people ask me why I went back to Iraq so many times (four trips in a year-and-a-half, all as a freelancer), I say that it's because it was so hard to get in the first time. Once I'd made that trip, every other trip seemed easy by comparison. I was committed to the story.

No one understood the risks we'd taken more than the Turkish Press Corps, who I'd met on my second night in Bagdad, while out looking for food. Bagdad was under curfew when Steve and I arrived. There was no food anywhere. A Jordanian interpreter for NBC snuck us some Cup-O-Noodles from their stash, which they were under strict orders to share with no one (although later, the NBC crew would be very generous, particularly with their whiskey). The Turks took me under their wing, fed me, and showed me the ropes in Baghdad, and even gave me a place to stay. In the last leg of the journey, the smugglers had handed us off to the Peshmerga—literally meaning 'those who face death', these Kurdish guerrilla fighters are legendary for their bravery and honour), but we had to pay them extra before they'd lead us out of the mountains. As a result, I was nearly out of money when I finally arrived in Iraq, and because of the war and the complete upheaval of the country's infrastructure, the banks were all shut and there was no way to get money from the outside.

An Unusual Embed

That all changed when I met Richard Pendlebury of *The Daily Mail*—the next person in a long line of individuals who helped me in Iraq. Richard hired me for a day rate, half paid in cash. I have him to thank for meeting 'Crazy Horse', the soldiers of Charlie Troop, 3rd Squadron, 7th US Cavalry Regiment, 3rd Infantry Division. On April 29th, *The Daily Mail* had sent us to cover Defense Secretary Donald Rumsfeld's visit to Camp Victory, the big US military base near Baghdad Airport. However, we weren't in the press pool and couldn't get past the Cavalry scouts guarding the front gate. It turned out Crazy Horse had a lot of stories to tell, so we hung out and talked to them instead. In March they had led the ground incursion from Kuwait into Iraq: in their parlance, they were 'the burning tip of the spear'. They claimed to have captured the first Iraqi flag, and to have killed over 1,000 Iraqi troops before reaching Baghdad. It was a definitive encounter for me: I didn't know it then, but I would end up spending most of the next three months with them.

I got to know Crazy Horse through regular visits to their compound near the airport. The compound had no electricity, no running water, no toilets, no fresh food, no internet or phones. They were waiting to go home, but instead they were called north to Balad where the insurgency was brewing.

At the same time, an event taking place on the other side of the world—the outbreak of the SARS virus—was about to change things for me again. I was living in Baghdad and only visiting Crazy Horse during the day, when I got word from journalists coming from Jordan and Kuwait that those countries had closed their borders to Canadian nationals because there had been cases of SARS in Canada. It meant that my only way out of Iraq was Turkey, and because of my illegal border crossing, I was rightly afraid to go back that way. I also had little money left, and no way to get funds into Iraq. When I told my story to the soldiers in Crazy Horse, they suggested I come and live with them, where I would have no expenses, and would be able to leave the country with them. Their commander agreed, and that was that.

Ironically, I eventually did end up going back to New York via Turkey. A few weeks after I'd moved up to Balad with Crazy Horse, my one DSLR seized up with sand. The trip back through Turkey was not good. I was detained overnight, interrogated, strip-searched, intimidated, and threatened by the Turkish border guards. But at least they didn't put me in jail. I went back to New York, replaced my gear, bought a satellite transmitter, and was back in Balad with Crazy Horse nearly a month later.

By the time I'd left, night patrols and skirmishes with insurgents were becoming a regular occurrence. One day (June 13th, 2003) before a particularly dangerous mission, it occurred to me that I hadn't taken a photograph of all of the 150 soldiers of Crazy Horse. At dawn I set about to remedy that, systematically going from squadron to squadron, beginning at dawn and ending at dusk (see pp. 92–3). It was the first time I'd taken posed portraits of the troop, and they were quick to recognise the grim motive of my endeavour (that I wanted to take their pictures in case they didn't live through the next day), but they complied. In most cases one frame was enough—'Relax and look into the camera', I said. Flash, then on to the next.

Detainee Photographs—July 15th, 2003

When I arrived back in Balad on July 15th, Crazy Horse was sharing the base with their replacements, soldiers of Alpha Company, 1-8 Infantry Battalion, 3rd Brigade Combat Team, of the 4th Infantry Division. Like me, the 4ID had arrived in Iraq after the invasion was over. They were the unit being denied access from the north by the Turks in March, and in whose wake I'd originally hoped to ride into Iraq. It seemed fitting I'd finally cross paths with them. It was through my relationship with Crazy Horse that, just by being there, I gained access to Alpha Company.

The 3ID soldiers made a big deal of the difference between their expectations of Iraq and those of the incoming 4ID soldiers who had arrived after the invasion, and had not seen combat. The 4ID soldiers did not feel the same sense of betrayal by their government, because they hadn't been lied to yet—at least that is how it was explained to me by some of the soldiers in Crazy Horse. Nor had they had time to gain respect for the Iraqis.

On the night of July 15th, I accompanied 4ID on patrol. There was one of the Crazy Horse soldiers I talked to a lot—Sergeant Jason Neely, who had a degree in psychology. He was angry at me for going on patrol with Alpha Company: 'What did I think I was doing going out on patrol with these fuckers, and taking photos of some poor farmers they'd mistaken as enemies?' More disturbing was hearing how the Alpha Company Commander, Captain Matthew Cunningham, on arriving at Camp Crazy (later renamed Camp Eagle) had ordered his men to kill Crazy Horse's pet dog, because it was 'unsanitary'. Nawatay, as they'd called the dog, was drowned and his corpse left smouldering in the camp garbage pit, where Crazy Horse found it the next morning. Five months later, Cunningham would be implicated in ordering and covering up revenge killings of three Iraqis on the night of January 2nd/3rd, 2004.

But that night, I went out on patrol with Captain Charles Sememko, an artillery officer temporarily stationed with Alpha Company. A half-hour into the patrol, the Bradley Fighting Vehicle ahead of us in the convoy was struck by a rocket-propelled grenade (RPG). We came to a stop. A second RPG struck, disabling another Bradley. Fortunately, no one was seriously injured. What followed was a standard cordon and search procedure of nearby houses,

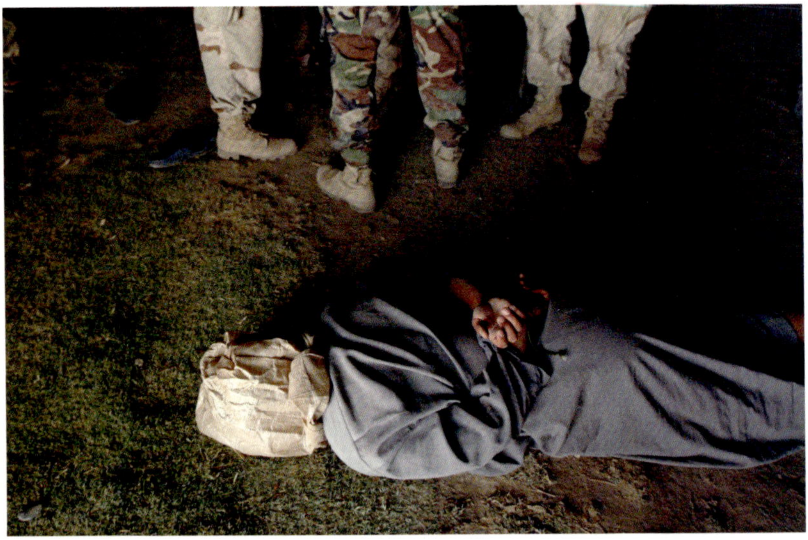

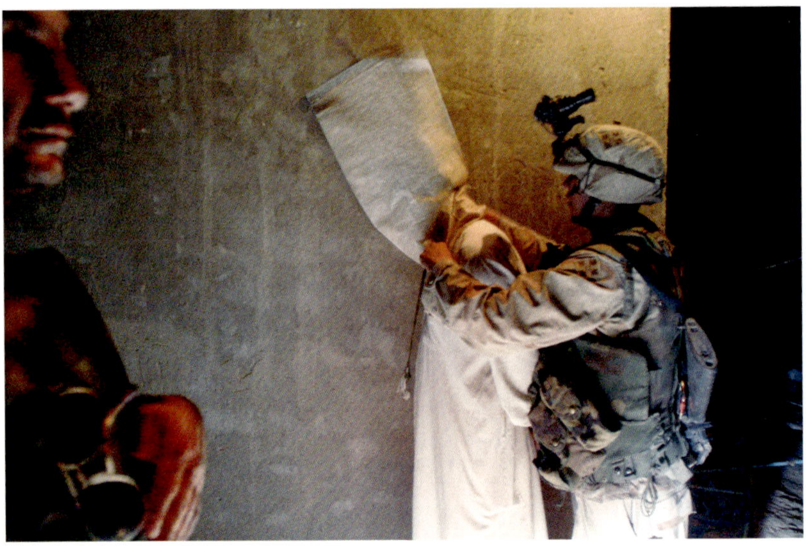

Top Detainee photographs—15 July 2003. Crossing paths with Alpha Company, 1-8
Bottom Infantry Battalion, 3rd Brigade Combat Team, of the Fourth Infantry Division

culminating in the detention of about a dozen Iraqi men. The soldiers entered a house near where the RPG appeared to come from, rounded up all the men inside, 'bagged and tied' them (which meant that white burlap bags were pulled over their heads, and their wrists were tied with plastic cuffs), and brought them back to the base. The base was an old Ba'ath military outpost, so the prisoners were put in the former Ba'ath Party jail.

This was very much straight journalism, spot news—I was simply there and I was photographing what was in front of me, things as they were. I added light, but that was it. There was a lot going on, and I had to make selections as I went. The old man being dragged off, the man sitting against the wall bleeding, the feet of the men in a circle—those images struck me as important details at the time. I'm sure if I didn't have photographs, I would have a hard time remembering what I'd seen because my memory can fail or play tricks on me in moments of heightened emotion—at least, that's what I fear, and I think is a big part of what draws me to photography. What I would have remembered most was the uncomfortable feeling in my stomach. No one was telling me not to shoot. The only thing that could have got in the way was my own feelings. In a situation like that, practice and professionalism really pay off. I was on automatic. The Iraqis probably didn't even notice I was there at that point because they were too afraid.

When I took their photos inside the base camp prison, it was a different matter. I didn't speak a word of Arabic back then. I can't imagine what they must have been thinking. These were people who had already lived lives of struggle and tyranny. By then, since they hadn't been killed, maybe they thought they were somewhat safe at the hands of their captors. There was much more I didn't see. After a few days, some of the prisoners were released. Others were taken away—I don't know where. A few days later, I left with Crazy Horse for Camp Udari in Kuwait to cover their return home—a decision I would later question: should I have tried to stay with the 4ID?

When you are on your own somewhere, there is a lot of responsibility to report the story. It's nothing like the media scrums at big urban events, like the bombings in Tyre I'd photographed in the summer of 2006, or the kinds of photos I've seen from the last days of apartheid in South Africa, with scores of journalists photographing the same thing (albeit often at great risk). You're all by yourself, and you know that if you don't take the photograph, no one else will. You step into the moment and shoot.

There is also a big difference between taking photographs of armed militants, and going with troops into someone's home, while they separate the men from the women and children and arrest unarmed civilians. It may be that the people being detained are insurgents, but you can't tell to look at them. Most of these raids are based on suspicion and the word of questionable informants.

It may also be that I did not feel the same sense of attachment to the soldiers of the 4ID as I did with Crazy Horse, who I'd been embedded with on-and-off for over two months. It's not that I lost total objectivity with Crazy Horse, but it's undeniable that living with people who are protecting your life creates a kind of allegiance. I didn't have that allegiance or sense of belonging with the soldiers of Alpha Company. Besides, Crazy Horse didn't like them.

I also think situations feel differently to different photographers. My personality, on a very basic level, seems to identify with the sympathetic side of a situation, and the vulnerabilities of those I am photographing—whether they are women wrestlers in the United States; loggers in Canada; drug addicts; the Lebanese during the Hezbollah–Israel conflict; Israelis living with the constant fear of being attacked; Palestinians confined behind walls and barricades; or soldiers fighting far from home. By July 15th, I was already on my second trip to Iraq. I'd been shot at and had seen bodies torn apart by rocket fire. Courtesy of the Turkish border patrol, I knew first-hand it what it felt like to be on the receiving end of an interrogation. I was a changed person from when I landed in Istanbul on March 15th, 2003, hoping to make it to Iraq to cover the war.

Over the preceding months, I'd been on a number of patrols (day and night), and had witnessed some altercations with locals, and the kinds of brief questioning that takes place at checkpoints. Everyone knows what it feels like to be in trouble: pulled over by the police for speeding, or sent to the principal's office as a child—these kinds of encounters with authority never lose that fearful sense of having your destiny in someone else's hands. It is the same uneasy feeling in your stomach. You can be scared sick. When the people in positions of authority are carrying weapons, when they are quick to point these weapons at you, when they are yelling at you in a language you do not understand, when you've already seen them haul off some of your neighbours never to return, and when maybe you've been tortured by Saddam Hussein in the past, the feeling must be intensified many times over. It always made me feel queasy and a little dirty just for being there. I hid behind my camera, wondering if it was comforting to the people being questioned to at least know that there was a civilian witness present (though many must have assumed I was part of the military, for why else would I have been there?).

Even routine checkpoint searches could be disturbing. In one photo (p. 91, top), soldiers are 'confiscating' money from Iraqis with the explanation that anyone carrying that much money must be using it to fund the insurgency. What the American soldiers did not know was that because of the devaluation of the Iraqi dinar, a huge stack of bills was not actually worth very much.

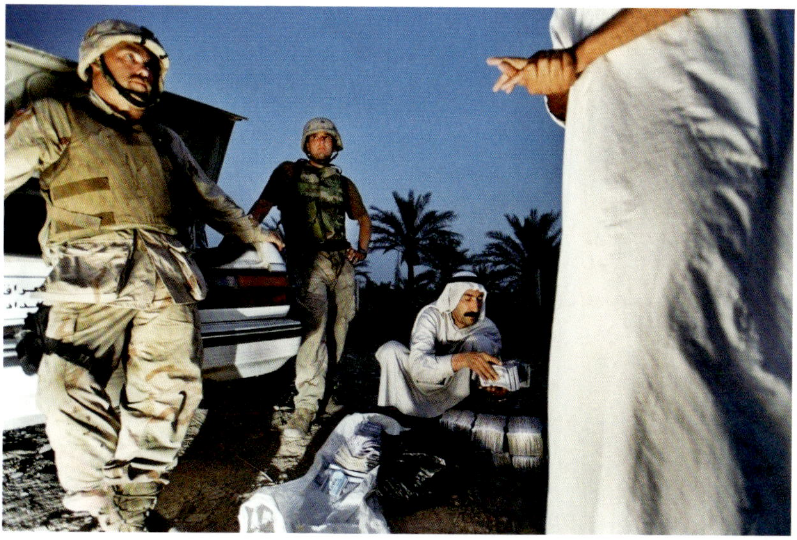

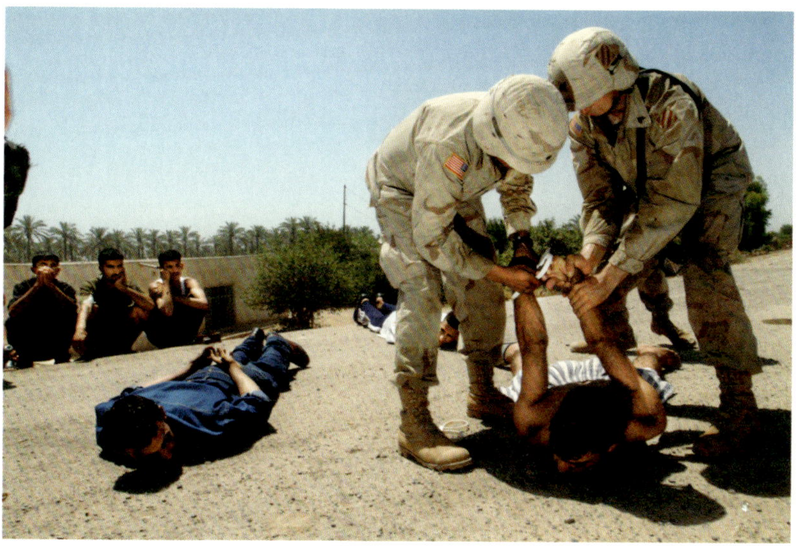

Detainee photographs—15 July 2003. Crossing paths with Alpha Company, 1-8 Infantry Battalion, 3rd Brigade Combat Team, of the Fourth Infantry Division

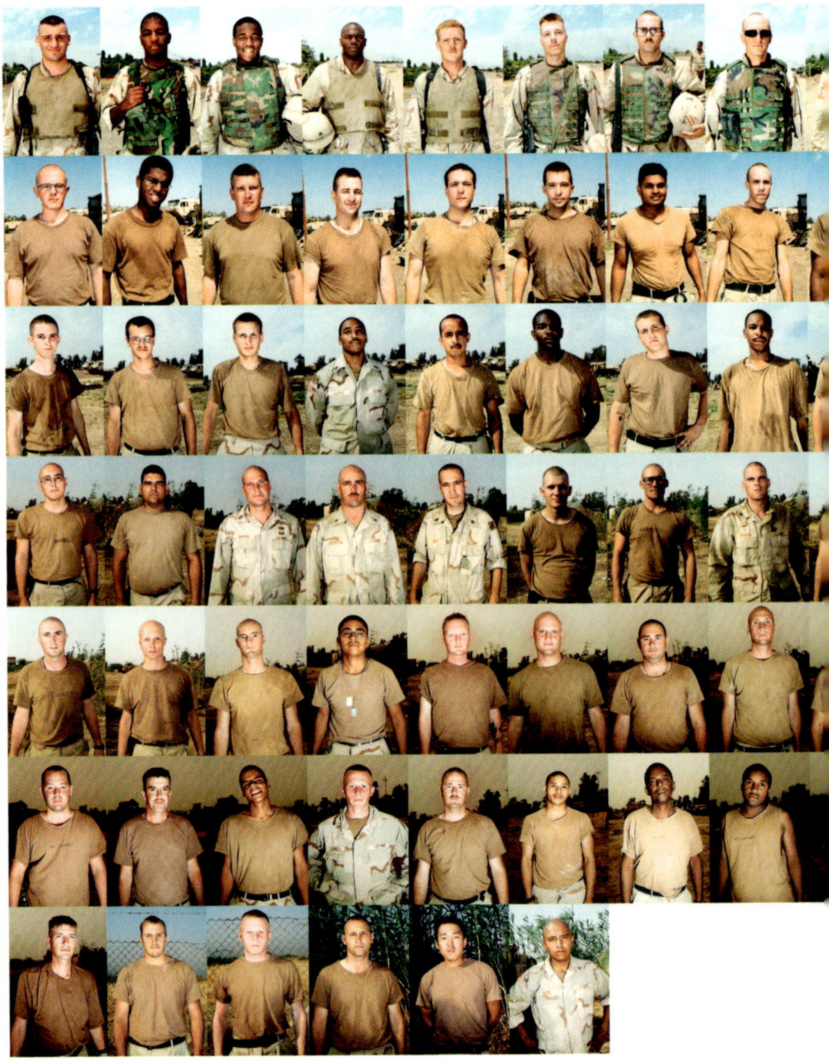

Composite portraits of Crazy Horse soldiers, Camp Victory, Baghdad, 2003

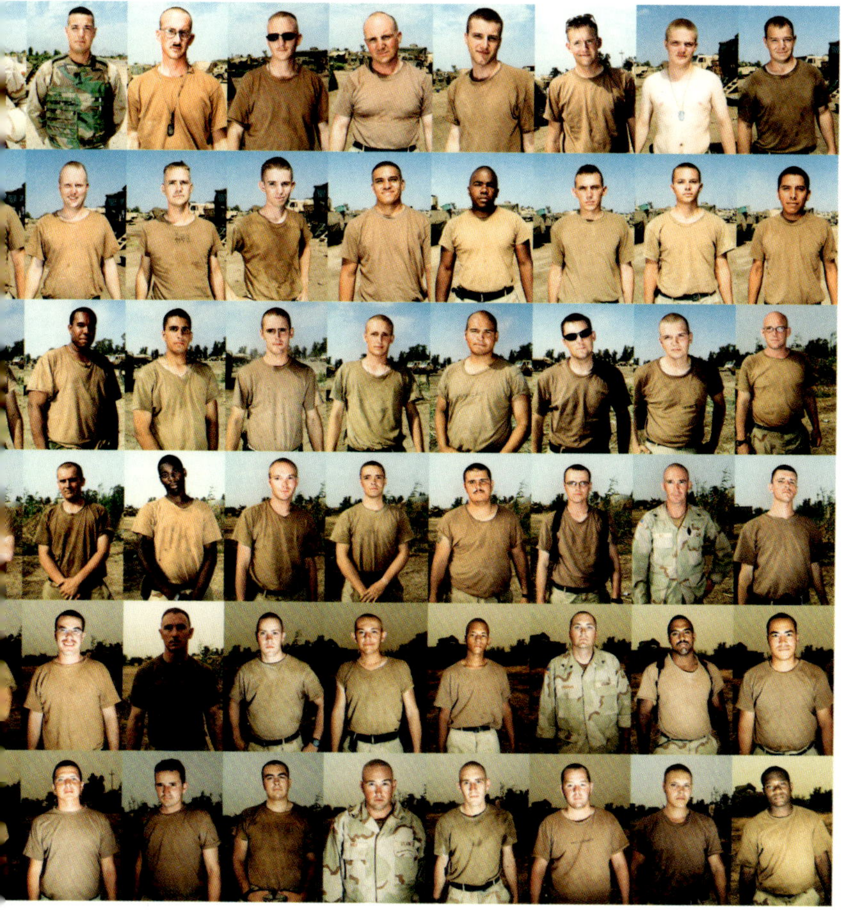

Moreover, because the banks had all closed, it was not so unusual to carry large amounts of money. The American soldiers never had enough information to really assess what they were seeing. Even if the soldiers wanted to know more about Iraq (and I met many who did), it was not part of their training.

On one occasion, a soldier at a checkpoint, citing the Geneva Conventions, told me I was not allowed to take pictures during arrests—on this scorching hot morning, a group of drunk young local men were being handcuffed and detained because they had 'insulted America'. There is a long history of perpetrators of violence documenting their victims for the purpose of further humiliating them by prolonging the moment indefinitely. I believe that the Geneva Conventions forbids such photography to prevent this type of humiliation.[2] However, much depends on the intentions of the photographers and the uses made of the photographs. When used as evidence, photographs say more about the perpetrators than the victims, and can be used to authenticate claims of mistreatment. At the time I took these photographs, and others of Iraqi detainees, I believed that the Iraqis I was photographing felt comforted that there was a photographer present, and may have felt this presence as a kind of safety net.

One of the most unsettling things about the scene at the house that night with Alpha Company was the imbalance of power, and what seemed to me the complete inability to tell one thing from another. Compared with my first weeks in Iraq, there was a lot of hatred on both sides. The soldiers I'd been living with for the better part of two months had voiced their disappointment at realising that not all Iraqis were happy at their presence. Even they knew how naive they were to expect to be 'greeted with showers of flowers'. But they didn't expect to be shot at either, not after they'd been told they had just liberated the country.

There is a popular image of troops living on the huge military bases with television, mess halls, McDonald's restaurants, showers, media centres and internet access. This is not the reality for many soldiers on front lines or remote forward operations bases (FOBs)—which could just mean a few tanks surrounded by some concertina razor wire and sandbags. In fact, when Richard and I first met Crazy Horse, they had had no contact with home for months, and so Richard lent them his satellite phone. One soldier called his wife, only to have her ask him for a divorce. He never recovered from the news, and was morose and distant for the remainder of the deployment, refusing to remove his wedding ring. In the first phase of my embed with Crazy Horse, I had no

---

2 Geneva Convention Relative to the Treatment of Prisoners of War of August 12, 1949 (Geneva Convention III), Article 13. The Article does not mention photography but it does state that prisoners should be protected 'against public curiosity'.

satellite transmitter, so I also had no access to news from the outside world either. It was not uncommon for journalists to have a poor sense of the news back home (pre-Twitter, pre-widespread internet), and I was often surprised when I did make visits back home, at how distorted a version of the war most people had.

The Use of Flash

Some photographers look down on the use of flash. Henri Cartier-Bresson famously said that a photograph should never be taken with the aid of a flash, 'if only out of respect of the natural light—even when there isn't any of it'.[3] I would not have been able to make any of these photographs without a flash. There were circumstances when the soldiers would have objected to me using flash. But here, because they were rounding up prisoners and had control over the situation, the flash did not risk giving away our position. I was charging my batteries off the Bradley Fighting Vehicles with an AC–DC converter. I also use a Quantum battery pack connected to my flash unit so that there is no recharging delay. You have to be able to use all your technology like second nature, so that you get it right in the intensity of moments when things happen quickly. As Cartier-Bresson says in another quote from his famous essay 'The Decisive Moment', 'We cannot do our story again once we've got back to the hotel.'[4]

I practiced a lot using the flash in total darkness. The new TTL (through the lens) brand-designated flashes have an infrared sensor that enables auto-focus in total darkness, but it was tricky to use the way I wanted, bouncing light so it wouldn't be so harsh against the deep black of the night. I practiced bouncing the flash off the sand to give it a softer feel and to avoid directing it straight at subjects. The soldiers had flashlights on their helmets which cast enough illumination to round-up their prisoners, but it wasn't enough light by which to take a photograph. Marshall McLuhan was right:

> *The electric light is pure information ... It could be argued that [activities that take place in the dark] are in some way the 'content' of the electric light, since they could not exist without the electric light. This fact merely underlines the point that 'the medium is the message' because it is the medium that shapes and controls the scale and form of human association and action.*[5]

Without the medium of electronic flash there would have been no message.

---

3 Henri Cartier-Bresson, *The Mind's Eye: Writing on Photography and Photographs*, Aperture, New York 1999, p. 28. 4 Ibid., p. 27. 5 Marshall McLuhan, *The Medium is the Message*, MIT Press, Cambridge, MA, 1994, pp. 8–9.

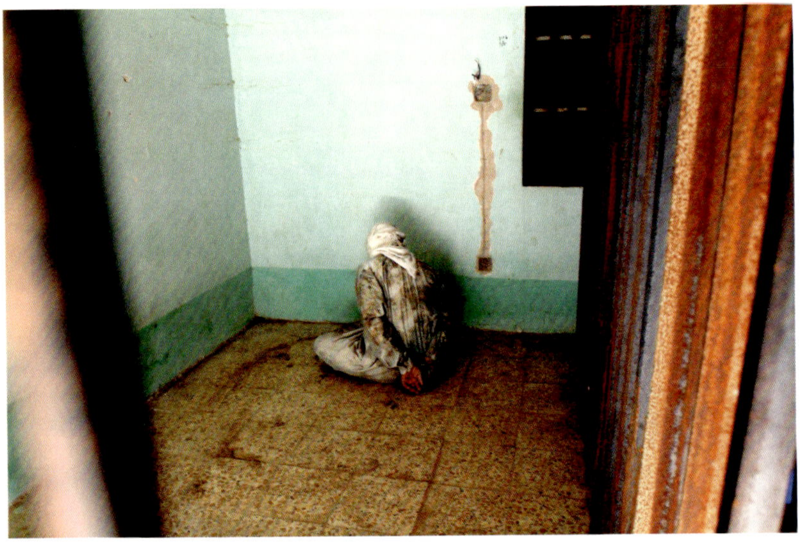

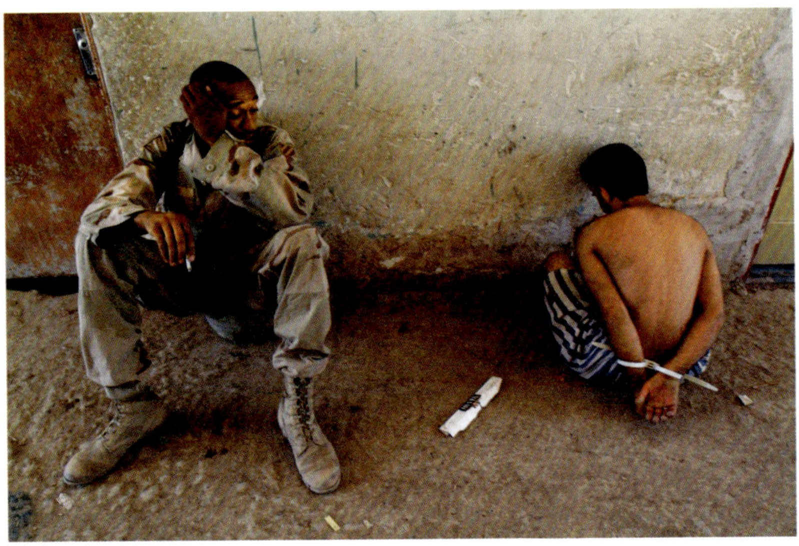

Detainee photographs—15 July 2003. Crossing paths with Alpha Company, 1-8 Infantry Battalion, 3rd Brigade Combat Team, of the Fourth Infantry Division

Publication

I thought these photographs were important enough for me to stay up late into the night under a clear patch of sky over the desert filing them from my Inmarsat RBGAN (Regional Broadband Global Area Network) satellite modem back to Sipa Press, my agency in New York. At $15 a megabyte, this was a significant expense for a freelancer.

It would be seven months before any of them were published (two were printed very small as accompaniments to a story I wrote about Crazy Horse in *The Walrus* in February 2004) and another three months before they were picked up by any international press. Antonio DeLuca, the brilliant designer who was then art director at *The Walrus*, had wanted to put the 'Hooded Prisoner' photo on the cover, but I thought it would be misleading, given that the photo was taken with soldiers of the 4ID, not with Crazy Horse.

There was so little interest in the detainee photographs, I didn't bother submitting them to World Press 2003. Instead, I submitted a series of atypically vulnerable portraits of the Crazy Horse soldiers. However, when the Abu Ghraib story broke at the end of April 2004 (nine-and-a-half months after I first filed the photos), there was a lot of interest in my detainee photographs from editors at *Time* and *Newsweek* who had remembered them from the Sipa news feed the previous summer. It was interesting that they did remember them—obviously, the pictures did have some merit, after all. I guess that when I took them, shortly after the swift and apparently successful invasion, the political climate was unfriendly to their publication. The Abu Ghraib story changed all that.

I remember that *Time* magazine was annoyed that Sipa sold them so quickly to *Newsweek*. The foreign desk editor at *Time* had emailed me directly. But, as it happened, the Abu Graib story broke when I was in the midst of my own personal crisis. On April 11th, along with my good friend and colleague Adnan Kahn, in the middle of a firefight in the town of Latifiya south of Bagdad, I'd been detained, threatened and interrogated by Fedayeen Saddam (paramilitary loyal to the Saddam Hussein's Ba'athist government). I was certain that we were going to die (they held guns to our heads, screamed insanely, and told us that they were going to kill us). When we did survive the ordeal, I was in shock and spent most of the next week drunk. The insurgents had taken most of my camera gear, so I was on my way back to New York to replace my gear, overland via Turkey again, when *Time* magazine was trying to reach me. In the meantime, Sipa Press had sold first rights to the whole series to *Newsweek* for $1,000, of which I would get my usual 50 per cent. *Newsweek* ran one interrogation photo on the inside, and *Time* ran a graphic by Matt Mahurin of a hooded prisoner on the front cover.[6]

When the Abu Graib accused went to trial in January 2005, there was another brief flurry of publications of my photographs. The 'Hooded Prisoner' was published for the first time on the inside of *Newsweek*. A series of the photographs was published for the first time in 2006 when John Knechtel, editor of *Alphabet City 10: Suspect* (2006) published six of the images alongside an essay by Slavoj Žižek—which I was very happy about, because I knew Žižek's work and had read his 2004 book *Iraq: The Borrowed Kettle*.[7]

The Drowning in the Desert

Subsequent events made me wonder if I should have tried to stay in Iraq with Crazy Horse's replacements. On the night of January 2nd/3rd, 2004, five months after I left Camp Crazy, Captain Cunningham's guys from Alpha Company 1-8 (the same company that I had photographed taking detainees in July) murdered three unarmed Iraqi men in orchestrated revenge killings. The afternoon of the killings, Captain Eric Paliwoda, a popular soldier, notably a favourite of Cunningham and of the Battalion Commander Lieutenant Colonel Nathan Sassaman, was killed in a mortar attack. The cover-ups (that went as high as Sassaman), and the military's efforts to thwart justice and deflect media attention from the killings, has been chronicled in detail in an extraordinary book by US Army lawyer Captain Vivian Gembara, who served in Iraq as the prosecutor and legal advisor for the 4th Infantry Division's 3rd Brigade Combat Team during the time of the killings.[8]

One of the murdered Iraqis was 19-year-old Zaidoun Fadel Hassoun. He and his cousin Marwan were stopped at a checkpoint for being out after curfew. Both were forced to jump, handcuffed, off a bridge in Balad into the Tigris River. Zaidoun, who couldn't swim, drowned (First Lieutenant Jack Seville was charged with assault in this case). Around the same time, another unarmed man, Zadan Khalaf was accosted in his home in Balad and executed. A bloodied gun found in his hand was later revealed to be a plant in the attempted cover-up. Cunninghman and Sassaman admitted to being present during the murder. No one was ever charged. A third man, Ismail Nasser, was killed by Staff Sergeant Shane Werst, the leader of a squad of engineers attached to Alpha Company, 1-8 Infantry Battalion. The third killing was not even brought to light until the Fall of 2004, when a soldier under Werst's command confessed to his wife and a psychologist about being part of what he described

6 *Time*, 17 May 2004. 7 Slavoj Žižek, *Iraq: The Borrowed Kettle*, Verso, London 2005. 8 Vivian H. Gembara and Deborah A. Gembara, *Drowning in the Desert: A JAG's Search for Justice in Iraq*, Zenith Press, Minneapolis, MN, 2008

as an execution. Werst was charged with the murder. In *Drowning in the Desert: A JAG's Search for Justice in Iraq*, Gembara wrote: 'I will always be disappointed by my chain-of-command's cowardly handling of the murders.'[9]

Gembara faced ostracism and hatred from many 1-8 soldiers for refusing to go along with their cover-up. She writes about how hard she'd tried to be accepted by the men in the first place, about 'the lure of camaraderie', especially for a woman who was already on the outside because of her gender and because she wasn't fighting on the front lines.[10] It must have been extraordinarily difficult to continue her investigations. She drew a lot of her courage to trust herself and to do the right thing from her father, a retired special forces officer.

On January 16th, 2004, just as Gembara's investigations in Iraq were making progress, the US Command released a terse statement to the press about investigations into abuses at Abu Graib. The Abu Graib story only broke four months later, but the statement meant the end of Gembara's murder investigation. Shortly after the January press release, the CID (Criminal Investigation Command) in Iraq denied her permission to secure crucial evidence, needed to effectively prosecute the perpetrators. This included exhuming the body of the drowning victim, Zaidoun Hassoun—without the body, there was no proof of murder.[11] So it is unsurprising that I wouldn't even hear of the murders until several years later, and had no way of connecting my photographs to the soldiers involved.

As we have seen, involvement in the murders and cover-ups went as high as the 1-8 Infantry Battalion Commander, Lieutenant Colonel Nathan Sassaman, his right-hand man, the Battalion Executive Officer, Major Robert Gwinner, and Alpha Company 1-8 Commander Matthew Cunningham who I'd filmed interrogating detainees, and who I'd written about in *The Walrus* ordering his men to drown Crazy Horse's pet. Within Alpha Company, the perpetrators were 1st Platoon, under Platoon Leader Sergeant First Class Tracy Perkins—who, according to his soldiers and Gembara's investigations, ruled his men by fear and intimidation.

When Gembara began to doubt the value of her own investigation, her friend and confidant in Iraq, Captain Tom Roughneen, reassured her:

> *They're murdering people! They went from soldier to executioner and no one blinked. When does it stop? ... Do you really think this was the first time for any of this? Of course not. Someone looked the other way the first few times, and 1-8 took that as a sign to do as they pleased.*[12]

---

9 Ibid., p. 298. **10** Ibid., p. 188. **11** Ibid., p. 226. **12** Ibid., p. 257.

Interview with **Ashley Gilbertson**

Julian Stallabrass

Ashley Gilbertson has produced some of the best-known images of the Iraq War, both on embeds and acting independently. He was embedded with the US Marines in the battle for Fallujah, in which much of the city was destroyed. He took some of the most considered and critical photographs of the war from within an embedded situation. His subsequent book, *Whisky, Tango, Foxtrot*, reflects on the war, embedding, photographic depiction, and the photojournalist's relations with the troops who were his hosts and protectors. This interview was made before an audience at the Brighton Photo Biennial in 2008.

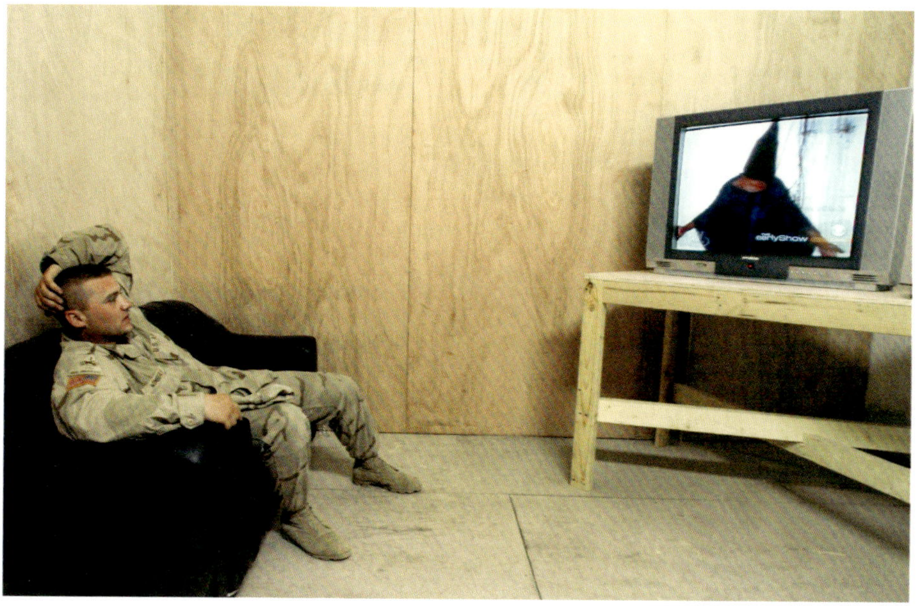

May, 2004. Specialist William Wimberley watches George W. Bush apologise on behalf of the US military for the torture that took place at Abu Ghraib prison

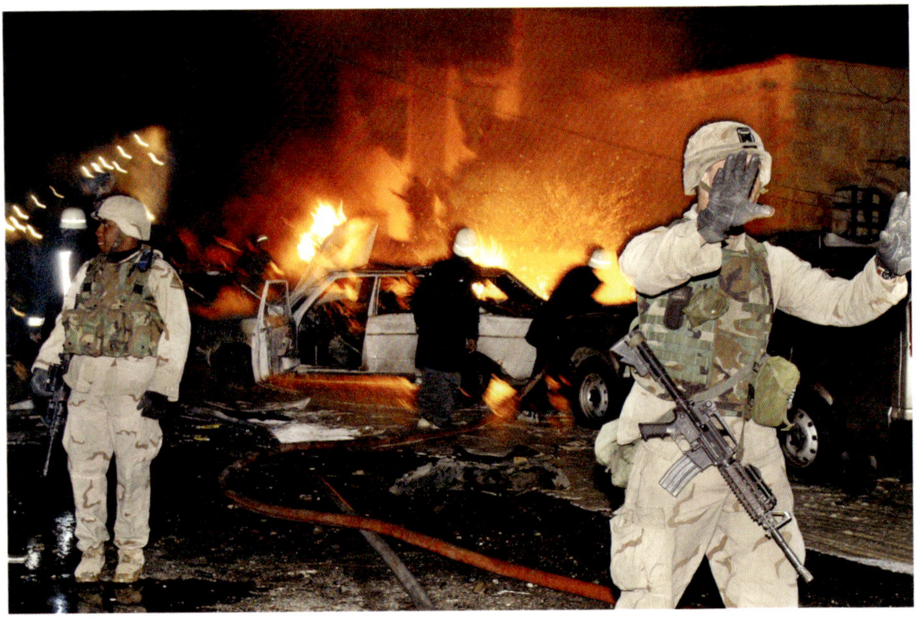

Baghdad, 2003. On New Year's Eve, 5 people were killed when a car bomb exploded outside the Nabil restaurant, and 40 more were wounded. The Nabil was popular with the press

Julian Stallabrass Maybe we could begin with the question of embedding, by which photographers and journalists are the guests of a particular military unit. You worked in Iraq as an independent photojournalist and on embeds. Why did you want to work that way, and how do you think the system affected you?

Ashley Gilbertson I think you need to be very conscious of what you're doing when you're embedding. I mean, I feel that I've embedded with pretty much every one of my subjects over the years. It's just the Pentagon came up with a really ugly name for what we do. I think you 'embed' with your loved one; you don't 'embed' with a group of Marines in Fallujah. Our goal as photojournalists is to spend as much time with a subject as humanly possible. We are living and breathing and eating and sleeping with them. You gain so much trust that way, and you actually start seeing more intimate moments of people's lives. So I don't think it's anything different from what we normally do. The reason to embed is for that reason, for the access, for that intimacy, to see what they see and to feel what they feel, although the Pentagon has put rules on what we do and how we work. Most of those rules are pretty much nonsense, except there's one clause that's been changing over the years, which is, I think, '13b'—it's like something from *Catch-22*. The rule stipulates in the case of dead or wounded soldiers or Marines you are to hold their photographs until the next of kin has been notified, which is, of course, fair enough.[1] However, they changed that in the last 18 months so that you can't take any photographs of anyone who's been killed or wounded unless you have a prior, written form of consent. So if you can imagine standing there, and this is the US military, and these guys are from Texas, so you stand in front of them and say, 'Hi, my name's Ashley Gilbertson, I'm from *The New York Times*'—what they hear is 'Hi, my name's Disgusting Pig Vulture, I'm from *The Jew York Times*, and I want you to sign this thing that says that it's OK that I photograph you in the case that you're killed'. That completely cuts out a *huge* amount of coverage of this war that we can't create anymore. I'm obviously absolutely furious about it. I think that it's actually denying the historical aspect of what's happening there. I mean, they're trying to gentrify what's a very, very ugly thing to be involved in. It's the whole thing of staying on message.

JS Critics of embedding say two kinds of things about it. One is that you come to identify with the troops you're with and maybe living with them for a number of months, you become too sympathetic; you really adopt the view of the military rather than that of the civilians. While I think that some of your photographs are proof of the opposite, there may be a tendency there. The other is that you necessarily have a very

1 The rule reads: '4.H.1. Media representatives will be reminded of the sensitivity of using names of individual casualties or photographs they may have taken which clearly identify casualties until after notification of the NOK and release by OASD(PA).' The initial embed rules are reproduced in Bill Katovsky and Timothy Carlson, *Embedded: The Media War in Iraq*, The Lyons Press, Guilford, CT, 2003, pp. 401–17.

narrow view of the war. Are you allowed to talk to civilians if you're on an embed for instance?

AG You can, except you're using military translators. That's why we at *The New York Times* take our own translators on embeds now. So you go through tapes—you do a quick interview with a civilian on the street, and the military translator will say, 'Oh—he's very happy to have the Americans here, he says that the Americans bring him fruit and school books', and you go back and he's like 'I want them to burn in hell', you know—so you need to bring your own translators. Some units are very, very open, and the translators are very good, except that's not all that common. But as far as getting too close to the unit, I only had that problem once in Samarra, when I realised I did not take a picture I could have out of sympathetic feelings towards the soldiers, and I have been very careful never to let that happen since. Mostly, soldiers realise you are just trying to do your job, and they let you get on with it. So I actually think we've been able to work very freely. I've never spent as much as a whole month embedded with any unit so as to actually get that close to it. I know there are some photographers who have spent 12 months embedded with one unit, which would drive me nuts. But as far as looking at things from a very, very small, like a pin-hole perspective—it's true, except this is also the case when you're working with Iraqi civilians—if you're working in Sadr City and you're on one street, that's only one street. There's an entire city of Baghdad out there, and the whole country beyond that. I mean, we have 100 Iraqi journalists and fixers working for us at any given time so that we actually can construct a picture of what's happing in Iraq. We're talking to high-ranking officers, we're talking to the prime minister every other day, to ensure that we know everything that's happening at every level of Iraqi society. I think to go in there now as a unilateral journalist without that support system, you would have enormous trouble.

JS How did the military tend to see you? You mentioned quite a cultural divide between you and these young American soldiers, but there's an officer class as well, there's the Pentagon itself, which was anxious to court the media for this war. Can you talk about your relationship with the media, the soldiers?

AG Well, as a photographer, I won't do an embed if they're going to take me on some dog-and-pony show. Well, of course I've done some dog-and-pony shows that are pretty funny—I mean, where they take out a gigantic pair of scissors and do a ribbon-cutting on a bridge in Tikrit that they had blown up during the war. But I've kind of got an advantage over an American reporter going in and talking to all these soldiers. I'm an Australian guy, I swear, like, a lot, I smoke a lot, I've got these fancy cameras they love playing with. They're immediately interested, they're like 'What the hell ... who the hell is this guy and what is he doing here?' Politics never comes into any conversations that I have because I'm not Republican or Democrat. I'm from some weird country in the South Pacific. So there's this sort of interest there that really puts them off-guard.

I won't do an embed unless it's with a unit that's actually out on the front, like, on point. There's no point being on the second line, or the third line because you don't see anything. You need to be with the very, very first unit. Then they can't stop me from seeing anything. When they shoot at civilians, they can't hide that from me. They can say 'Don't pick up your fucking camera or we'll shoot you in the head'. For example, when a Marine is killed and I go to take pictures and they freak out, I actually feel like I've had my life threatened by soldiers or Marines when that happens. I understand that it's an intense, emotional experience that they're going through, and to have some jackass photographer try to take pictures of it—you're going to react strongly, except back then rules said I could do it. So it's basically only when someone has been killed or wounded that I've had difficulties working.

JS And to look at the other side of the picture, what about the attitudes of Iraqi civilians to your presence and to being photographed?

AG I think at the outset they were happy to talk to us and they were interested that maybe we could help them. You need to think of the history of Iraq, the recent history of Iraq. Any media working in Iraq was answering straight to Saddam. It was all state-controlled media. So when we came in, and showed our press cards that said we were independent reporters, that didn't really click. They thought that when they're telling us something, it's going straight back to George Bush. So initially I think they were actually quite happy to talk to us because they felt that President Bush would listen, and say, 'OK, look we need to change this, we need to do this'. After a couple of years they realised that in fact we're a pretty useless bunch and that the President doesn't read *The [New York] Times*. And then it got to a point where if Iraqis were seen talking to foreign reporters or inviting them into their house, they'd be killed, which again made access a lot more difficult. Now we can talk to civilians again, but you need these stupid pieces of paper from the Ministry of Defence because apparently it's an Iraqi operation now, which makes it almost impossible to get into a neighbourhood, and when you do get into that neighbourhood that you've been waiting for weeks to get into, the Iraqi military follow you everywhere you go. So if you can imagine pulling up outside someone's house with three Humvees behind you and all these guys with guns, like, hanging outside their house, it doesn't really make for a good open dialogue.

JS Amazing. I mean it's one of the big contrasts with Vietnam I think, because the National Liberation Front and the North Vietnamese Army were aware of the effects these images were having, and even went out of their way to protect photojournalists to an extent. It seems that in Iraq the opposite is true.

AG Well we're targets, we're infidels. We're the spokespeople for the infidels coming in and trying to conquer the Middle East. I mean that's how they see us. We've got communiqués from [Abu Musab] al-Zarqawi himself that say 'We're going after the Western press'.

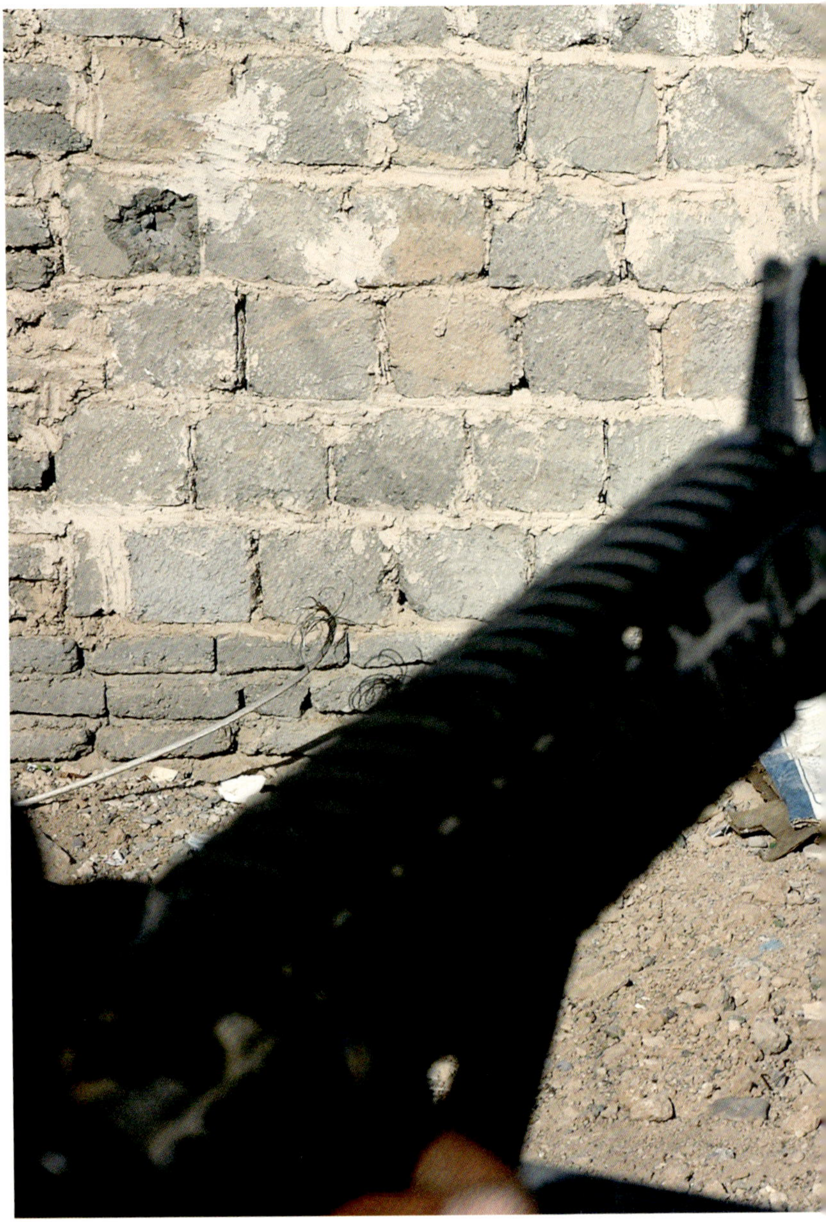

March, 2004. A man and a boy venture outside to assess the damage to their Samarra neighbourhood. The boy carries a white flag to show that he is a non-combatant. Most residents carried flags like this, but that didn't stop US soldiers from aiming weapons at them

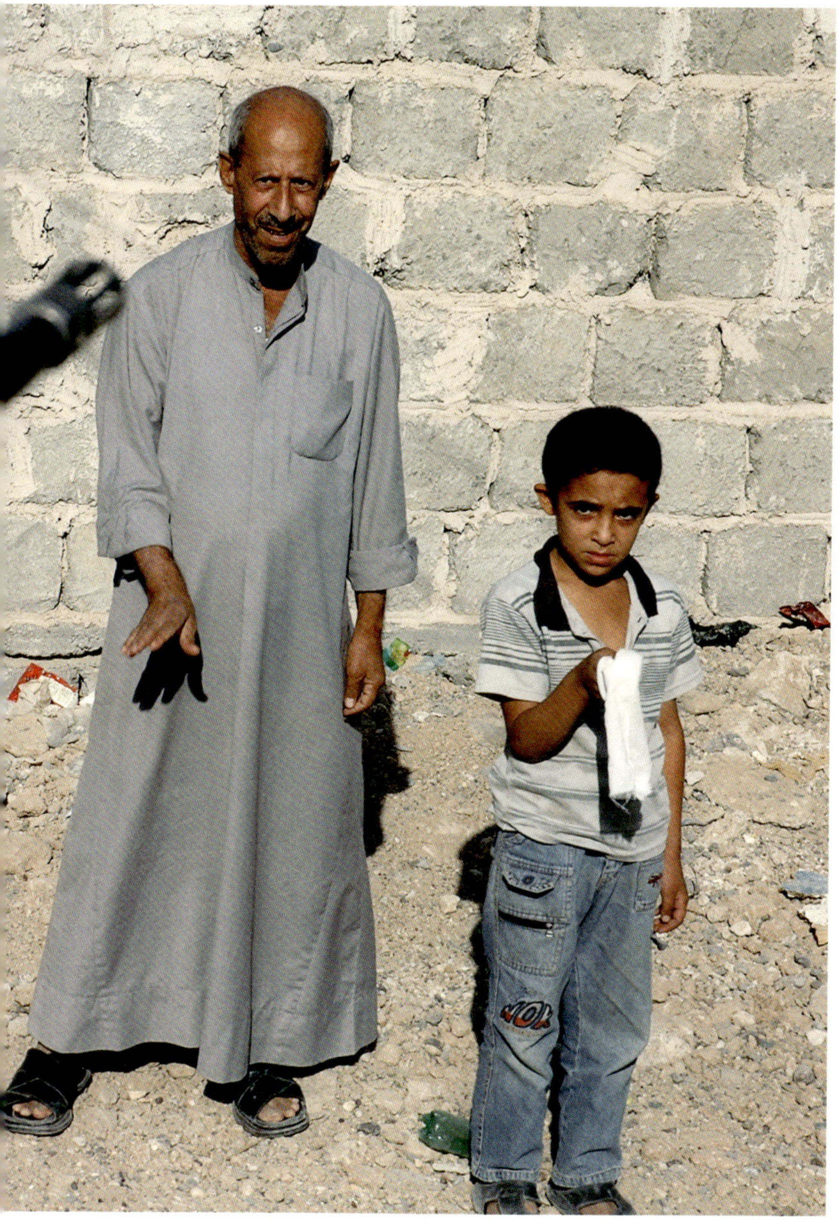

When they double suicide-bombed the Hotel Palestine, they were trying to take out the Associated Press. That was a direct attack on them. They've killed, they've beheaded reporters ... there have been more reporters killed in this war than any other war to date, and that's because we are targets.

JS Do you know why the Iraqi resistance is not at all interested in Western public opinion, or influencing it through the media?

AG There's certainly websites, I mean they're constantly changing them. We've got one guy in the newsroom whose job it is to keep track of where these websites are going, and there are entire institutes dedicated to this, in both London and Washington that track Jihadi and nationalist websites. If you're in the loop, if you sitting in Peshawar, it's not very difficult to find those websites, but for us non-Arabic speakers, they are very, very difficult to find. They don't want to reach out to us. In the case of Al-Qaeda, they just want us finished. In the case of the nationalists, they did finally reach out, but there's no unified front. I mean, we're talking about sheikhs in villages who haven't got water, let alone cell phones and computers. The nationalists were a disenfranchised group of Sunnis that had no other choice but to fight. Now that they've been brought back into the fold with the awakening councils, that's somewhat changed, but again, any settlement is very, very fragile.

JS I wonder if you could talk a little about changing demands of the press. What it is that the press wants from you as a photographer?

AG Lots of pictures, as often as possible, and digital technology has made that a hell of a lot harder. We used to be able to tell a lot of white lies and say we can't get the film out today, and that would give us a couple of extra days to work on a story and create stronger pictures, but now we can't do that. Now we've got satellite phones, satellite special internet connections, we have laptops, we have little things we can charge all of our equipment from car batteries, and of course the digital cameras—we've got no excuse any more. And I think the pressure on photojournalists has actually become a lot more intense. I mean we have to do all of our own editing, all of our own captioning, we have to file. I mean, I never did this in Iraq, but in America for example I covered the hurricane in New Orleans, and I had to file five times a day for the website. It was nonsense, I could hardly work. This is the problem. Even so, newspapers are still superior to television, because television is so busy, standing in front of cameras doing live updates every 15 minutes, that they can't report. I was told by mast-head editors at *The Times* before I went on this last trip that 'we'll no longer judge by your front page stories and pictures. We'll now judge you by what you put on the website and on the blog'—which is crap. I also think that that level of pressure, when there are so many photographers working and transmitting that often, means that some photographers buckle under the strain. There is the case of the photographer with *The LA Times*, who had two pictures, that were great by themselves, of the British Marine telling a civilian to sit down, and then the civilian

trying to get up with his baby and run. They were both good pictures but he felt they were even better spliced together as one. So he did a pretty good job in Photoshop putting these things together. It landed on the front page of the paper, and an Iraqi back in LA picked up the paper and was looking for relatives and found the same guy twice, and called the paper, and they fired the photographer.[2] I think that we need to be more careful, I mean, we have to do less work on our pictures than we used to do in the darkroom. The unofficial rule was if you can do it in your darkroom you can do it in your pictures in Photoshop, but I think you actually have to do less than that now, because there is so much manipulation being done out there we actually need to stand back and be above that as press. Our role and our credibility is constantly being threatened and undermined, so I actually think that we have to be more credible, and do less work on our pictures to increase that credibility.

JS To continue with this 'demands of the press' issue, has it ever surprised you which of your images have been picked up and been successful, and are there images that you've taken which you would have liked to have seen out there but were killed or just not used for various reasons?

AG The picture of the MP photographing the dead Mahdi Army soldier never ran, and I thought that was one of my strongest pictures. Every picture of wounded and dead American soldiers that I've shot, which is only a handful, have all run, except they only run in *The Times*, they don't go in *Time* magazine or *Newsweek* or anything like that, but they often pick up the softer pictures. One picture that I shot quite literally as a joke, of this soldier standing in the sunset with his gun raised and looking like a frigging hero—it was such a stupid picture ... but I filed it and sent it back to the paper, and it's, like, I guess this running joke that we have with the picture editors, and they're, like, 'Yeah that's great, Ash, thanks a lot'. The picture has sold so many times, every three months when I get my stock, my quarterly stock thing from the agency, you know, it's 'Soldier in Sunset', 'Soldier in Sunset'—everybody loves it, it's crap, I shot it as a joke! The difficulty is you look at the images from Vietnam, and those pictures have had 40 years to actually gain traction and become iconic, images that we all know very well. The pictures in the Iraq room are all very, very fresh, and I wish that people would pick up more stuff from the war that's been shot over the years, except pretty much all editors in both Europe and the States want stuff that was shot last week. They're looking for the really fresh stuff, and stock stuff very rarely gets used.

JS That's very interesting. You live in the States now. What has been the public reaction to your work? Of course, you have a reputation obviously as a photojournalist, but do you have much understanding of the broader reception of your work, and do you

2 Brian Walski, an *LA Times* staff photographer, was fired in April 2003, and *The Times* published a note describing the manipulation and reproducing its component images.

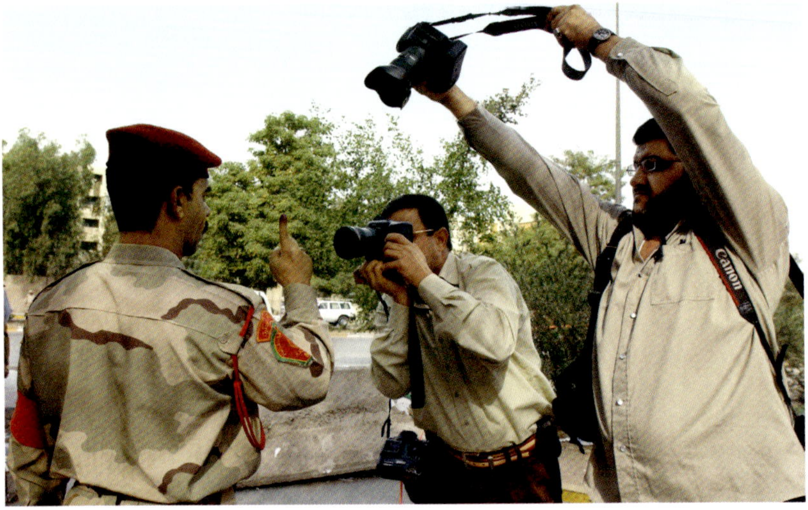

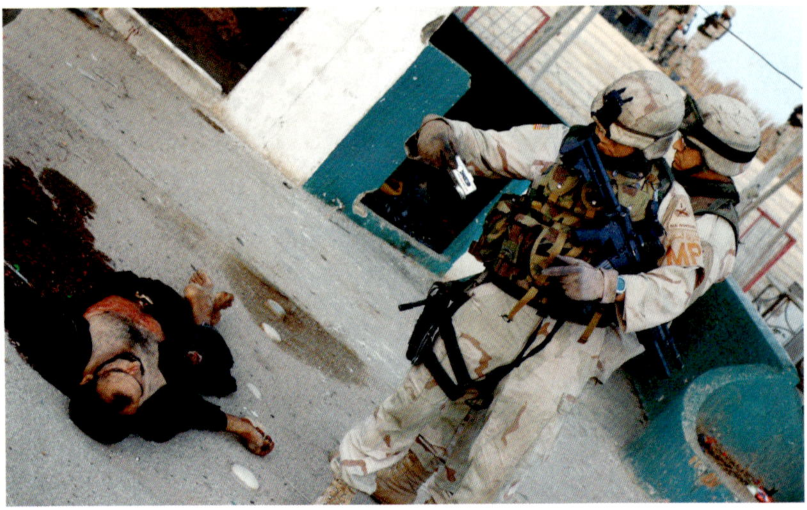

Top Wire photographers pose a soldier to photograph his ink-stained finger, signifying that he had voted in the December 2005 national election
Bottom Army policy is to leave dead Iraqis for other Iraqis to recover and bury. The body of the Madhi Army fighter was an object of curiosity for GIs, one of whom takes a snapshot with his digital camera. March 2004

get communications from members of the public, particularly in the States?

AG **Yeah, especially when I launched my book—I actually got a lot.[3] You get emails while you are away, and people write to you with, like, 'Thanks a lot for your job' or they say you're a scumbag or a pig, get out of Iraq or whatever, but when I did the book tour I got a lot of reaction from people both at readings and when I did a radio or television appearance, with a flood of emails, and largely people were glad for the role that photojournalists are playing in Iraq. I mean, these are actually people who take time to write so they obviously feel pretty strongly already—they're really appreciative that we're actually there doing a job. I think that a *lot* of the American public realise there's very few of us left doing this anymore—at any given time you've got half a dozen photographers working in Iraq, and you've got maybe a dozen foreign reporters working in Iraq. This is the largest story that our generation is going to cover, and there's almost no reporters covering the thing. In fact, I was out to dinner the other night with the ABC Bureau chief for Saigon during the Vietnam War, and he said, 'Your newspapers are falling to pieces, there's not enough ink being put into the Iraq story any more', and I said 'Well, was there much more airtime devoted to Vietnam towards the end?', and he said, 'Right, there are parallels'. People were just exhausted, and there was very little space on TV or in print devoted to the conflicts as they dragged on for years.**

JS No, that's true. But the character of those reactions—you're saying that they're mostly supportive. So you don't get large amounts of mail from right-wing pro-war activists?

AG **I do get some. I try to control myself and not write back, but you get some really crazy ones, people who are really angry. One of these jackasses went through my book and took every single fact, all of which had been reported in *The Times*—I use that as my benchmark—took every single fact, like, questioned the thing, sent me this furious email swearing at me, and I take it all really personally as well, so it makes me pretty mad. And I think for every ten positive emails you get one crackpot. But a lot of the Right have supported the book as well. I mean, both Left and Right, soldiers and civilians, have liked the book. The soldiers say, 'You told it like it was', and for all the stuff that they did wrong, that they're responsible for, they realise that I'm not out there to paint a bad picture of them; I'm there to paint *a* picture of them as I saw it. This whole idea of objectivity and subjectivity, I think it was Gene Smith who said subjectivity, no, but honesty, yes. Or objectivity, no, honesty, yes. That makes more sense, doesn't it?[4]**

---

3 Ashley Gilbertson, *Whiskey Tango Foxtrot: A Photographer's Chronicle of the Iraq War*, University of Chicago Press, Chicago, IL, 2007. 4 'The journalistic photographer can have no other than a personal approach; and it is impossible for him to be completely objective. Honest—yes. Objective—no.' W. Eugene Smith, 'Photographic Journalism', *Photo Notes*, June 1948, p. 4.

Overleaf Kael Alford, A father shows his hand to snipers as he carries his terrified child across the front line between US forces and the Madhi Army at the wrecked outskirts of the old city. Najaf, 21 August, 2004

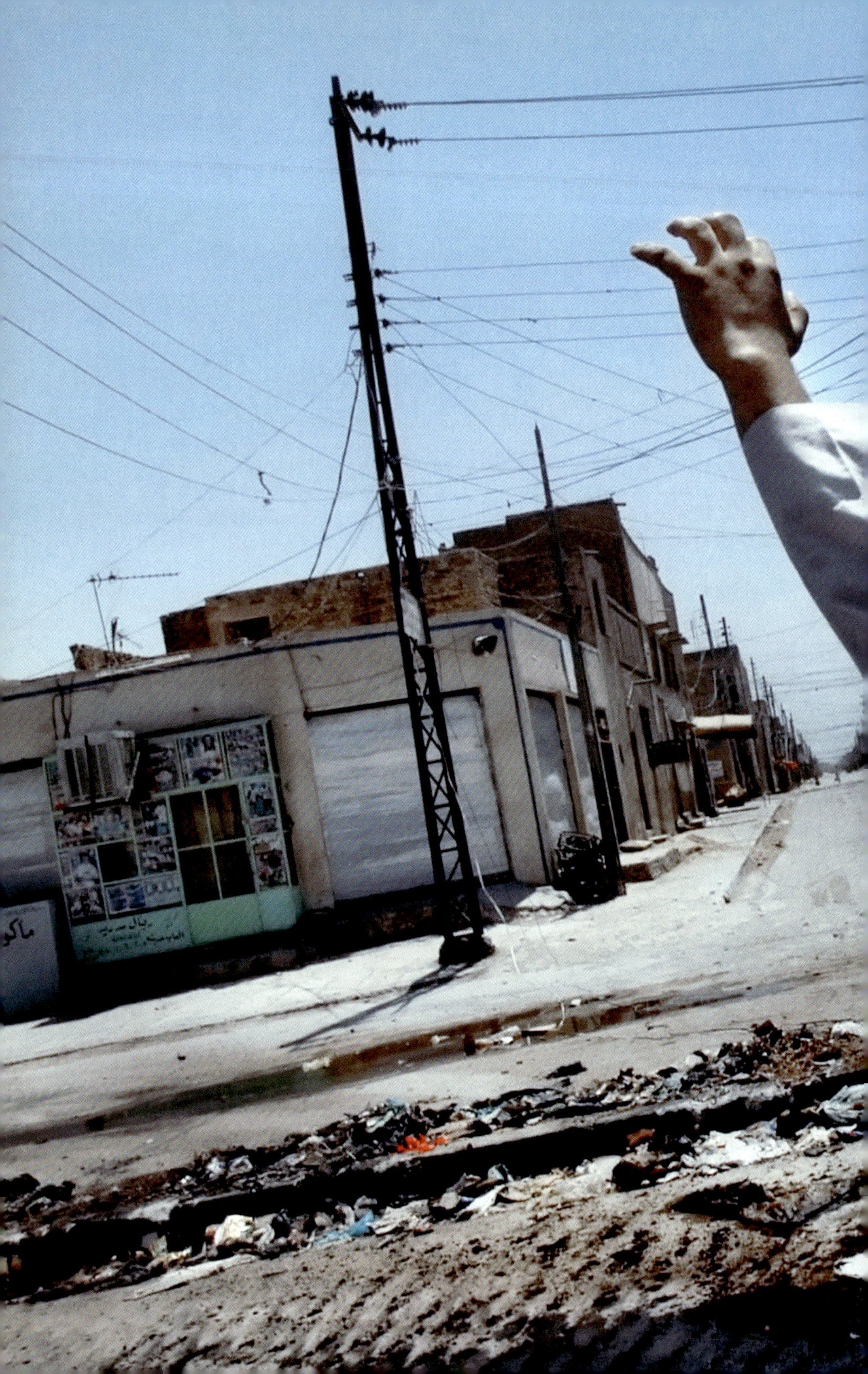

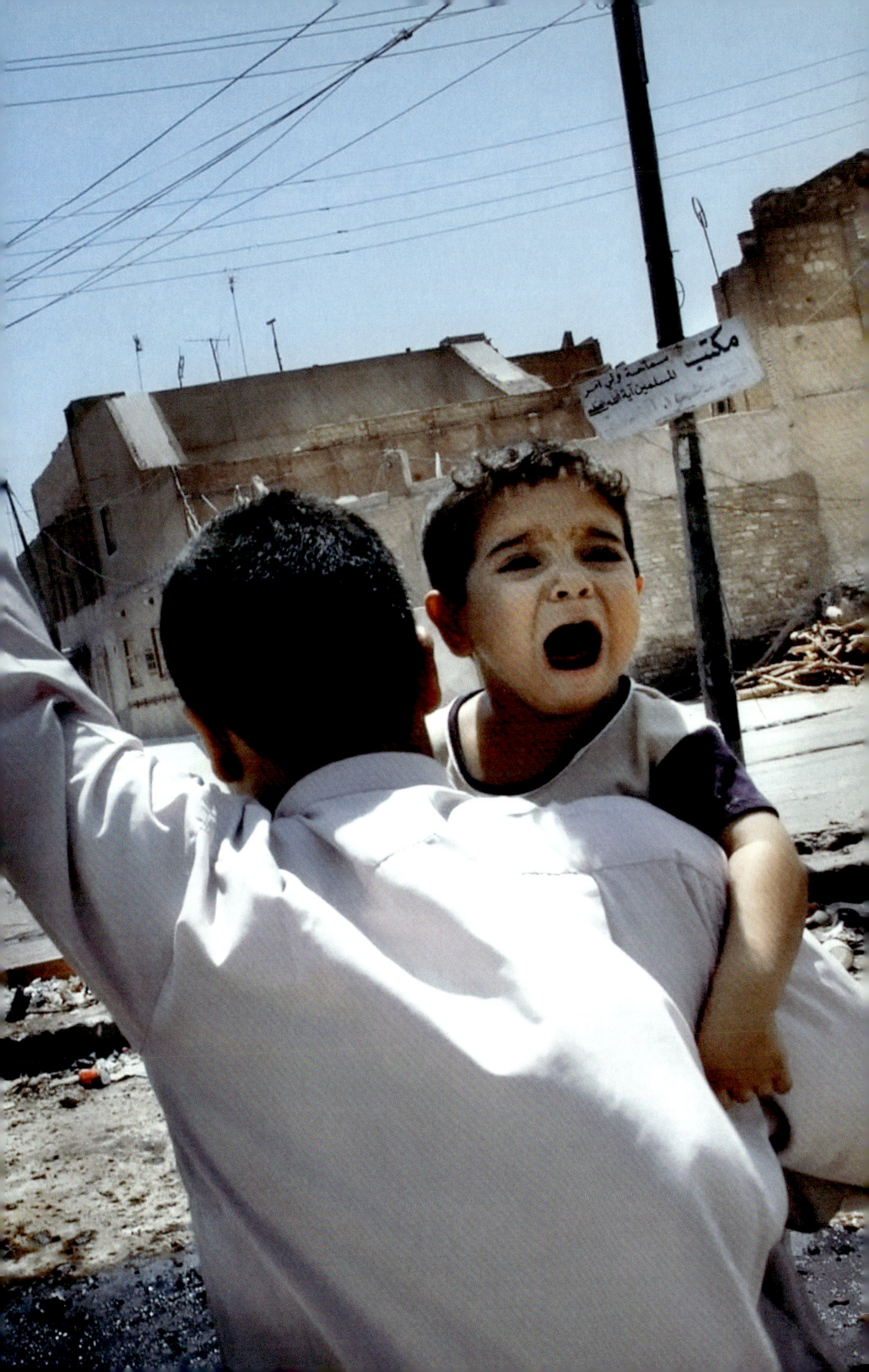
مكتب
سماحة ولي امر
المسلمين آية الله

Making an Ugly World Beautiful? Morality and Aesthetics in the Aftermath

Sarah James

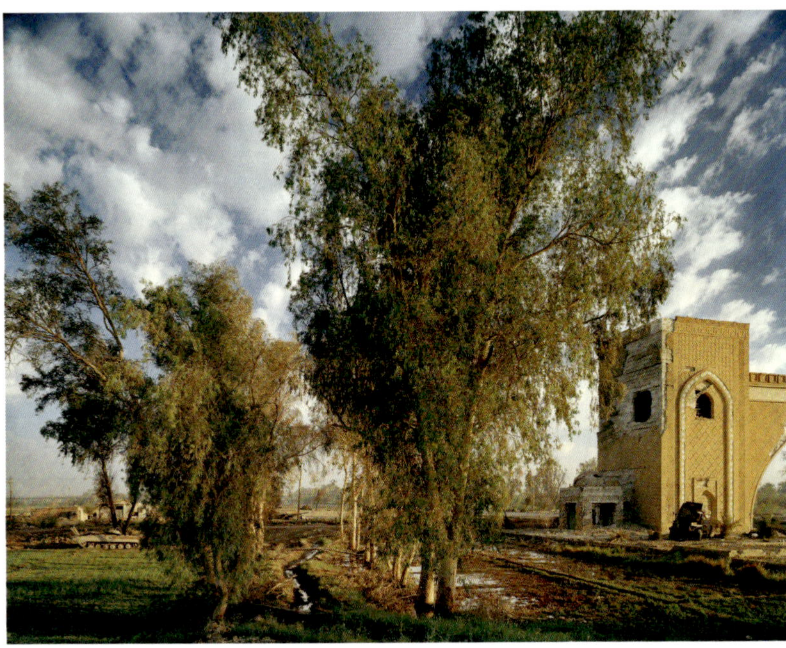

Simon Norfolk, *The North Gate of Baghdad, the scene of fierce fighting during the invasion, 19-27 April 2003*

Throughout history, war has confronted photography with the limits and possibilities of its aesthetic and means. The relationship between war and photography mirrors that crisis of representation synonymous with modern times, the ever-deteriorating link between experience and knowledge, and the destruction of traditional fields of perception. Today, war photography in the museum has turned into a medium of the aftermath. This is because the technological nature of today's warfare has resulted in a war that is nearly impossible to document as it happens. Surveying sites ruined by war and catastrophe—Bosnia, Iraq, Afghanistan, Kuwait, Beirut, Baghdad, Lebanon, Palestine, or Manhattan's Ground Zero—photographers such as Simon Norfolk, Paul Seawright, Joel Meyerowitz and Sophie Ristelhueber have developed this strange new genre. Each works in saturated or subdued colour, often on a monumental scale and with thrilling precision, capturing the surfaces of the destroyed city of Baghdad, the snow-covered sites of Serbian mass graves, the barren post-war wastelands of Beirut, or depicting the Lebanese refugee camps and Israel's everyday militaristic cult of the dead. The surreal landscapes and alien environments charted by these photographers are as abstract, inhuman and incomprehensible as the wars that caused them.

Many of these sites are synonymous with the 'war against terror' waged by America and its allies against the forces which they perceive as threatening 'liberty' as defined by neo-liberal democracies, and their precious economies. Beginning in Kuwait in 1990, and continuing to this day, such warfare has now gone beyond even the simulacra and spectacle of the heavily televised 'Operation Desert Storm.' It follows a post-Cold War military doctrine of 'rapid dominance' based on overwhelming power, dominant manoeuvres, and spectacular displays of force. Defined by Harlan K. Ullman and James P. Wade, America's new mode of warfare attempts 'to affect the will, perception, and understanding of the adversary to fit or respond to our strategic policy ends through imposing a regime of "Shock and Awe".'[1] Now five years of the war in Iraq have passed—as opposed to the 48 hours originally suggested by the Pentagon—and it is horribly clear that the aim of a rapid domination has failed. Yet this violent military assault is certainly of a horrific magnitude, costing thousands of lives and trillions of dollars. A form of terrorism itself, it is designed to impose an overwhelming level of shock and awe, so as to paralyse one's enemy, to overload their perceptions, rendering them incapable of resistance at both tactical and strategic levels. Ullman's shock and

---

1 Harlan K. Ullman and James P. Wade, *Shock And Awe: Achieving Rapid Dominance*, National Defense University, Washington, DC, 1996, p. xxiv.

awe operates in the mass media just as it does in international politics, via an aesthetic of violence. The staging and representation of key events are exploited so as to supersede cognitive assimilation, and are used to provoke a dangerous range of powerful and war-mongering emotions.[2] This is not only a war fought to control territories but one waged over meaning. In the equivalent of a grotesque hermeneutic Hiroshima, America seeks a position of total moral and cultural superiority. When meaning is at stake to this degree, photography's representation of war could not be any more ideologically loaded, aesthetically volatile and morally precarious.

The work of Seawright, Ristelhueber and Norfolk is not war photography as we know it. Their images portray environments of surreal devastation as epic, highly aestheticised, and often depopulated landscapes. Norfolk's pictures present the debris of rapid domination, superbly composed and theatrically framed: graveyards of wrecked Afghan airlines jets; the fragile, circus-like victory arch entrance to a local commander's headquarters in Bamiyan; a clutch of space-age Soviet cluster bombs; the concrete screen of an outdoor cinema, pock-marked by artillery fire; and a track of a destroyed Taliban tank laid out, serpentine, like a dinosaur's skeleton. Huge purple sunsets and open vistas of pink clouds hang behind bombed-out villages, and sunlight ripples across the decorative surfaces of mortar rounds. The same intricacy, ornament and dramatic horizons abound in Ristelhueber's work. Giant, derelict towers in Armenian ghost towns lean like peculiar monuments; aerial photographs taken after the Gulf War make curling sand patterns out of trenches and tank tracks; and armies of beheaded Iraqi palm trees extend endlessly into a bleached-out sky. Not only mapping the aftermath of war, photography such as Norfolk's crucially makes visible and surveys the otherwise invisible national and corporate empires that support such wars, and increasingly control the world. ECHELON, the global computerised surveillance system of the US National Security Administration, super computers such as IBM's 'Blue Gene' (which designs America's nuclear weapons), and the technology of fibre-optic fencing, radio systems and motion detectors that are used to violently police America's Mexican border have all been recorded by his camera. His photography valuably resists the possibility of such invisible forms of warfare disappearing from the popular imagination. These crisp and highly precise photographs are suited to such subjects, depicted in all their minute detail and sinister glory.

---

2 See Roland Bleiker and Martin Leet, 'From the Sublime to the Subliminal: Fear, Awe and Wonder in International Politics', *Journal of International Studies*, vol. 34, no. 3, August 2006, pp. 713–37.

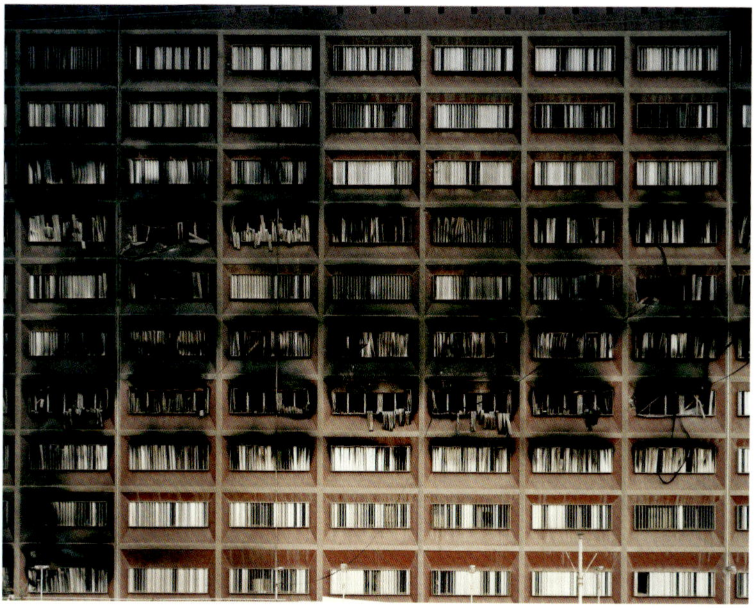

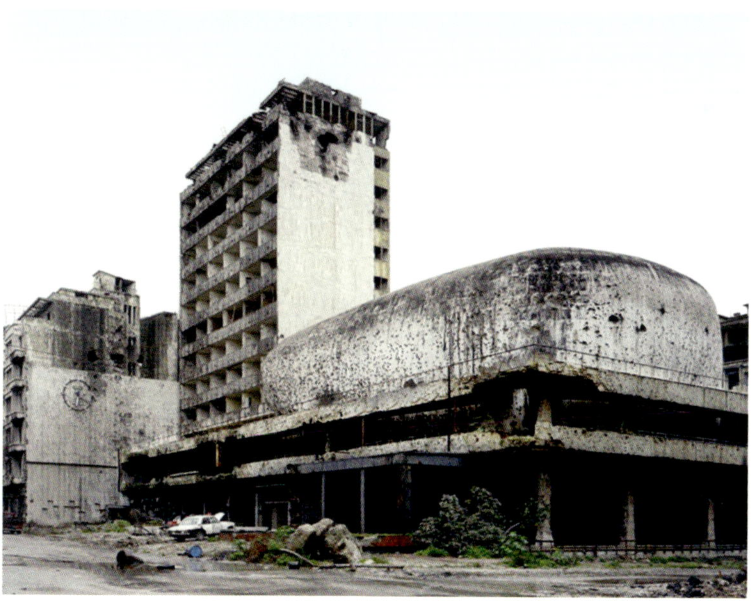

Top Simon Norfolk, *The bombed, burned and looted Ministry of Planning, Baghdad, 19-27 April 2003*
Bottom Gabriele Basilico, *Beirut*, 1991

The recent work of Norfolk, Seawright, Ristelheuber and Meyerowitz could not be further from the black-and-white traditions of the social documentarian, or the often gruesome shots of photojournalism. In many ways, the images by these photographers are closer to the medium of landscape photography than they are to the documentation of war. If photography gave warfare a face during the Vietnam War, these photographers produce almost abstract monumental scenes, frozen on slick surfaces, which are undeniably commensurate with the incomprehensibility of capitalism's pure war, waged against unknowable and abstract 'terrors'. Within this largely depopulated photography, 'human beings seem to have even less of a place, and a concept of experience seems to be ever more atavistic'.[3] But if aftermath photography has moved away from the humanistic tenets of the documentarian, what aesthetic and what experience does this monumental, beautiful photography of destruction and surveillance call upon? Photographing Ground Zero, Meyerowitz has spoken of his recognition that his subject matter required a new definition of the sublime. Norfolk has named this perplexing subject that his photography also seeks to document as the international 'military sublime'. Thus, a contemporary version of this past universal category emerges as perfectly analogous to the unfathomable, awe-inspiring and horrific nature of today's globalised, technologised warfare.

The radicality in the aesthetic projects of these aftermath photographers lies in their taking beautiful photographs of gruesome subjects, which are necessarily asked to be read against themselves. One could argue that against the blindness of universalism, in a dialectical fashion photographers like Norfolk, Seawright and Ristelhueber rely upon a process which sublimates the seduction of beauty into the horror of violence. Their work exploits this violent dialectic at the moment of realisation. So that an aesthetics of sublimity serves not to transcend violence but to collapse into it, prompting a strange revelation or reflection upon the real that would otherwise be buried. Further, such *a posteriori* photography allows these images a certain politicality. Their carefully composed nature, often lengthy exposure time and beautifully printed form contrasts starkly, and consequently also offers an ideological alternative to the cheap current of 24-hour live coverage endlessly relayed to our living rooms via the world's news agencies, and the form of spectatorship this promotes.[4] In moving against the shocking televised images that are assumed to have lost their power, these careful, slow photographs force a

---

3 Bernd Hüppauf, 'Experiences of Modern Warfare and the Crisis of Representation', *New German Critique*, no. 59, Spring 1993, p. 75.

deeper kind of reflection on important subjects too often lost in the media's glare. Equally, heightening the aesthetic and artistic status of the photograph enables a withdrawal from the medium's purely documentary function, and consequently an unburdening of the image from photojournalism's truth claims. This very definite move away from the snapshot or documentary image also enables such 'museum' photographs to be freed from the ambiguity of the former's easily choreographed form. It releases them from the exploitative or instrumental context that sees photojournalism manipulated by the largely conservative and nationalistically biased media organisations that determine its context and reception.

But what does it really mean to make war beautiful, to depict the 'military sublime'? The sublime—in representation, or under interrogation—has too often been a hiding place for postmodernists. In his 'Postscript to Terror and the Sublime', Jean Francois Lyotard declared that there could be no politics of the sublime, only terror.[5] But, he conceded, there is an aesthetics of the sublime in politics. Even he, however, could not have imagined the sublime as orchestrated by the Bush administration. Nor perhaps could Lyotard's libidinal economy have accounted for an American market that can reincorporate and ruthlessly rebrand an already morally indefensible war, exploiting the military doctrine of 'shock and awe' for trite commercial purposes.[6] Indeed, as Len Finlay has observed, 'the military sublime works in tandem with the market sublime in an often obscene symbiosis to direct the fortunes of war and the diversification of violence, including cultural violence'.[7] Can a photography that pictures this process also police the line between military and market sublimity, while resisting the commodification and fetishisation which sometimes hides in acts of aestheticisation? Does the photography of Norfolk, Seawright, Meyerowitz and Ristelhueber make this military sublime more real, more tangible, and more difficult to stomach?

---

4 See François Debrix, 'The Sublime Spectatorship of War: The Erasure of the Event in America's Politics of Terror and Aesthetics of Violence', *Journal of International Studies*, vol. 34, no. 3, August 2006, pp. 767–91. 5 See Jean Francois Lyotard, *The Postmodern Explained: Correspondence, 1982-85*, trans./ed., Julian Pefanis and Morgan Thomas, University of Minnesota Press, Minneapolis, MN, 1992, p. 71. On the problems of thinking a political sublime, see Ned O' Gorman, 'The Political Sublime: An Oxymoron', *Journal of International Studies*, vol. 34, no. 3, August 2006, pp. 889–915. 6 Following the United States' invasion of Iraq in 2003, the term 'shock and awe' has been used for a wide range of commercial purposes. The United States Patent and Trademark Office received around 29 trademark applications in 2003 for exclusive use of the term. Sony registered the trademark for use in a video game title, but later withdrew the application, stating it was 'an exercise of regrettable bad judgment'. Other equally distasteful uses of the term include fireworks, golf equipment, an insecticide, bowling balls, shampoo, condoms and baby's cot toys. 7 Len M. Findlay, 'When I hear the word "culture": State Syntax, Cultural Vocabularies, and Violence', paper given at the conference *Culture and State*, held at University of Alberta, Edmonton, Canada, 2–5 May 2003, p. 18.

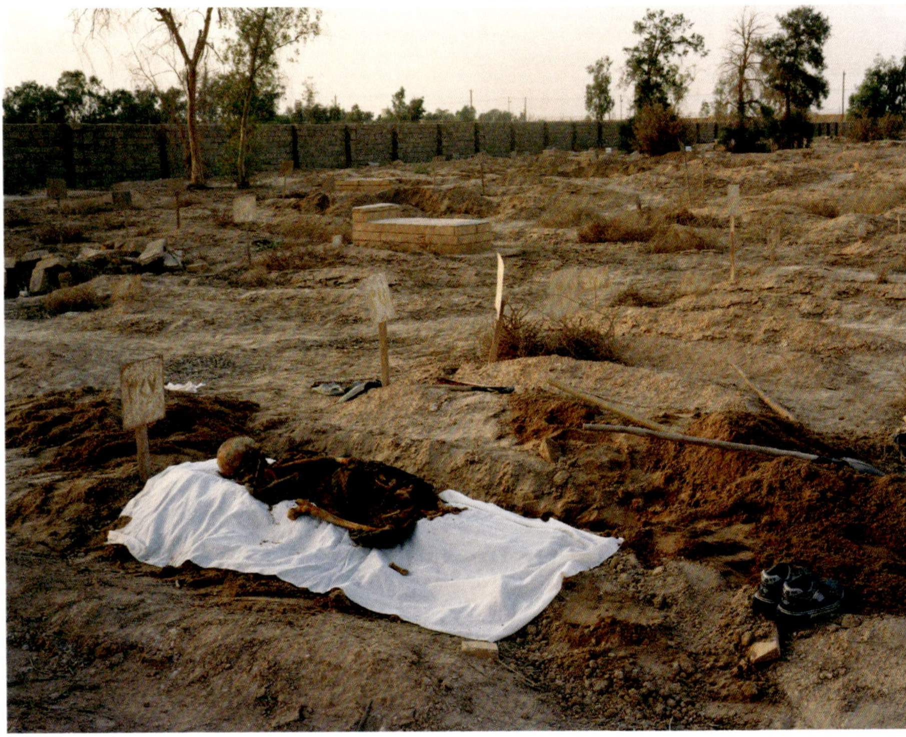

Simon Norfolk, *Grave Number 327*. The body of Shalal Moussa Al-Zubeidi from Amarra, jailed in Abu Ghraib in a June 1993 for Islamic political activity. He was killed in September 1993 and his body buried in a secret part of Abu Ghraib cemetery in a numbered grave. His family have come to dig up his remains and move them to the family plot in Najaf. Baghdad, 19–27 April 2003

Or does it actually make it dangerously unreal, strangely theatrical, detached, inhuman and perilously close to those universal abstractions mobilised in international politics and neo-liberal culture? Is it not dangerous to cast ourselves as helpless in the face of abstract, monolithic, neo-liberal, capitalist, military and corporate might? Is, in fact, the sublime effect of the work a way of bringing into focus the dangers and seductions of the military sublime?

It is impossible to argue that these photographers have not, to some extent, engaged in the representation of warfare's beauty. Norfolk has spoken of the 'astonishing creation' at the heart of war's unspeakable destruction, of the 'strange beauty' found in 'the way a mortar shell tears a "splash" into tarmac as it cuts down a Sarajevo bakery queue; the graceful turn of a falling anti-missile flare...'[8] It is hard to know what that post-Auschwitz philosopher and aesthete Theodor Adorno would have made of this photographic aestheticisation of destruction. If he argued that form transfigures and stylises horror; sentimentalising it, he also believed that 'perennial suffering has as much right to expression as a tortured man has to scream'.[9] For Adorno the Holocaust was too profound a violence to allow aestheticisation; an anti-sublime of unthinkable proportions. If Auschwitz occurred again today, would it be absorbed into the military sublime, photographed by a large-format camera, in colour, minute detail, and on a monumental scale? The beautiful, detached photographic imagination of these 'aftermath photographers' is arguably more at ease with supercomputers than it is with mutilation, death, displacement and genocide. When the images of the dead or horrifically injured occasionally puncture these otherwise depopulated landscapes—the bloody and fragile face of 18-month-old Zainab Tharmar, seriously wounded by an American controlled explosion of Iraqi missiles (p. 5), or the crumpled body of a dead soldier in the dirt—they bring with them a whole new and horrible tension. Such images interrupt the ghostly smooth surfaces of war's aftermath with humanist shudders of reality and fatalities. Pictures of the Lebanese Red Cross and Hizbollah units storing dead bagged bodies in refrigerated lorries jar violently with the panoramic shots of empty swimming pools, or the unreal rainbow patterns on burned filing cabinets in the Iraqi National library. These images challenge the thesis that a war photography of intimacy is no longer possible. For it is still possible to take pictures of the dead. The dead, after all, share an almost ahistorical equality. Today, just as in the previous century. Children's bodies are still torn

---

8 See Simon Norfolk's text, 'Refuge: The First Safe Place', http://www.simonnorfolk.com. **9** See Theodor Adorno, *Negative Dialectics*, trans., E.B. Ashton, Continuum, New York 1973, p. 362.

apart by mortars. Broken families still cluster in refugee camps. Corpses are still heaped in mass graves. The only difference is that documentary as a valuable and vital medium is now understood as dead.

Yet even if many photographers have moved away from depicting the human face of war, the popular visual imagination still seems to demand it. Look at how the iconic masked face of an injured office worker became emblematic of the 2005 London bombings, or how the 'We're Not Afraid' movement retaliated with a bizarre campaign based on the collective utilisation of photographic portraits. There is also a sense that the humanitarian documentary vision has not been completely relinquished in this aftermath photography, nor the pristine aesthetic of these museal works totally reconciled with their subject matter. For example, in Norfolk's series *For Most Of It I Have No Words: Genocide, Landscape, Memory*, 1998, he revisits both historical sites of genocide, and their traditional documentary mode of photographic representation. These pictures, in stark contrast to most of his other works, are in black and white, and have a grainy quality. Images of hundreds of skulls found at the church of Ntarama in Rwanda are indistinguishable from 1970s images of the mass graves in Cambodia. His dramatic pictures of Dresden recall *Dresden, a Camera Accuses*, the photobook by Richard Peter which recorded the horrors of the city's deathly destruction in 1945. The series also includes portraits of the Vietnamese offspring of Agent Orange victims, images of Auschwitz, and the Ukrainian forests used for mass shootings. It is impossible to imagine these images large scale, or in slick, crisp colour. Norfolk insists that he is 'using the visual economy of black and white and the austerity of the square format', but that these images are 'not documentary in the traditional sense'. Instead, he argues that they are 'documents like forensic traces at a crime scene'.[10] Norfolk's vocal rejection of traditional documentary in this context is intriguing. We are left unsure of the status of the documentary look of these images. Yet even in this series documenting atrocities, Norfolk includes pictures of Armenian poplar trees and Namibian sand dunes that could easily—and, in this context, uneasily—be mistaken as the modernist abstract and aesthetic works of Albert Renger-Patzsch or Edward Weston. Norfolk's expert use of different photographic aesthetics brings one back to the uncomfortable partnership of aesthetics and politics. His emphasis on the evidential function of the medium suggests a proximity to the work of Gilles Peress. Peress has stressed that he

---

10 See Simon Norfolk, *For Most of It I Have No Words: Genocide, Landscape, Memory*, essay by Michael Ignatieff, Dewi Lewis, Stockport 1998. 11 Hüppauf, *New German Critique*, 1993, p. 56.

seeks to work as a 'forensic photographer', collecting evidence and taking still-lives, like a police photographer. Yet while problematising the boundaries between documentary and aesthetics, his black-and-white photography still seems to stray less from the domain of photojournalism than Norfolk's.

In his series *Archaeological Treasures from the Tigris Valley*, 2003, Norfolk performed what he describes as 'cursory excavations' at battlefields in Iraq. There is a tension within this form of photography that is proffered more as a kind of archaeology than documentary, when its subject matter is so very far from being historical. Fashioning a makeshift studio, he recorded these objects—mostly soldier's personal affects and weaponry; photographs of loved ones, sandals, bullets, pliers and cigarette packets—so that 'they might be studied by scholars at a later date'. Each artefact is represented in a disturbingly beautiful and detached manner which seems to problematise their already impossible standing as evidence. While the task of redeeming the historical evidence of a war that might otherwise be forgotten is a noble one, as is the attempt to deepen moral ties with distant and anonymous victims, it is odd that Norfolk frames this endeavour so historically and aesthetically. Although documentary is engaged in history, it surely achieves its power in the ways that it bears directly upon the social of the present. Yet Norfolk seems happy to offer his already historicised finds to a distant and academic future.

If documentary photography is no longer a medium capable of representing today's technological warfare, the paradox that lies within these representations of the technologised military sublime is that it is not upon a contemporary sublime that photographers such as Norfolk are drawing. The discourse of the sublime has long encircled war photography. With the aerial photography used during the First World War, the medium emptied the landscape and the battlefield of its traditional points of orientation, and the discourse of the sublime was mobilised. As Bernd Hüppauf has suggested, from such a perspective, scenes of destruction could now be seen as grandiose spectacles or places of horror which 'no longer arouse feelings of empathy, pity, or sorrow, because the potential for experience was reduced to a barren functional space'.[11] But the sublime called upon by contemporary practitioners such as Meyerowitz and Norfolk is even older than photography's invention. If the archaic and idealised form of social documentary has been rejected, perplexingly these photographers restate strong links to the aesthetics of the 19th century. This is true not only in the choice of apparatus—Norfolk uses a large-format 4x5 wooden field camera and tripod, and Meyerowitz is known for working with a Deardorff 8x10 wooden field camera—but also in terms of the approach, composition and framing of their photography. Norfolk has stressed the importance of the 17th- and 18th-century European landscape painting of Claude Lorraine and Nicolas Poussin, particularly in terms of their characteristic golden light and the symbolism of ruins. Similarly, Meyerowitz has spoken of his 9/11 images in terms of the influence of Vermeer's Delft views and Casper David Friedrich. For Norfolk, this excursion into romanticist aesthetics is justified by the re-emergence of the ruin, and the philosophical and political notions surrounding the sublime, and the vanity of empire in the context of today's new global empire.

Yet, wedding long-derided and derelict 19th-century aesthetics with a subject matter that in most ways could not be further from such lofty ideals seems to be to attempt an ill-fitting union. Such romanticist aesthetics have been comprehensively critiqued, and today seem obsolete, like 'an edifice which stands still, but on rotten foundations, propped up by vested interests'.[12] In aligning itself with the elitist aesthetics of the Enlightenment—albeit motivated by a leftist agenda—does this photography not risk creating a meta-level of artificiality? Does it not in fact empty warfare of its moral content, picturing it instead in terms of a 'dreamlike landscape, like a furnace,' as Ernst Jünger called the aerial images of the First World War?[13] The question of the representation of extremely political subjects in an aestheticised form arises most forcibly when we look at Norfolk's series *Bleed*, 2005, taken of the Crny Vrh mass graves in Bosnia. Many of these pictures are almost completely abstract. Only the picture of the aluminium waste pond at Petkovici seems to possess some of the violence we might have expected, as a vast pool of red, wound-like, leaches into the snow. But this is still a highly composed, beautiful violence, prompting the question: can we not criticise Norfolk's images in exactly the same way that First World War photographers such as Frank Hurley's works have been?[14] Do representations of the military sublime also risk articulating a moral realism that could turn into 'an iconographic apologia of a philosophy of harmony in the face of total destruction'.[15] Doesn't the dividing line between the beautification of war, and a photographic realism in which the intention to make visible the destructive might of contemporary warfare is involuntarily consumed by the coherence and consistency of the surface, blur?[16]

---

12 Jonathan Dollimore, 'Art in Time of War: Towards a Contemporary Aesthetic', in John J. Joughin and Simon Malpas, eds, *The New Aestheticism*, Manchester University Press, Manchester 2003, p. 40. **13** Hüppauf, *New German Critique*, 1993, p. 59. **14** See Hüppauf, 'Hurleys Optik. Über den Wandel von Wahrnehmung', *Medien/Kultur. Für Friedrich Knilli zum sechzigsten*, ed. Knut Hickethier und Siegfried Zielinski, Spiess Berlin 1991, pp. 113–31. **15** Ibid., p. 55. **16** Ibid.

If the aftermath photography of Norfolk and Meyerowitz strikes definite relations with 19th-century landscape photography, romanticism and aesthetics, it has a more troublesome relationship with that century's war photography. In the 19th century the public were appalled at the photographers of the American Civil War for bringing the dead to their doorsteps. Thus by the Second World War a prohibition on showing dead American soldiers had emerged; a prohibition bound-up with a conservative, nationalistic, patriotic ideology, and was broken only on very rare occasions.[17] The contemporary military sublime, however, is largely a corpse-less photography. Can it pursue the same prohibition against the dead, while avoiding a nascent conservativism? Norfolk has argued that he prefers to photograph people-less pictures, because 'people gobble up the photograph', stressing that they are unimportant in terms of the 'panoptic process' that his photography engages in.[18] In focusing upon landscapes of the aftermath of war, Norfolk, Seawright and Ristelhueber are perhaps in danger of displacing violence from the political (carried out by subjects and inflicted upon subjects) to the natural. In this context, photography cannot but objectify and universalise the sublime experience, forcing the beholder of the sublime moment into a position of moral and subjective superiority. The symbolic environment of an empty landscape that pervades this military sublime, like the contemplative sublime of Schiller, is deprived of nearly all bodily substance. Schiller's sublime necessarily demands the disavowal of the other.[19] Any radicality in the sublime surely lies in the ability of its beholder to produce the image of the suffering in himself. The contemplative sublime cannot accommodate flesh, bodies or selves. How then can it produce empathy, or awareness of fellow suffering? The hidden truth of the sublime is that its archaic threat is posed less by natural phenomena than by other human beings. Picturing a depopulated military sublime can only perpetuate the myth that the sublime, and therefore terror, is inhuman, something neo-liberal states and technocrats want us to believe.

One of the main features of the aftermath photography of Norfolk, Seawright and Ristelhueber is a strong sense of detachment from the scenes under their lens. A detachment which is a million miles away from the social documentarian in the field. Edmund Burke argued that the sublime

---

17 An example of the exception was George Strock's *Life* photograph of dead US soldiers on Buna Beach in New Guinea, published in September 1943. **18** See 'War/Photography: An Interview with Simon Norfolk', on BLDG BLOG, November 2006, http://www.bldgblog.blogspot.com/2006/11/warphotography-interview-with-simon.html. **19** See Charles H. Hinnant, 'Schiller and the Political Sublime: Two Perspectives', *Criticism*, vol. 44, no. 2, Spring 2002, pp. 121–38.

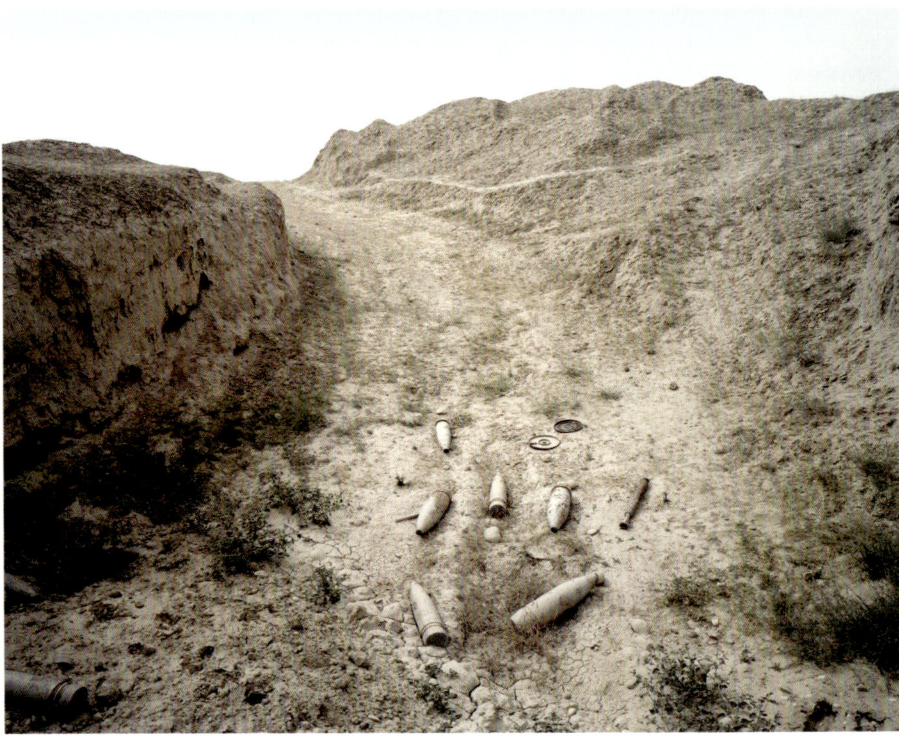

Paul Seawright, *Valley*, 2002

is governed by terror but also that terror becomes sublime only 'when it does not press too close'. Perhaps this is the strangeness we might feel when viewing such photography. In courting the sublime, it does not ever 'press too close' to the real human face of war. Surely if death is absent from the photograph, then so is sublime terror. The almost surreal nature of the pictures by these photographers, and their depopulated surfaces, makes one feel doubtful of whether such a thing as the military sublime can exist in the most radical form—that of a fearful terrible and threatening sublime—when it is viewed from such a safe cultural, moral and political distance. If there is any sublimity in death, it is in its terror. If the terror of death can no longer be photographed, and is no longer representable, surely only the aesthetic and disinterested sublimity of abstraction can remain? The sublime necessarily requires theatricality, and arguably yields a rudimentary typology of heroic and tragic protagonists. In Norfolk's work, the occasional characters that emerge—such as a solitary Afghan man with a caged bird, a balloon seller in Kabul's wastelands—are either used as theatrical props or are forced to represent more abstract ideas. In some senses, Norfolk's images of war are not so far from Andreas Gursky's vast typologies charting globalised capitalist culture: both are more interested in the macro than the micro, in the surfaces and systems of today's society, and the photography of both suggests the difficult place of humanism within it. Meyerowitz's Ground Zero photographs do not so easily fit into this military sublime. Many heroic characters are captured by his camera. Although these portraits act as homage and human document, because of the highly aesthetic nature of them, many critics have made uncomfortable parallels with figurative paintings by Rubens or Titian.[20] In some respects then, in mostly avoiding the representation of people the depopulated images by photographers such as Norfolk and Ristelhueber avoid such issues.

In the face of such epic political, cultural and military destruction, which has rehabilitated the category of the sublime, what is the status of Meyerowitz and Norfolk's photographic representations of this sublime? Does such photography interrogate the category by entering into it? Is it possible to find a radical political position within a photography that purports to chart and represent the sublime? Unity is clearly related to the maintenance of order that the West is presently trying to posit against the 'terror' and rupture of the Islamic other. So, is the harmony and unity associated with the sublime

---

20 See 'Echoes at Ground Zero: Lawrence Weschler in Conversation with Joel Meyerowitz', 7th April 2003, http://www.joelmeyerowitz.com/photography/Images/Meyerowitz_Weschler.pdf.

and constituted in the perfectly composed, beautifully printed image not itself morally dubious? While it is clear that this photography is embedded in the subjective and political, the question remains: does a war photography that seeks to represent the inhuman, abstract and even horrifically beautiful world of this contemporary military sublime offer any resistance to it? Kant argued that the dynamically sublime is experienced when we recognise our helplessness before, for example, the terrible physical power of nature, but nonetheless discover within us a power of resistance of quite another kind. For a truly terrible sublime to operate in photography it requires a collective subjectivity still capable of imagining disaster. Can we read a critique of the limitations of humanism into this work, akin to the materialist challenges to the limitations of aesthetic humanism? Perhaps this photography, which seeks to represent the inhuman military sublime, acknowledges that humanism itself and its enlightenment project must be seen as culminating in genocide and holocaust; as being complicit with, or even leading to, barbarism. So that the human is from the outset the institution of its double—the inhuman. Today the tradition of aesthetic humanism has been superseded by multiculturalism. Global capitalism nurtures and replaces derelict humanism with violent cultural, military and economic imperialism, anchored in the mass media and the corporate world. If the unilateralism and exceptionalism of the Bush administration's own construction of a military sublime prefers not to provide a space for the suffering individual, or human experience—favouring instead abstract universalisms—should a photography bent on a more critical representation of this sublime refuse to be complacent, or compliant with this prohibition? Like the category of the sublime that Adorno critiqued and reinstated in a post-Auschwitz world, a political sublime must surely be one of negation and shudder, one that restates the body and inter-subjectivity as central to aesthetic experience. Yet those who argue for the need to reinstate the world of aesthetics into a cultural theory that has too readily debunked it suggest that the central challenge of such a move is to understand the tension between the aesthetic and humane.[21] Jonathan Dollimore, for example, has argued that the aesthetic vision is most captivating precisely when it exceeds and maybe violates the humanitarian one.[22]

For the sociologist—perhaps a closer partner to the photographer than the archaeologist—the category of the sublime is to be avoided because it unites what should be sundered.[23] As Judith Huggins Balfe has suggested, 'the usage of the term is understood as a strategy for the re-enchantment

---

21 Dollimore, 'Art in Time of War', pp. 36–50.

of particular aspects of the social world, and thus for status enhancement of both the subject and object of the experience. Like whistling in the dark, the claim of sublimity is a self-fulfilling prophecy.'[24] It is hard to accept that the humanism of the documentarian does not still have an important place in photography's representation of war. There is a humanism in this photography of the aftermath, but perhaps instead of one anchored in the horror of empathy, it emerges in those moments which force the individual beholder to face the limitations of his or her own rationality and perception, while at the same time maintaining the possibility for new and less alienated forms of experience. Most importantly, the success of such work lies exactly in reminding us that the sublime is the peculiar place where aesthetics and ethics merge, and that it is an uncomfortable coalition at the best of times.

22 Ibid., p. 42. **23** See Judith Huggins Balfe, 'Sociology and the Sublime', *New Literary History*, vol. 16, no.2, Winter 1985, p. 239. **24** Ibid., p.242.

Interview with **Adam Broomberg and Oliver Chanarin**

Julian Stallabrass

War, Photojournalism and Art Photography

In a sustained series of interrogations of the documentary form, Broomberg and Chanarin have produced a wide variety of combinations of photography, text and, occasionally, video. Their early work strikingly illumined its subjects though portraits and interviews. Works such as *Chicago*, while remaining documentary in form, also pointed to things that could not be seen or represented. In more recent work, Broomberg and Chanarin have turned towards more direct intimations of the unseen and all that is suppressed and censored, along with exploiting discrepancies between text and image. In their series *The Day that Nobody Died* they exposed a roll of photographic paper to the light of the 'front line' in Afghanistan while on an embed with British troops. The interview was held at Paradise Row Gallery, London, in October 2008.

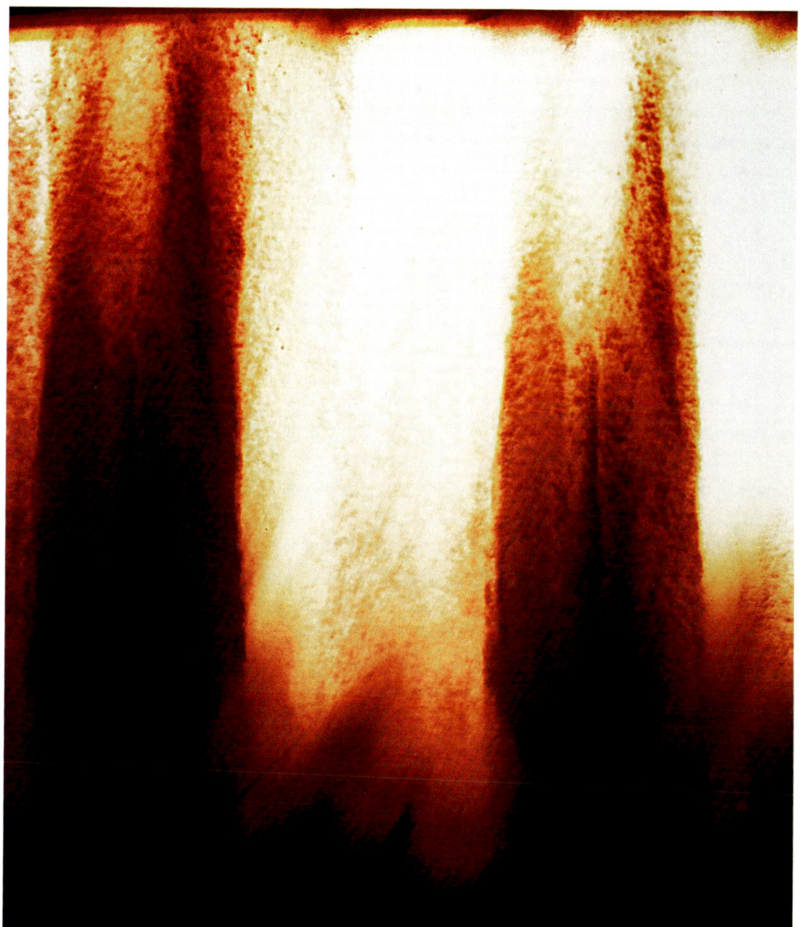

The Fixer's Execution, 2008

Julian Stallabrass You have presented us with some extraordinary objects in the next room, with your show *The Day Nobody Died*. Perhaps you could tell us how they were made?

Oliver Chanarin This started way before we went to Afghanistan. Adam and I were invited to visit Hedley Court to photograph and interview soldiers who have returned from Afghanistan and Iraq having lost limbs. We learned there that there are more amputees in Britain now then there were even during World War I. This is because military medicine has become so advanced that more are surviving. We met a number of soldiers, some of whom as young as 19, who had come back from Afghanistan some just a week or two before, some had lost an arm, some both legs.

Adam Broomberg It wasn't just the type of physical injuries that intrigued us but also the psychological; the type of conflict that they are experiencing is also similar to WW1 in the particularly passive nature of injury or death that they experience. During WW1 they compared the psychology of fighter pilots with those who were stuck in trenches. Even though the fighter pilots had a greater chance of dying every day, they would return emotionally more intact because, in the conflict, they had a greater sense of control, even if it was just over when they died. Whereas those stuck in the trenches had a passive sense of waiting which led to a particular type of trauma. This is the kind of shock we encountered in Hedley Court. As you know, we have spent the last few years navigating conflict zones, always concerned with how to represent trauma in those zones and how complicit representation is in these conflicts.

JS Are you going to use those images of the amputees?

OC We realised immediately that the images failed and would always fail to represent any of the trauma. They were hopeless as representatives of that experience.

JS Your previous response, as in *Mr. Mkhize's Portrait*, for instance, would have been to interview them, and use extracts alongside the photographs.[1] There were people who were quite badly brutalised in that book. You now felt that inadequate?

AB It's a different setting. Here we were talking very much about a conflict zone in which photojournalists are the image-makers. That is something we have never claimed to be, and it is a language we were taking head-on for the first time.

OC It's interesting to compare *Mr. Mikhize* with this more recent work. There are some similar concerns in terms of the role of photography as evidence, the power relations between us and our subjects, representation of human trauma and, in particular, the navigation of authority. In the

1 Adam Broomberg and Oliver Chanarin, *Mr. Mkhize's Portait & Other Stories from the New South Africa*, Trolley, London 2004.

case of *Mr. Mikhize's Portrait* we were commissioned by The Constitutional Court of South Africa; a relationship that turned out to be fraught with problems. Our strategy there, the approach you describe of presenting portraits and interviews, feels naive to us now. Nevertheless, compared with Afghanistan we were relatively free. As embedded journalists there are hundreds of restrictions. We were forbidden to photograph soldiers who were injured or even the results of enemy fire.

JS Is that one of their stipulations?

OC Yes, we also couldn't photograph in the morgue, in any of the hospitals or in officers' tents. You are actually forbidden to photograph anything which resembles a sign of war.

JS Can you talk about the experience of embedding and what the army was expecting of you and how you did or didn't fulfil those expectations

AB Olly and I have done a lot of lying in the last few years. When we worked with the Israeli Defence Force we spent eight months phoning once a week, speaking what Hebrew I could muster up and trying to win them over. After eight months of negotiation we got half an hour access to Chicago, a fake Arab village in the middle of the Negev desert built for military training.[2] Because we are Jewish they expected a sympathetic representation of their crisis. We approached this project in a similar way—we were not totally upfront about what our real concerns were.

OC As the soldiers who were chaperoning us realised we were more interested in our box than the spectacle surrounding it, we started to slip down their priority list. At a certain point, they made sure they got us to Kandahar, which is basically like being nudged out of the war. As they realised what we were doing, they slowly manoeuvred us away from the frontline.

JS Where there any soldiers who were curious about your project? Or some to whom you manage to explain it?

AB There were. The head of media operations, Colonel Matthews, was hilarious. The class system in the British Army was astounding, probably more for us as outsiders. It feels like the 19th century. Colonel Matthews would swing between being completely intrigued to completely paranoid and suspicious. On the third night we were there, he barged in and asked us: 'Do you actually have MoD [Ministry of Defence] clearance?'

OC Watching that mechanism at work was fascinating. Despite the fact that we were there, on the ground, in the midst of a war, events still came to us like distant newspaper headlines, and that disjuncture was surreal. For example, we heard about the 100th death not from the military or the colonel but from a journalist from *The Sun* newspaper, who had heard about it from his editor back in London.

2 Adam Broomberg and Oliver Chanarin, *Chicago*, SteidlMACK, Göttingen 2006.

Where had this information come from? It was shocking to discover that the newspapers have their own intelligence network in the army, a network of spies that is gathering information all the time.

AB The MoD use combat shooters. The British military has around 40 professional soldiers who are also professional photographers. They carry an M16 and a Nikon D3. They are on the frontline, spending up to three weeks on patrols, their first duty being to take photographs, and their second to engage in combat. When the combat shooters get back to the base they hand over their digital chips to Media Operations, and anything deemed unnecessary or too contentious is deleted and the rest is held on file or made accessible to the public, but they don't own anything. This is remarkable because photography is so concerned with ownership and copyright.

OC If you think of a sliding scale of witnesses, with a soldier on the one end and a journalist on the other, the combat shooters inhabit this ambiguous zone in the middle. This starts to raise questions about the role of the embedded journalist in that situation. What became clear to us, to be an embedded journalist inevitably involves more collusion than collaboration. You work together with the army to create images. The strategy we adopted—to not show anything—felt like the most subversive way to engage.

JS At the Brighton Photo Biennial, there is a show that displays many of these US Army photographs, and again, although all the photographs are credited, they're copyright free because they are part of the state archive. They are fascinating because many of them say things which you would think the army wouldn't quite want to communicate. There is an amazing image, for instance, of American troops in an occupied house, photographed through a tarnished mirror. It is a very sinister image, and there it is on the US Army site available for download. More typically, these photographs are very generic, as you would expect, with lots of pictures of US forces being nice to Iraqi kids or playing football. Anyhow, I am still unclear of how you go from interviewing these amputees, realising they were in incredibly dangerous, traumatic and passive situations, to then getting it into your heads to say we are going to put ourselves in that same situation.

AB We have always skirted around conflict, the show we are in that you curated at the Brighton Biennial is about what has become known as 'aftermath photography', images made just after the fact. We went to Iraq during the war but not to the centre of the conflict, the same with Rwanda, Darfur. We felt it was time to place ourselves in the centre to examine how representation is produced in that space.

OC This year we were invited to be on the jury of the World Press Photo Awards, which are very much for photojournalists, awarding news images. There we looked at thousands and thousands of images of war. One was particularly interesting, it won first prize in the 'Spot News' category, and was taken during Bhutto's assassination by a photographer who was right there at the scene of the explosion, only a few

yards away from the detonation. It all happened so quickly he hadn't been able to focus, the camera was askew. The picture is not really a picture—more a blur of colour and light, there was nothing to discern in it. It was interesting because it was mostly evidence of the witness having been there. We started to think about what constitutes a photojournalistic image.

JS We know of some photographers, James Nachtwey would be a good example, who if they had been there, would have got it right, would have made a record.

AB But what does that mean, 'got it right'?

JS He would have done what he is professionally engaged to do, maybe produce something interesting formally but certainly produce something which could have been used as evidence.

OC Nachtwey is a good example. Nachtwey doesn't call himself a war photographer but an anti-war photographer. We feel, quite strongly, that that is a conceit because as a journalist embedded in a conflict you are essentially part of that machinery, you're a cog...

AB Not only embedded journalists suffer this. Nachtwey, I would imagine, resists being embedded but even so he is inevitably a part of the war-waging machine. Image-making and war-waging are congruent activities. Now to get 'good images', whatever that means, of combat means you have to collaborate with the military. If you want real access, you need to be embedded, which brings with it a whole set of obstructions including self-censorship. This collusion gives you remarkable access and the possibility to create spectacle, images the public and photo-editors demand: like a soldier silhouetted against a desert sunset.

OC I don't think our project is intended to be set up in opposition to Nachtwey or even in opposition to photojournalism. We are not trying to undermine photojournalists who go to war zones, who risk their lives trying to bring back images of war. What we are asking photographers in those situations to do is to think a little about the kind of images they are making and what aesthetic rules they engage. There are a whole set of aesthetic rules that Nachtwey or any Magnum photographer uses.

AB I think we also need to look at the relationship between photographer, photo-editor and the market. Maybe we can put some responsibility for the problem on the market. Thomas Hirschhorn is an artist that you also included in the Biennial. His piece is an 18-foot-long banner which is a collage of images showing the effects of modern munitions on the human body. The most horrific thing you have ever seen. For me the best way to make radical work now is to construct a two-pronged attack. The first is what you have done, to display images that the media is not prepared to show, to show the reality of the war and the physical effects it has on the body. And the other is to withhold

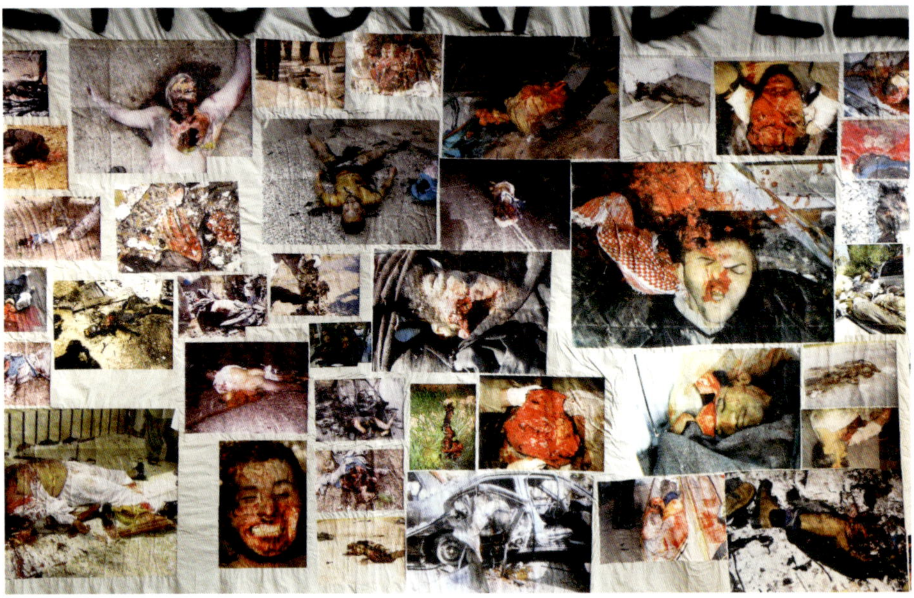

Thomas Hirschhorn, *The Incommensurable Banner*, 2007, detail

images, which is what we have tried here. To collude, but to expose that process of collusion.

JS We should also talk about the viewer. With the Bhutto image, there is an abstract spectacle of light and colour that you project into because of the caption. Your work seems to be similar in that you are given a caption, so how do you see this projection working? Is it something you want to encourage or frustrate? What do you expect people to get out of looking at these? Visually, they are quite curious, looking a bit like Morris Lewis's abstract paintings. They have colours which are redolent of the sky but also of blood. So where do you want to put the viewer?

AB I have had my mother walk around them going: 'Ooh, that looks so violent or that is so exquisite.' Let's face it, these show the marks of light on paper. Of course we are playing on the pictorialist and sublime notion of beauty, that there is something beautiful about it or violent because red denotes blood and therefore violence. But for us the most important part of the work is not what the viewer sees in the rolls of paper but rather their reaction to the film. I don't think we would ever show one of those rolls without the film which describes the process of production—this performance is most important. I don't care what the paper looks like.

OC Images of other peoples suffering are designed to elicit a sense of shame. But in this project we are questioning that... What use do these images actually have, other than to act as a catharsis of some kind? Looking at images of war can actually short-circuit any kind of immediate call to action. We get this every time we turn the page of the newspaper. One aim of our work is to try to put the burden of looking back on the viewer. To rob the viewer of the cathartic effect of looking and ignoring images of human trauma.

AB Our images are not wholly useless though. They are not useful because they are beautiful, or useful as a blank canvas onto which you can project. They are useful because suffering does require a witness. To bring back a piece of paper that has been right there. To bring back that piece of paper, not a photograph but that same piece of paper, and to pin it to the wall is to bring back some visceral form of evidence, more than that Bhutto image constitutes evidence.

JS Maybe you would like to elaborate on that more. Talking to people at the opening was an interesting experience because some where very taken by the images and intrigued by the combination of text and image, and others were quite angry. One woman described it to me as a 'conceit', which I thought was an interesting phrase because it was not necessarily condemnatory. You could see it as a literary conceit, an 18th-century game with words or images, maybe an allegory. The reactions were mixed, and so it would be interesting to hear why you think that evidential character or the presence of the paper at that place was necessary or interesting. You could have exposed these things right here in Hoxton and no one would have been any the wiser.

OC I think it would be useful to go back to the experience of being there and to carrying this box around with the British military. Of course the word 'conceit' comes to mind. You have a war going on, soldiers risking their lives, and there we were asking them to carry this heavy cardboard box around while we filmed them. There is something subversive about that. There was an article in *The Times* about this project. When the journalist first arrived for the interview she was really angry about us having made soldiers engage in this absurd performance, about us having co-opted the military. The journey of the box shows the mechanism, the workings of the war.

AB I think anger is an important response. Why do images in the paper not anger them? What range of emotions could they go through looking at an image of the war: they could go from total revulsion, which will stop them buying the newspaper, so of course editors won't publish pictures showing the real effects of war on civilians. What they do publish are all these inoffensive images. There is an agreement between editors and advertisers which allows only certain images—none of which would anger people.

JS There is a performative element in all of your work, and you are made to think, not only about the image but your goal in recording it and what you do with it. One way of looking at the images on show here would be to project into them a sublime spectacle of violence and destruction or even of the appalling progress of the war in Afghanistan and all that has occurred in the last few years, but the video puts a very different light on it and almost presents you as latter-day surrealist jokers. Would you talk about the contrast between these two things?

AB We discussed it in Brechtian terms, the way his epic theatre was based on a series of interruptions. That the performance was so obscured that you became aware of the mechanisms, the workings behind it. An actor plays out the script but also makes you very aware that he or she is an actor. The fact that the box carrying the photographic paper appears in each scene undermines the spectacle. The unfolding of the conflict is constantly interrupted by this mute, comical witness that literally blocks your view during the whole journey.

OC The box acts as your proxy, takes you on this journey and shows you this war that you would never normally see in a journalistic context. To see the mechanisms is to see something ultra banal, the way the whole machine is constructed to allow the war to function.

AB The editing was very important; we made the takes as long as possible. None of the montage decisions were based on trying to entertain, the same way the images are not, but it's actually about drawing it out so you feel the mundanity and the banality of war.

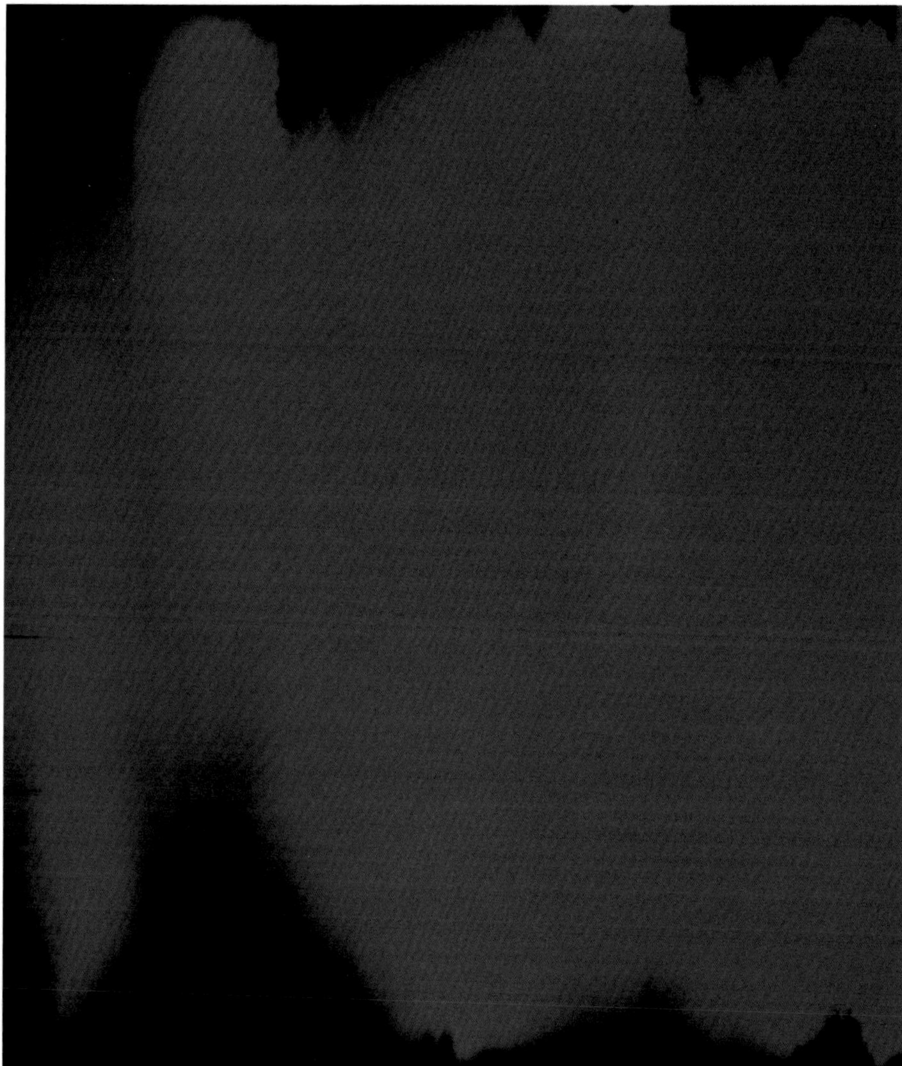

The Repatriation, 2008
Overleaf Thomas Hirschhorn, *The Incommensurable Banner*, 2007; as displayed at Fabrica, Brighton Photo Biennial 2008. Photograph by Julian Stallabrass

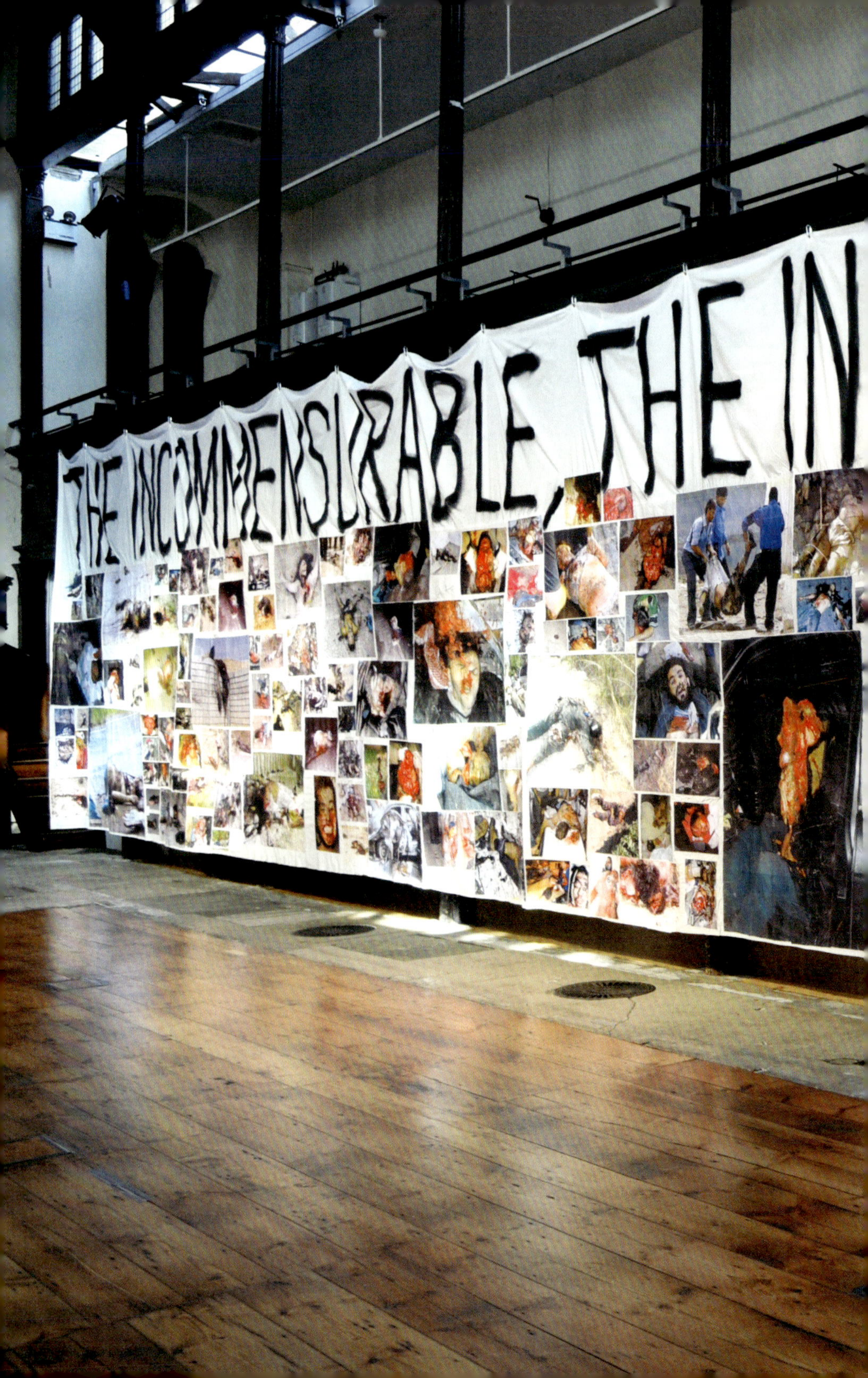
THE INCOMMENSURABLE, THE IN

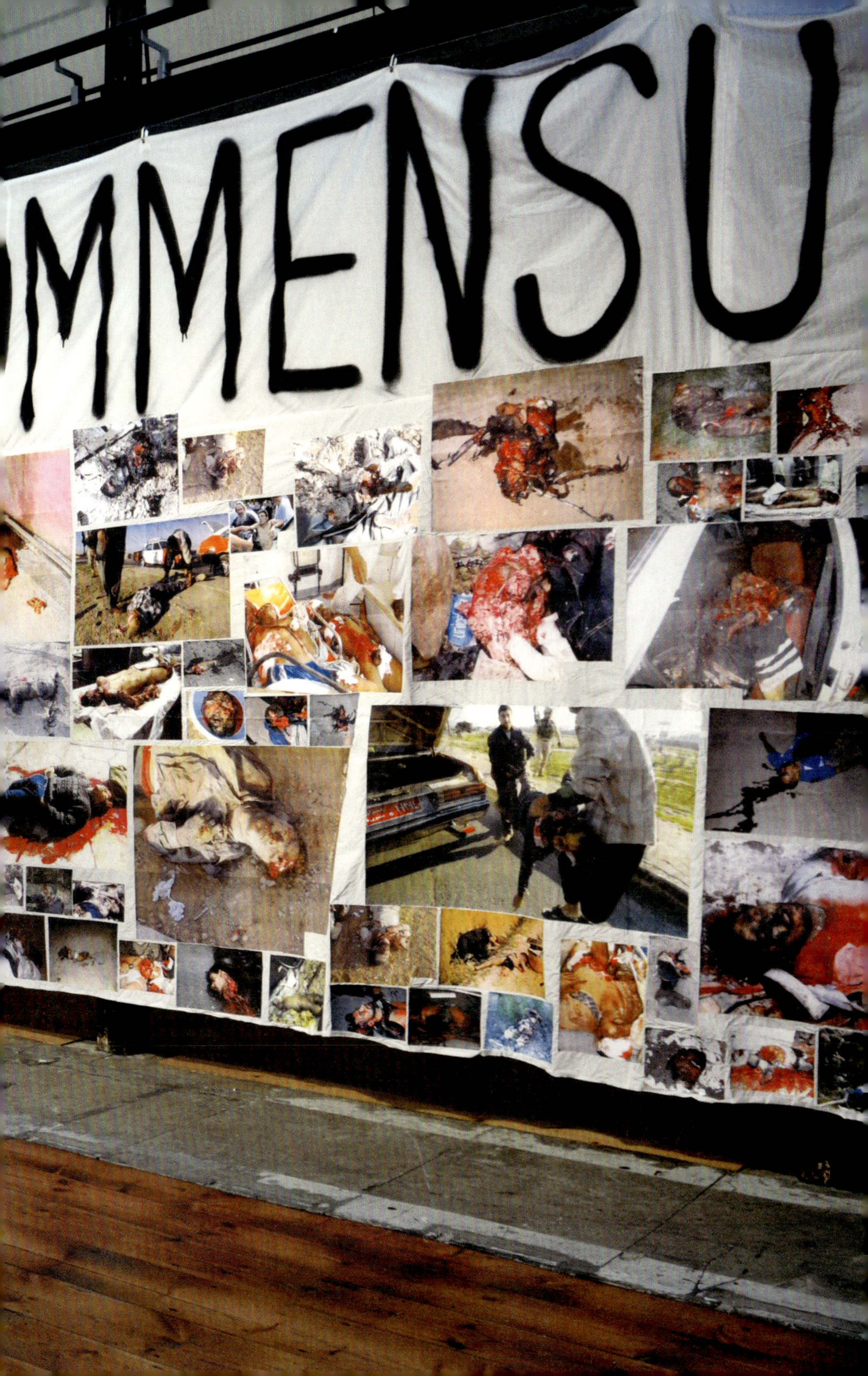
MMENSU

Now You See It, Now You Don't
Coco Fusco

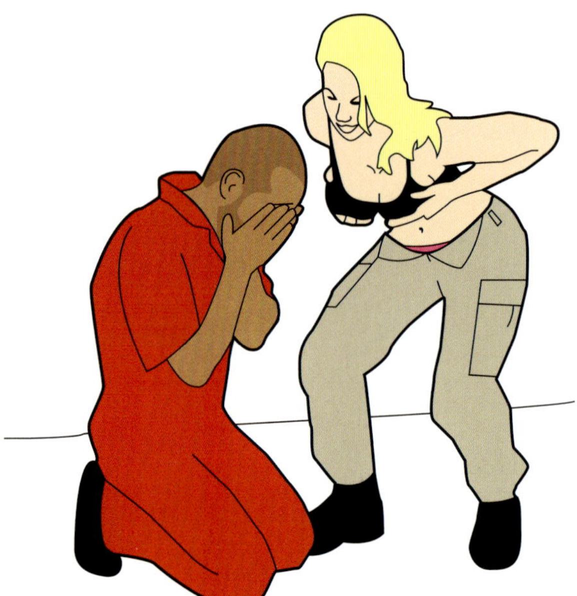

Coco Fusco, 15. Fear Up Mild. While most sexual explicit gestures may induce guilt, the ones that violate religious doctrine are most likely to push your source to the crisis point where he will either confess, collapse, or both

You may be fuming by now, Virginia, because I have not made an effort to catalogue all the obstacles that female soldiers face in what remains a nasty line of work in an excessively masculine and misogynist milieu.[1] Quantifying adversity, however significant a feminist exercise, is insufficient means for understanding women's relationship to power in a neo-conservative state. Focusing exclusively on women's experience of hardship may actually give the military more ways to obfuscate its excesses toward others. I'm not trying to suggest that sexual aggression as a form of torture is the only thing that should concern those who decide to think seriously about the war. But it would be unwise to overlook it. Torture dominates the discursive field of this war as a public image crisis for the US military, as a practice to be rationalized through the verbal gymnastics of legal theorists, and as the paradigm through which the rights we grant our enemies are formulated and the righteousness of our own use of force is measured. The gendered and sexualized character of most publicized abuses gives its current incarnation a particularly sensationalist character. I doubt the practice of torture by agents of a presumably democratic state has ever been so visible or that that feminine visibility has contributed to its normalization.

How did it happen that torture took center stage? It wasn't simply the result of an unanticipated scandal. The more information comes to light, the clearer it becomes that torture is an integral part of the overzealous reaction to an unanticipated insurgency and an unfamiliar enemy. An apparent lack of information about our opponents and their motives led to indiscriminate round-ups and long-term detentions, turning military prisons into a central theater of operations. Most military interrogators who have gone public insist that they can do their jobs without crossing the line, and that they are taught not to torture. At the same time, they all acknowledge that the particular conditions in this war have created a slippery slope. Psychology experts have enumerated the factors that increase the potential for torture's occurrence at the hands of American soldiers: a hierarchical culture demanding obedience to authority, the isolation and dislocation of soldiers, insufficient supervision, frustration, fear, and the pressure to produce quick results. Whistleblowers and critical commentators have pointed to the confusion about permissible tactics generated by frequent alterations of policy and its interpretation along the chain of command. They have also noted the irregularity of putting military

---

1 This essay is an excerpt from "Invasion of Space by a Female," in Coco Fusco, *A Field Guide for Female Interrogators* (New York: Seven Stories Press, 2008). Reprinted with permission of the author and Seven Stories Press, http://www.sevenstories.com.

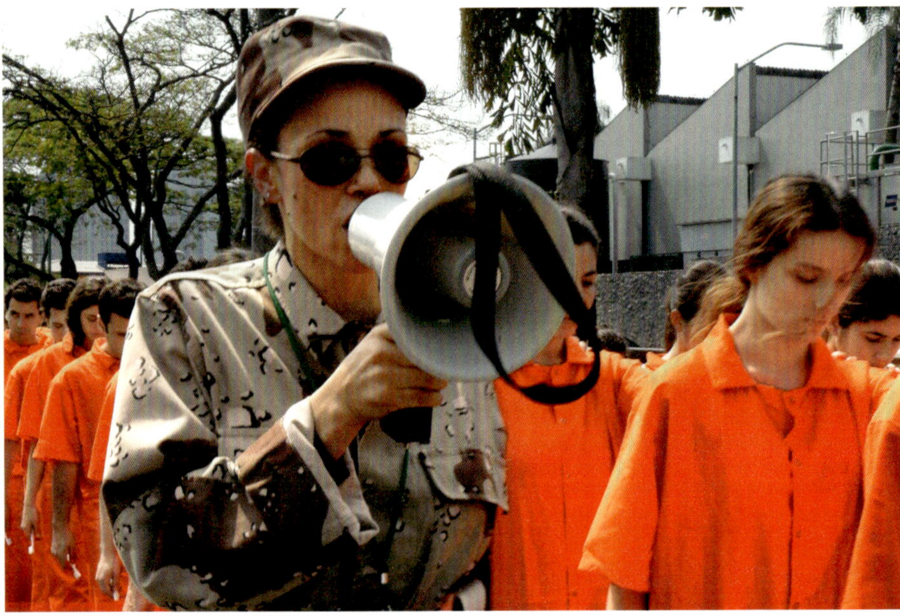

Coco Fusco, *Bare Life Study #1*, VideoBrazil Festival of Electronic Art and Performance, São Paolo, September 2005

police under the control of military interrogators, a scheme devised by hard-liner General Geoffrey D. Miller at Abu Ghraib to transform the physical management of prisoners into punitive aggression that would induce cooperation in the interrogation booth. Disgruntled soldiers suggest that their working in proximity to the CIA and private contractors who are not bound by the same restrictions led to coercive methods spreading virally into the military's repertoire.[2]

Much speculation has taken place over the last three years about whether the intelligence community developed these sexual tactics because of cultural stereotypes about Muslims and Arabs that have achieved the status of truisms in military circles. Veterans of military intelligence who received training in the early stages of the war have noted that they received lectures on the so-called "Arab mind," in which it was argued that when it comes to sexuality, Muslim men are more vulnerable than Westerners.[3] Outdated anthropological arguments become the basis for the development of tactics that manifest themselves in the roles interrogators assume for themselves and impose on their sources. Male interrogators tend to degrade male prisoners by forcing them to perform homoerotic acts presumed to be humiliating, threatening and insulting them, but stop short of performing these acts themselves. On the other hand, women interrogators use sexual insults, force them to engage in humiliating acts, and also perform sexually for them. Their most infamous antics include gyrating half-clothed atop seated prisoners and smearing them with fake menstrual blood in an attempt to break them by invoking a cultural taboo. Apparently, when male interrogators perform sex acts on non-consenting subjects it is understood as sexual assault, but when women do it, it can be authorized as invasion of space.

Torture is not a new element of war. Interrogation has invariably been crucial to military efforts to thwart insurgencies, and rare are the instances in which information is obtained from captured enemies without some degree of physical or psychological violence. Nevertheless, the presumed moral superiority of democratic governance and modern warfare is based on the

---

2 Tony Lagouranis makes this argument throughout his memoir, *Fear Up Harsh: An Army Interrogator's Dark Journey Through Iraq* (New York: New American Library, 2007), pp. 17–18. Chris Mackey also complains in *The Interrogators* (see note 8 for full citation) about the deleterious effect of the presence of OGAs (other government agencies). In addition, investigative journalist Seymour Hersh and military historian Alfred McCoy have both argued that sexual torture as a tactic originated within the CIA as a special access program and that its implementation by US soldiers is the result of the presence of both the CIA and private contractors inside military prisons. See Alfred McCoy's *A Question of Torture: CIA Interrogation from the Cold War to the War on Terror* (New York: Henry Holt and Company, 2006) and Seymour Hersh's *Chain of Command: The Road from 9/11 to Abu Ghraib* (New York: Harper Collins, 2004). **3** Lagouranis and Mikaelian, *Fear Up Harsh*, pp. 17–18

criminalization of the indiscriminate killing of non-combatants and of torture. Our public discourse of the last fifty years has defined torture as an antiquated practice of non-democratic regimes that is antithetical to our values and that endangers our own troops. At the same time our political goals on the world stage continue to make torture expedient when accepted means within a democracy are deemed to be too expensive or contrary to US interests. The US has maintained a conveniently duplicitous attitude and approach toward torture: we tell ourselves that we don't do it, and at the same time we clandestinely support and work with others who do. We deny our involvement, outsource most of the nasty labor to proxies abroad, and invest locally in the development of psychological coercion methods that leave fewer visible scars. That is the disingenuous hide and seek game we play with torture, pretending that we don't do it if we can't see it. Now that our involvement has become visible, we continue the ruse by trying to call it something else, or saying we are not sure what it is. The hairsplitting in legal discussions of what might or might not be torture would certainly strike you as being as utterly perverse, Virginia, as it does me: how is the actual filling of the lungs with water in waterboarding only a "simulation of drowning"? By what insidious logic can it be that threats of death and prolonged isolation are not torture because the psychological pain induced cannot be equated with organ failure?

When I speak of the current debates in the US about torture in countries where that outsourcing has taken place, I am invariably reminded by audiences that only fools believe that Americans do not engage in torture. They've seen it and lived with it up close; it's not just a tidbit from a high school history lesson or a cop show rerun, and when dolled up versions show up in porn or advertising, people complain—loudly. For those in proximity to the practice, torture is experienced as a real life political drama that ritualizes the violence of occupation through excruciating compulsory performances of mental and bodily submission. We, on the other hand, are experiencing torture in this war as a spectacle from a faraway place. That spectacle has a peculiar relationship to it own indexical representation. By this I mean that even though the idea of torture dominates the media sphere and public consciousness, we are compelled to imagine the full range of what it is through personal and collective fictions, because most of us don't get to see much of the real thing. Despite the widespread circulation of the Abu Ghraib photographs that depict military police abuse of prisoners, the public does not see most visual documentation of proceedings in interrogation rooms in military prisons. Over the past four years we have been informed that such images have been classified, destroyed, lost, or censored in the interests of national security—but who complains

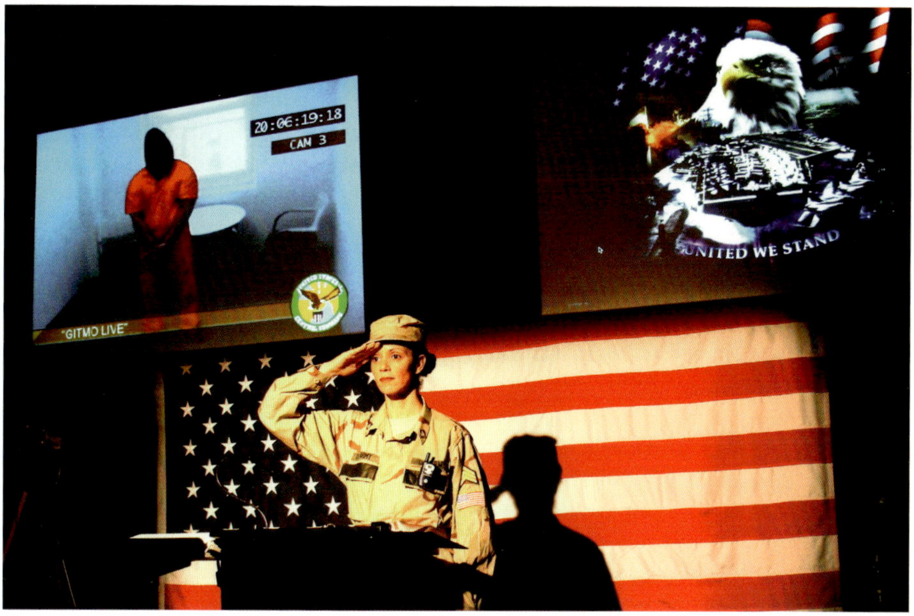

Coco Fusco, *A Room of One's Own: Women and Power in the New America*, 2005, performance-lecture

besides lawyers who want to make a war crimes case against the state? Congressional hearings and human rights investigations feature protracted semantic struggles to determine, in the absence of pictures, what happens in those stark rooms. That dearth of publicly available documentary images of military interrogations contributes to the inflation of value of testimonials and "expert" speculation.

Sexual harassment performed by female interrogators is not something that the American public has actually seen. Several months after release of the Abu Ghraib photographs, a story appeared in the news about a former Army translator whose eyewitness accounts of interrogations at Guantánamo featured a female interrogator who had smeared fake menstrual blood on a detainee.[4] Shortly thereafter, the Pentagon publicly confirmed that "sexual tactics" had been used on detainees. Subsequent detainee testimony from Guantánamo and Abu Ghraib contained numerous references to women in the prisons, sometimes described as prostitutes, who sexually taunt them. Other stories have surfaced from time to time about male interrogators' use of sexual tactics as well. None of these reports has sparked the same degree of controversy, probably due to the absence of photographs.

For every revelation of excess by a remorseful perpetrator, angry prisoner, or troubled witness, there are ad hominem attacks on whistleblowers and "untrustworthy Muslims," defensive rebuttals from other soldiers, and byzantine rationalizations from the military. On top of this, the White House continues to issue flat out denials: we don't torture, no matter how much evidence there is to the contrary. I don't know at this point what is more sickening—the photos from Abu Ghraib, the use of denial as a tactic of persuasion, or the ways that our military codes can actually be construed to permit much of what would "shock the conscience" of many a civilian and soldier. What else should I feel when I read a Department of Defense memo from a staff judge advocate (who happens to be female) recommending that military members who use death threats or waterboarding against detainees should seek prior permission or immunity since they might be construed as violations of the Uniform Military Code of Justice?[5] The government has turned legal debates about torture into exercises in semantic subterfuge so that the practice can continue take place while the decision makers deliberate duplicitously about what it "really" is.

Whereas obfuscation seems to be the rule for the policy makers, the

---

4 Erik Saar and Viveca Novak, *Inside the Wire: A Military Intelligence Soldier's Eyewitness Account of Life at Guantánamo* (New York: Penguin Press, 2005), pp. 223–7. 5 Staff Judge Advocate Diane E. Beaver, "Memorandum for Commander, Joint Task Force 170, Department of Defense," *Administration of Torture*, eds. Jameel Jaffer and Amrit Singh (New York: Columbia University Press, 2007), p. A-93.

fictional visualizations of local and global policing that pervade tele-visual space follow a much clearer trajectory, assuaging fears about unpredictable people with interrogations that are swift, violent and effective. Watch *Sleeper Cell, 24, The Unit*, or even the abundant cop show reruns that fill our airwaves. Suspects are routinely beaten, lied to, and threatened with death and violence to family members, and lo and behold, the needed data emerges. Torture is thus normalized in popular culture as an effective means of eliminating the unknown. Criminals, whether they are motivated by politics or driven by psychopathology, all succumb to the male protagonist superheroes of contemporary terror-inspired fantasies about world domination. Could it be that in our hearts we want the full protection offered by authoritarian rule, while in our minds we seek to deny our acceptance of its means? Could that be why fresh-faced young women hovering over brutalized bodies symbolize the real American drama surrounding the practice of "torture lite?" They hardly seem to be capable of masterminding anything like an illegal covert program functioning on a global scale.

Singling out the hapless "torture chicks" from the rest of the soldiers who authorized and committed abuse is as an expedient distortion of the mistreatment of detainees and prisoners. It has helped the military to make the case in early stages of the Abu Ghraib scandal that abuse was the result of personal flaws in a few low-ranking soldiers rather than the wrongdoing all the way up the chain of the command. It has diverted attention away from the influence of a culture of sexual humiliation that is integral to military social life. The female soldiers who were court marshaled were not only not alone or in the majority, but the media's honing in on them with greater intensity made torture at the hands of the US military seem a lot less frightening. Yes, Lynndie England had a guy on a leash, but in the picture she wasn't choking him by pulling it. Yes, the prisoner in the picture with Sabrina Harman is dead, but her smiling presence in the shot does not indicate that she killed him, only that she was responding inappropriately to his death.

Here's how the implicit argument goes: How bad can torture really be if performed by a member of the "weaker sex?" Doesn't torture require something more aggressive than insults and humiliating acts? Aren't most women in the military struggling to survive and get ahead in an overwhelmingly masculine environment where they are frequently subject to unwanted sexual advances? Can poor, uneducated women who themselves are victims of their boyfriends in addition to being tools of an authoritarian power structure like the military be blamed for violating human rights as part of their job? If torture involves women doing things to men of a sexual nature, which has been the case in numerous interrogations in Guantánamo, Iraq and Afghanistan, can it even be called torture?

Military investigators have determined that some female interrogators' sexual taunts fall under the authorized tactic called "futility," meaning that they contribute to convincing a prisoner that all his efforts to resist are doomed to fail. Other actions were found to fall under permissible "mild non-injurious physical touching." More extreme actions such as the smearing of fake menstrual blood were deemed excessive, but a crucial rationalization was added that absolves the chain of command.[6] Those actions were also characterized as retaliatory, enabling the military to blame the individual who did not seek prior authorization, which, it is implied, she would not have received. Nonetheless, no formal disciplinary action was taken against the interrogator, who also refused to be interviewed. The ostensible reason given was that too much time had passed and the interrogator was no longer in the armed forces. However, in not taking action, the military implicitly invites others to continue the practice as long as they can keep it under wraps.

While the state and the media may use cultural perceptions of women to temper the image of Americans as torturers, their presence also serves a larger agenda. That agenda is emblematic of the ways that the Right has marshaled the discourses of identity politics in the twenty-first century to serve conservative causes. As the number of women in the US military grows, the ways to capitalize on them by transforming their particular assets into weapons increase. Cultural perceptions of women can be used strategically to humanize the current US military occupation of Iraq, in that women are assumed to be less threatening. Women's presence also creates the impression that American institutions engaging in domination are actually democratic, since they appear to practice gender equity. On the other hand, specific use of women as women in military interrogations to provoke male anxiety actually corresponds to an authorized tactic called "Invasion of Space by a Female." The existence of this standardized term is testimony in itself of the state's rationalization of its exploitation of femininity. Despite all the handwringing in the media about why some military police at Abu Ghraib could not prevent themselves from brutalizing prisoners, little attention has been given to the implications of formulating strategies that turn female sexual exhibitionism into a weapon.

There are many different ways that women function as a mitigating and punitive force in the military carceral scenario. The testimony of several

---

6 The Schmidt Report, *Investigations into FBI Allegations of Detainee Abuse at Guantánamo Bay, Cuba Detention Facility*, published June 9, 2005, pp. 7–8, http://www.cfr.org/publication/9804/schmidt_report.html.

detainees suggests that they are frequently confused by the presence of women soldiers in military prisons. Sometimes they assume that the women are sex workers who are brought there to provide services to Americans, or simply to sexually torture them. Testimony also indicates that some prisoners are particularly sensitive to the effects of sexual taunting and insults by women soldiers and that this vulnerability is exploited.[7] But there are also plenty of ways that the routine duties of military police can be experienced as humiliation by prisoners: they control prisoners' movements, strip and search them, shave and shear them, and survey them as they bathe and relieve themselves. The interactions with MPs are disciplinary performances of subjection, and gender can easily be used to intensify the experience without it appearing to be intended or considered sanctionable. An account by one interrogator noted that female MPs have at times been assigned in order to soften the experience of adolescent detainees. On other occasions their presence is intended to irritate male prisoners who it is assumed will perceive it as an affront to their dignity.[8] That effect is not inevitable however: former detainee Moazzam Begg writes in his memoir that he developed a fairly amicable rapport with one military policewomen who guarded him.[9]

The level of gendered provocation rises when women soldiers are used in interrogation to coerce and delude prisoners by representing sexually charged cultural stereotypes of femininity. This includes using women as bait: one interrogator recounts, for example, how he created a scene designed to entice a young detainee into becoming a potential informant by allowing him to sit unshackled in front of a television playing an American movie with a blond female soldier.[10] The same interrogator maintained in his account of his experience supervising an intelligence team in Afghanistan in 2002 that women were best at assuming the roles of the "befuddled interrogator" or the compassionate solace-provider: in other words, the bimbo who can't do her job, or the sympathetic mom who wipes your tears.[11] He also sent a female interrogator out to question Afghan women after their male relatives were arrested, assuming she would be less threatening and that this would lead to a naturally favorable rapport.[12] One of my teachers in the interrogation course commented that female interrogators could leverage their gender

---

7 The most comprehensive account of detainee experiences I have found is Andy Worthington's *The Guantánamo Files: The Story of the 774 Detainees in America's Illegal Prison* (London: Pluto Press, 2007). 8 Chris Mackey and Greg Miller, *The Interrogators: Task Force 500 and America's Secret War Against Al Qaeda* (New York: Little, Brown and Company, 2004). 9 Moazzam Begg and Victoria Britain, *Enemy Combatant: My Imprisonment at Guantánamo*, Bagram and Kandahar (New York: The New Press, 2006). 10 Mackey and Miller, *The Interrogators*, p. 377. 11 Ibid., pp. 481–2. 12 Ibid., p. 422.

and elicit confessions best by pretending not to be interrogators at all, posing instead as nurses or even girlfriends. These sorts of scenes can turn into the starting point for pointedly sexual aggression, but it appears that in many instances, the gendered exchanges have remained relatively controlled. Those who call for the use of women in this manner claim to believe that the cultural particularities of Muslim prisoners will make them more sensitive to their presence. However, I would argue that it is equally likely that the decision to use women in this way is also informed by American perceptions of women. The personae described are recognizable types drawn from an American cultural context. The American military milieu is often characterized as hostile to women because of the prevailing tendency among the men to sexually objectify them: the roles women are asked to play in order to harass the prisoners correspond to sexist characterizations that are leveled at them by male soldiers in other contexts as forms of denigration.[13]

The tenor of the interactions between male prisoners and female soldiers changes when they are intended to destabilize prisoners by demeaning them. Several accounts by detainees mention that female soldiers humiliated them by looking at them when they were naked and hurling insults about the size of their genitals. This performance of "the castrating bitch" is described in Sergeant Kayla Williams' account of her contact with interrogators in Iraq. Though she herself was not an interrogator, she was called upon to help with interrogations at Mosul because she speaks Arabic and is female. The male interrogators on hand brought in a prisoner and removed his clothes, and then instructed her to "mock his manhood," "ridicule his genitals," and "remind him that he is being humiliated in the presence of a blond American female."[14] While she felt uncomfortable with and unfit for the role she was asked to play, she found greater fault with the male interrogators who slapped and burned the prisoner in her presence. To Williams, their actions violated the Geneva Conventions, but apparently sexually humiliating words did not. As she details her own discomfort with what she was asked to do, she also speculates on what kind of training one would need to perform the role effectively, which suggests a degree of acceptance of the legitimacy of such actions.[15] Williams later met the female interrogator she had momentarily replaced and discovered that

---

13 Several internal and Congressional investigations of sexual harassment in the US military have been conducted in the past fifteen years in response to widely publicized incidents, such as the Tailhook scandal of 1991. The Air Force maintains a website with a bibliography of internet sites, books, periodicals, and documents relat¬ing to the issue at http://www.au.af.mil/au/aul/bibs/sex/haras.htm. **14** Kayla William and Michael E. Staub, *Love my Rifle more than You: Young and Female in the US Army* (New York: W.W. Norton, 2005), p. 247. **15** Ibid., p. 248.

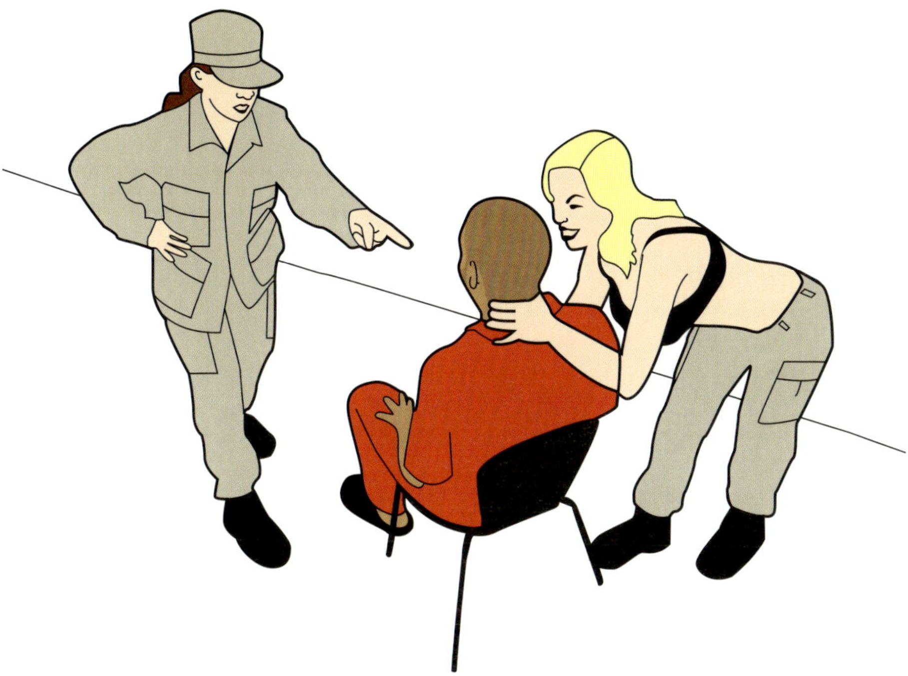

Coco Fusco, 7. Mutt and Jeff. One of the oldest tricks in the book, but it works like a charm.
Basically, he's gotta go for one of you

she defended the tactics as legitimate. For the most part, so have her superiors.

Up to now, there is only one publicly known instance of a female interrogator being sanctioned for tactics used on a prisoner. Stationed at Abu Ghraib in 2003, she was cited for forcing the man to walk through the prison hallways naked in order to humiliate him into cooperating.[16] According to many accounts, however, the level of sexual provocation of male prisoners by female soldiers reaches far greater heights. Womens' words and actions have been combined with costumes and make-up: tight shirts left unbuttoned, high heels, sexy lingerie, loose hair, and garish makeup have all been mentioned in detainee and eye witness accounts. The sexual language used is apparently not restricted to insults; several detainees have claimed they have been threatened with rape. Pictures of semi-naked women were hung around the neck of the alleged "twentieth hijacker" in an attempt to unnerve him.[17] Reports have circulated that female soldiers have fondled detainees' genitals, and that they have forced detainees to masturbate in front of them. Female interrogators have also been described as using many forms of sexually aggressive behavior in booths, ranging from touching themselves and removing their clothing, to touching the prisoners. Some of the provocateurs have worked in teams of two or three, all sexually harassing the same prisoner. All the actions are combined with sexual language to enhance effect: sometimes the language is accusatory and demeaning, other times it is designed to effect arousal. A Yemeni detainee claimed that when he refused to talk in an interrogation, a female interrogator was dispatched to his booth in a tight t-shirt; she asked him what his sexual needs were, showed off her breasts, and simply stated, "Are you going to talk, or are we going to do this for six hours?"[18] Another account from a detainee held at Guantánamo affirmed that his interrogator combined sexual provocation with politically inflammatory statements, baring her breasts while reminding him that his attorneys were Jews and that "Jews have always betrayed Arabs."[19]

Key to all these deployments of female sexuality as a weapon is that they are planned. To me they are indicative of the state's instrumentalist attitude toward gender, sexuality and cultural difference. In other words, if the military is going to incorporate women, it is also going to capitalize on their particular assets and take advantage of permissive societal attitudes regarding sexual exhibitionism. The effort to gather information about another culture

---

16 Spec. Luciana Spencer of the 205 MI Brigade was cited in the Taguba Report for forcing a prisoner to strip and walk naked in front of other prisoners at Abu Ghraib. See http://www.washingtonpost.com/wp-srv/world/iraq/abughraib/timeline.html. **17** Worthington, *The Guantánamo Files*, p. 205. **18** Ibid., p. 198. **19** Kristine A. Huskey, "The Sex Interrogators at Guantánamo," *One of the Guys: Women as Aggressor and Torturers*, ed. Tara McKelvey (Emeryville, CA: Seal Press, 2007), p. 176.

is turned into an opportunity for using gender and sex as punishment. The purported sexual freedom of American women becomes something with which to bludgeon imprisoned men from supposed less permissive cultures. The fact that reports of such activities have come from several military prisons makes it virtually impossible to dismiss individual instances as aberrations or the invention of an isolated eccentric. The most widely circulated theory that has emerged to explain why these tactics have been implemented—that intelligence experts latched onto outdated Orientalist views of Arab men as sexually vulnerable in the scramble to extract actionable intelligence as quickly as possible—is supported by interrogator accounts of how lectures on the so-called "Arab mind" were integrated into their training once the insurgency began.[20] Military investigations into reports of such actions have either justified them when performed under the rubric of an authorized interrogation plan, or blamed individuals for supposedly failing to obtain authorization prior to execution of the acts. Like every other "coercive tactic" that has come under scrutiny through recent human rights investigations, female sexual aggression toward prisoners is not unequivocally condemnable by the military's own legal standards.

That may explain why female intelligence officers would authorize and accept orders to deploy sexuality as a weapon. It is not clearly understood as a infringement of military conduct, nor is it seen by the military as a violation of human rights if there are legitimate state interests. So a female agent of the state who sexually accosts prisoners to root out terrorism is just doing her job. For civilians accustomed to a certain degree of autonomy regarding their bodies, the idea that one could be ordered to behave sexually may seem to be beyond the call of duty, but soldiers have in theory already agreed to sacrifice their lives, so sexual aggression in the service of a greater cause may appear mild by comparison. In theory, members of the military are entitled to question and refuse what they believe to be unjust orders. The question here would be how to define the injustice. Kayla Williams didn't find fault with the order; she found herself to be lacking in ability to perform. In other words, she personalized an ethical and legal issue and thus avoided confrontation regarding the legitimacy of the practice. From what I have been able to gather, it does not seem that this is an uncommon position among women in the military. When I asked a few young women who had served how they felt about being asked to use their sexuality as part of their patriotic duty, they seemed to have difficulty understanding the question, or perhaps they thought it was too sensitive

---

20 Lagouranis and Mikaelian, *Fear Up Harsh*, p. 17.

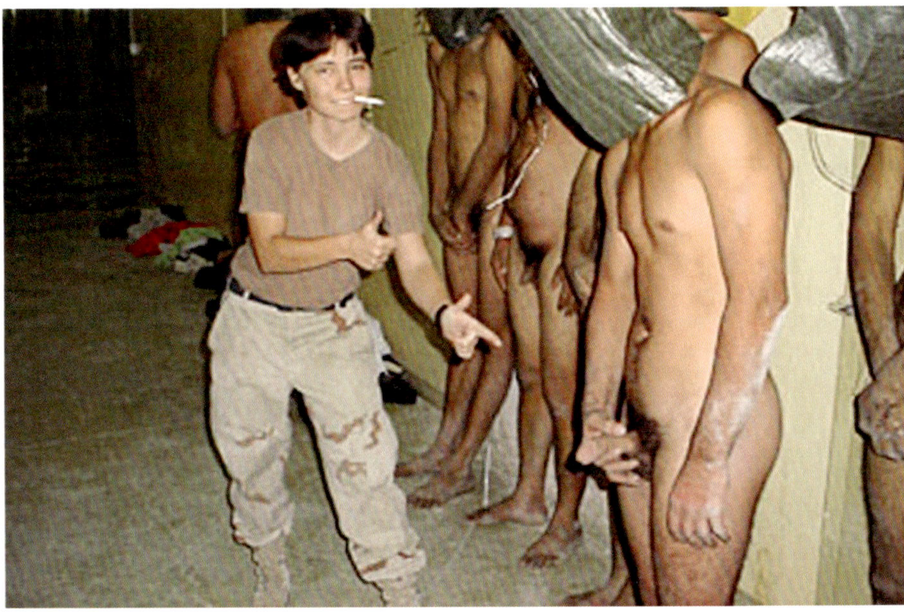

Abu Ghraib 12.14 am Nov 8 2003. SPC England points to the penis of one of the detainees

to answer. Only one said it made her think of Playboy bunnies dancing for soldiers in the USO—a famous scene from *Apocalypse Now.*

I don't think the sole issue here is the way that the codes of conduct in war can be construed to justify unconscionable acts. It seems to me that our culture lacks a precise political vocabulary for understanding women as self-conscious perpetrators of sexual violence. We rely instead on moralistic language about virtue, privacy, and emotional vulnerability to define female sexuality, or on limited views that frame women's historical condition as victims. Since the 1970s, feminists have tried to undermine the repressive moralistic language by arguing that female sexual assertiveness should be understood as a form of freedom of expression. While I don't disagree with that position, the sexual torture dilemma is making its limitations glaringly apparent. Flaunting one's sexuality may indeed be a form of self-realization, but it doesn't happen in a vacuum, nor is the only context for its appearance democratic. The absence of consent from the recipient turns the display into an act of violence. And when this imposition has been rationalized as part of an interrogation strategy, the act ceases to be strictly a matter of personal responsibility. We don't like to look at ourselves that way. Our popular culture represents female violence as the product of irrationality—the spurned lover, the irate mother, the deranged survivor of abuse. So the picture of what we are becoming in war cannot be not clearly drawn.

The photos of prisoner abuse from Abu Ghraib that were made public are profoundly disturbing. The grainy snapshots document political performances of American-ness that both the state and the citizenry may seek to distance themselves from, but that were nevertheless carried out in our name. Whereas photographs of murdered civilians once stood for the injustices not only committed by Franco's forces in Spain but also those of US troops in Vietnam, it is the images of American soldiers torturing helpless Iraqi prisoners that have come to stand for the illegitimacy of the occupation. We've tempered the implications of those pictures with explanations for the misconduct that enable us to condone the occurrences. According to officials who have seen the additional images that were censored from public view, the ones we saw represent the tip of the iceberg, and other abuses depicted include urolagnia, rape, and sodomy. But that is not what we see Charles Graner, Sabrina Harman, and Lynndie England doing. The ubiquity in the media of photos of them posing with Iraqi prisoners has helped to limit the understanding of sexual torture as a calculated practice. The absence of presiding authorities and the shocking gratuitousness of the violence make it difficult to determine who controlled the scenes, or even imagine that there would have been a director for this theater of cruelty. In that sense what the MPs are shown doing in those photographs is somewhat different from what has been described in numerous testimonies and investigative reports as the carefully orchestrated coercive sexual tactics that have been used in recent military interrogations.

The parade of sadism featured in the Abu Ghraib photographs has a riotous quality, exacerbated by the looks of glee and upturned thumbs of the MPs. Regardless of who told the perpetrators to do what they were doing, their apparent excitement was probably intensified by the communal character of the brutality. Interrogators, on the other hand, are trained never to allow themselves to emotionally engage their sources since this would impair their ability to maintain control. The female MPs involved participate in the sexual humiliation of the prisoners, but not through exhibitionist display of their sexuality. Their non-sexual demeanor combined with the looks of complicity make them seem to be asking to be viewed as "one of the guys"; their performances are directed at other (male) soldiers rather than detainees. Their diminutive presence creates the impression that less harm occurred because women were involved. On the other hand, the female interrogators who sexually harass detainees manipulate male anxiety by enacting their submission to female power as a monstrous, if not grotesque, sexual experience. While human rights experts, lawyers, and cultural theorists are still arguing about whether the Muslims are indeed more culturally sensitive to sexual harassment from women, there is testimony from some prisoners and witnesses that indicates that they found this tactic to be extremely disturbing and degrading, leaving them with psychological scars.[21]

Although the once popular comparisons to "frat boy antics" supported the erroneous characterization of the acts at Abu Ghraib as evidence of bad behavior by a rogue element, the MP's performance of sexual degradation resembles the ritualized humiliation of soldiers by other soldiers that has been an accepted convention of military sexual culture for a long time. Scholars of the military have noted that among the consequences of a military culture that has historically condoned many forms of sexual aggression are the toleration of heterosexual rape, the exploitation of sex workers, and homophobic violence.[22] "Mock rapes" may occur as part of training for survival as a prisoner of war, while simulated and real acts of sodomy are accepted as part of informal initiation rites.[23] While it is highly likely that Charles Graner

---

21 Riva Khoshaba, "Women in the Interrogation Room," *One of the Guys*, pp. 179-87. See also the letter from T.J. Harrington, deputy assistant director, FBI Counterterrorism Division, to Major Gen. Donald J. Ryder, Department of the Army, relating three incidents in which military interrogators used "highly aggressive interrogation techniques." Jaffer and Singh, *Administration of Torture*, p. A-127. **22** Elizabeth Hillman, "Guarding Women: Abu Ghraib and Military Sexual Culture," in McKelvey, *One of the Guys*, p. 113. **23** Ibid.

and company were following orders from interrogators, it is also likely that, lacking specific training in intelligence or interrogation, the MPs took recourse to ritualized forms of aggression that they already knew from military life.

There doesn't seem to be a consensus as to whether the use of sexual tactics was instigated by interrogators from the CIA, private contractors, military intelligence officers, or all three. Nonetheless, all three entities appear to have been involved. From what I have been able to glean from official reports, witness and detainee testimony, and the stories of interrogators themselves, sexual tactics in interrogation involve sexual humiliation and homophobia, but less man-handling than what was depicted in the Abu Ghraib photos. This would conform to standard regulations restricting physical aggression in military interrogation, and also reflects the American predilection for psychological coercion versus physical force. Sexual tactics in interrogation are usually directed at one prisoner at a time, in isolation. Whereas the purpose of posing prisoners in explicitly sexual ways for photographs was to create embarrassing evidence that could be used to coerce prisoners into becoming informants, the use of sexual tactics in interrogation is aimed at "breaking" detainees by means of an open attack on their masculinity.

The use of American female sexuality as a weapon against Islamic enemies exploits a number of cultural biases and archetypes. The stereotype of Arab masculinity as fragile leads to treating it as a point of vulnerability, while the stereotype of women as less aggressive makes their sexual harassment of detainees seem to be milder and more acceptable than other forms of torture. We don't really have a language for comprehending female sexual aggression as rape, which diminishes our ability to perceive it as such. Soldiers are trained to rationalize any form of violence against the enemy that is permitted within given rules of engagement, and measure all demands made of their bodies against the ultimate sacrifice of death. At the same time, the proliferation of erotic exhibitionism both as subcultural practice and as popular cultural entertainment in late capitalist America generates a dominant interpretive framework for the participation in and witnessing of sexualized torture that favors a reading of it as something else: erotic play and illicit pleasure, for both the viewers and those viewed.

Interview with **Geert van Kesteren**

Brigitte Lardinois

Geert van Kesteren's book, *Why Mister, Why?*, is one of the most eloquent photographic documents of the Iraq War, which examines many aspects of civilian and military experience. Aside from the innovative design and presentation of the book, van Kesteren has experimented with multimedia installations which integrate his photography with sounds and data feeds. Faced with the impossibility of continuing to make serious photographic work in Iraq, he turned to examining Iraqis' phone-camera pictures. When selected and arranged interpretatively, they say much about life under the Occupation, sectarian violence and the continuing depredations of everyday existence in a nation of extreme insecurity and failed infrastructure. The interview was made before an audience at the Brighton Photo Biennial in October 2008.

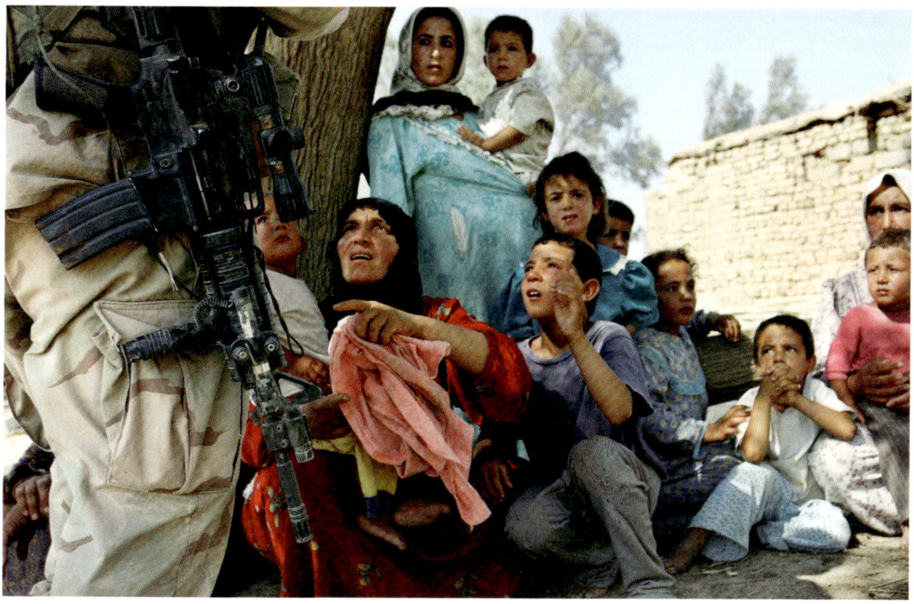

Geert van Kesteren, US Army on the hunt for terrorists, Baath supporters, weapons and Saddam Hussein. Engineers of the 4th Infantry Division raid a farm near Tikrit where they found several weapons and a field phone. Six men were arrested and brought to an improvised prison on the base. Women and children were kept aside, under the shadow of a tree. Tikrit, Iraq, 4 August 2003

Brigitte Lardinois I'll very quickly introduce myself—I'm Brigitte Lardinois. I worked for about ten years as an exhibition organiser in the Barbican before becoming the cultural director of Magnum, where I worked from 1995 until 2006. Then I took a senior research fellowship at LCC, where I am working now. I have great pleasure to be here with Geert van Kesteren. We had rehearsed a joke which was that we were going to say that, as this talk is sponsored by the Dutch Embassy, we are going to have it in Dutch, with Arabic translation, but it seemed a bit too stupid, and I have said it now anyway. But we are indeed both Dutch, but we met when I was working at Magnum, and Magnum had invited Geert to join as a nominee. That was immediately after the Geert publication of the book *Why Mister, Why?*, which really blew everyone away, and rightly so.[1] *Why Mister, Why?* is a book about which Martin Parr and Gerry Badger write, in their book of books, that it has the same importance as, or that at least it's in the tradition and on a par with a book like, *I Protest!* by David Douglas Duncan.[2] One of my first memories of Geert, and also of Julian Stallabrass, who is the curator of this really unbelievably well put-together festival, is when the three of us interviewed Philip Jones Griffiths the year before he died.[3] Out of all those connections, then, comes the invitation for Geert to show here, and my role is to have him talk to you, and also to give you the opportunity to ask him questions.

Just so you know how we have vaguely structured this talk, I would like to first ask Geert to tell us about *Why Mister, Why?*, then to talk about *Baghdad Calling*.[4] They are two different projects made at different times, and it's very important that he has decided to show them together. However, before we go there I want to say that I'm very aware that Geert works very closely with his wife, Connie Luhulima. Now that his arrangement with Magnum has come to an end, Connie and Geert together form the independent production team that has actually put the show together with the Lighthouse Gallery here in Brighton.

That's quite enough of me. Geert—*Why Mister, Why?* It wasn't your first book; it was in fact your second book because you had done a book on AIDS in Zambia. I don't think the time-frame gives us time to talk about that, so... Iraq gets invaded, what do you do?

Geert van Kesteren Nothing.

BL Nothing?

GvK No, I had to stay at home. I couldn't go to Iraq. Previously I was in Iraq back in 1998 and again in 2000. In 2000 I got the opportunity to be the photographer for *Stern* magazine for an interview with Uday, a son of Saddam Hussein, who was well known for being very sadistic and a playboy. Strange interview because, before I entered the room, I had to leave all my cameras behind, and when we came into the room there were huge TV cameras and we were on the national Iraqi TV, and the programme was repeated for about

1 Geert van Kesteren, *Why Mister, Why? Iraq 2003–2004*, Artimo, Amsterdam 2004. 2 Martin Parr and Gerry Badger, *The Photobook: A History*, vol. 2, Phaidon, London 2006, p. 258; David Douglas Duncan, *I Protest!*, The New American Library, New York 1968. 3 See this volume, pp. 56–81. 4 Geert van Kesteren, *Baghdad Calling: Reports from Turkey, Syria and Iraq*, Episode, Rotterdam 2008.

three weeks, every day, three or four times! But that interview also gave us a bit of access in Iraq. We simply said to the Ministry of Information—'Uday said it was OK', so they let us do certain things which were generally off-limits. When the story was published, a businessman from Oman told us that Uday was really mad about it, so they said, 'as long as they are in power you shouldn't go back to Iraq'. So I didn't go during the invasion, and just after Bush declared that the war was over, I went directly back to Iraq, and that's where *Why Mister, Why?* started.

BL Because you were there for something like six months or...?

GvK Yeah, like six and a half months in a time-frame of ten months.

BL And were you embedded with the US military...

GvK For six weeks.

BL For six weeks only?

GvK Yes, I did an embed for two weeks in Tikrit, and that was in August 2003. Then in 2004, I did an embed in Samarra, in February and January. The thing about these embeds was they were interesting to do because in my first week in Iraq, in one of the old palaces of Saddam, an older CIA officer took me aside and asked me if I worked for German TV, and I said I worked for *Stern* magazine. Out of the blue, he started to explain a lot of things which were very important for the upcoming ten months over which I stayed in Iraq. He told me that he was the interrogator of Tariq Aziz, and that he had also interrogated Mr [Amir] al-Saadi. Al-Saadi was a rocket scientist working for Saddam, and he urged me to go to his wife, a German lady called Helma al-Saadi. He urged me to go there and take her to the International Red Cross to let them know that her husband was being treated really, really badly. I wouldn't even...

BL He asked you to do that?

GvK He asked me to do that, yeah. And he said that, 'well, I wouldn't even cage my own dog like this', and he gave me all the details: they were questioning Tariq Aziz in such a brutal way that he was on hunger strike for a few days, things like that. So very early in that war, I had a quite clear picture of what was going on in the prisons, and ever since that day I've tried to get images from those scenes.

BL And... can you just decide 'I'll be embedded now'? Surely there's a lot of paperwork?

GvK My luck was that, on the one hand, I was working with *Stern* magazine, a German magazine, and Germany was against this war, so if I was with Iraqis and I could tell them I was working for a German magazine they welcomed me very much. Also, being Dutch helped, and if I needed an embed with the Americans, I was also working there for *Newsweek*. It was much, much easier. I had an army nickname, 'G-man', because they couldn't pronounce 'Geert'.

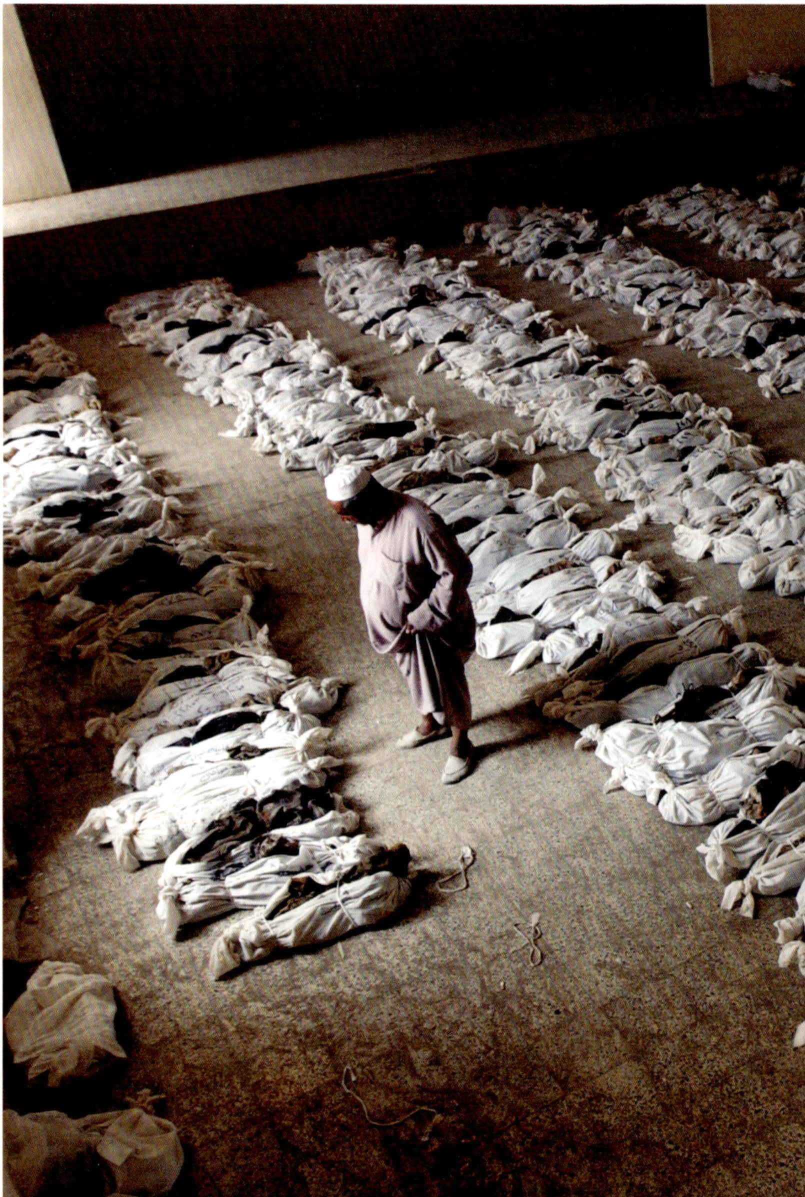

Locals search among the remains that were found in a mass grave near Jurff aq Sukhr for their loved ones, missing for more than ten years. Hundreds of bodies were found in this mass grave, where an unknown number of Shia people were executed after their rebellion was crushed by troops loyal to Saddam in 1991. Many skulls were blindfolded. Some

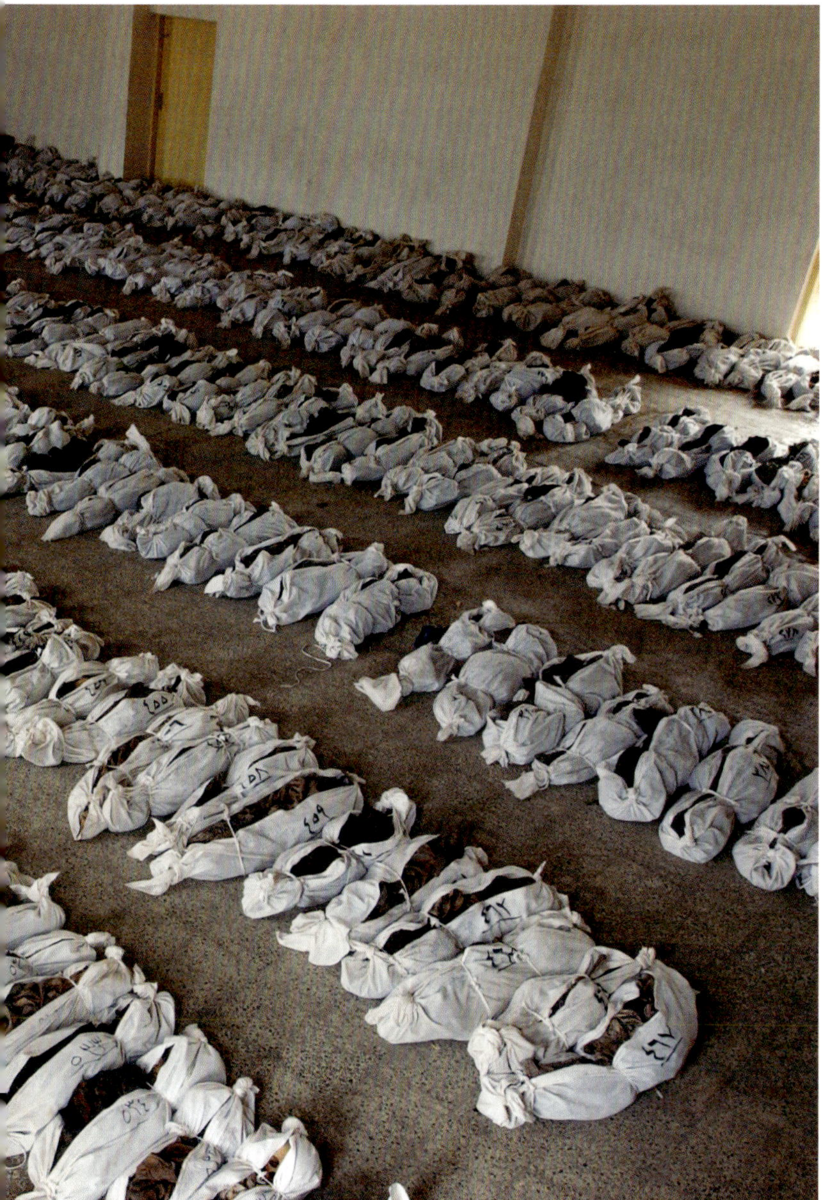

could be identified, but most bodies were reburied without identification as there was no official forensic research. After the bodies were counted and when possible identified, they were wrapped in white sheets and brought back to the town hall of Musawyyb, where relatives could claim the remains. Iraq, May 2003

BL They can't here either!

GvK So it would be 'Hello, it's G-man from *Newsweek*!' And they gave me an embed quite easily.

BL I guess that you had the book in mind as you worked, since increasingly even very traditional photojournalists work towards the making of a book, but at the same time you were actually shooting for the magazines and probably for Dutch papers as well. You were wiring photos back?

GvK Yeah, there in the middle of the desert you were sitting with a laptop and next to it a satellite phone, and you were transmitting to New York. On the screen behind us is a sequence of the nearthing of the mass graves made by Saddam who killed, apparently, up to 200 to 300,000 Iraqis who rose up against him in 1991. Yes, but of all these images, only one ever got published. It was a spread in *Newsweek*, and that was it.

BL Was that because they were so gruesome or because there were other photographers there as well?

GvK It was a gruesome and important happening: Saddam crushed the revolt after the First Gulf War with mass executions. When these people were digging up the mass graves in June 2003, the US had not found weapons of mass destruction, nor was it proven that Saddam had any links with Al-Qaeda (and of course neither was ever found). The discovery of the mass graves could give the Bush administration some 'credit' for invading Iraq, and it was the first time the Arab world was confronted with its own crimes, but the newspaper I was working for did not think my images were interesting.

The most important thing for me is that by the end of the war I would end up with a whole stack of photographs and stories that didn't get published. If I can go back a bit to those embeds, what was so interesting about the embeds for me was to be really close with these soldiers, and being close to them meant that with all the information I had from Iraqi people, telling me—I'll give an example—on an Arab channel it was reported over and over again how a male American soldier was body-searching a Shia woman on a bridge in Baghdad. So people were really upset about this in Iraq...

BL And they had images of that?

GvK Yeah, that was featured on the news over and over again. So, about these embeds, what was so interesting to me was that I could really ask these soldiers, 'OK, what is going on here?', and their answers also made very much sense in a way, because they were sent on a mission by politicians, but their answer was: 'Well, forget winning hearts and minds, because the Iraqis will never like us, so they'd better fear us.' And that, for the 4th Infantry Division in Tikrit, in Samarra with whom I had some embeds, was their main way of acting, and their main way of thinking.

BL Already so early on?

GvK Yes, that was only half a year after the invasion. And in August I did an

embed, and these guys were looking for Saddam, or one of his nephews, weapons of mass destruction or 'terrorists', as they called them, and they busted into houses without a translator and without anyone knowing a word of Arabic. So they simply arrested every male. As a photojournalist, I simply reported it and wrote it down and thought it was quite important to know.

BL It's right that you describe yourself as a photojournalist, but what I find particularly interesting in working with you is that you're actually much more than that—you're also a journalist who writes and, if the truth were told, a bit of a campaigner as well. It's very much that you come across something that you witness and really feel people should know about, so you must have wanted to scream from the rooftops that this whole thing about befriending Iraqis was nonsense. I mean, how quickly were you actually able to convey what you found there? Because there is a time lapse of course, between being there and actually getting the book out. How does that process work?

GvK I never photographed in Iraq with the idea of making a book. But then I saw a lot of upsetting things, while my images and stories were hardly published. I saw myself as photographer, not a writer or maker of books. I did not understand that my opinion would matter. But I felt more and more the need to tell that significant story. How, I did not know then, but the longer I spent there, the more I understood how the magazines were not the right space to give voice to my experiences.

BL So you go for several stints, and then you have all this knowledge, and then you decide, 'OK, *Stern* has had it, *Newsweek* has had it, the Dutch newspaper *de Volkskrant* has had it.' I want to know that moment when you start on this seriously important book, I want to know more about how you began.

GvK It became more and more dangerous in Iraq. It had become very dangerous in the weeks before the infamous incident on that bridge in Fallujah, when some US contractors were killed and burned alive and hanged on the bridge.[5] Every month you felt the tension rising in the country. At first, you were welcomed everywhere you went, would be given tea, eat with all sorts of people, yet eventually we ended up living in hotels with blast walls around them, and driving around in armoured cars with bodyguards.

BL This happened in a relatively short time?

GvK Yes, it happened very, very fast. When I came home that very week of the Fallujah incident, Harald Menk, the *Stern* picture-desk man, called me to say: 'Geert, don't go there anymore; make a book', and I said: 'I can't make a book! Come on, I don't have the war, Saddam hasn't been found and hanged yet, and this and this and that.' And he said: 'No, no, no—you'll get your work, make a book.' So then I slowed down, and I was viewing the work again, and I was discussing it with my wife, Conny Luhulima, and with my dear friend, photo-consultant Edie Peters, and

5 Four contractors working for a private security company were killed at the end of March 2004.

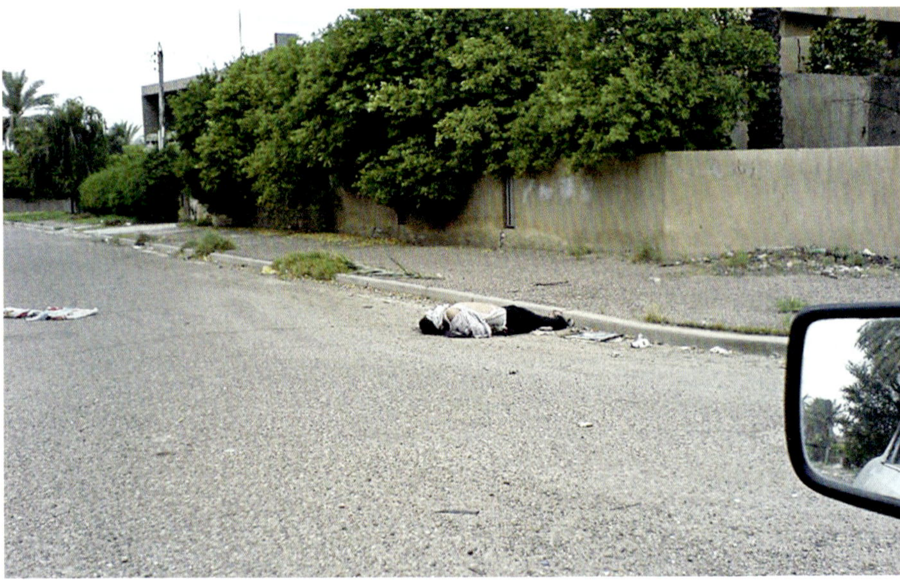

Geert van Kesteren/Collection Baghdad

we quickly figured out that this was a very, very important period of time, and, yes, it's true, I was very frustrated that so many stories weren't published and so many photographs were unseen, so that's when I decided not to go back to Iraq but instead use my own money to do the book.

BL And it must have been very, very gratifying to all of you that it was so well received.

I would like to move to *Baghdad Calling*, which is a book that Geert did when he couldn't go back, when indeed everything was becoming far too dangerous, and I remember having meetings with him in Utrecht in Holland where he said 'I want to go. I want to actually go and talk to the people who are no longer in Iraq, to the refugees.' There were an incredible amount of them, *millions* of people in Jordan and in Syria, and he said 'I have to be able to interview these people, take their photographs and tell of their plight', because in fact—and we were monitoring it—there was very, *very* little about it in the press. So Geert set out to do that. And then I remember him being incredibly frustrated having been there and saying: 'But, you know a refugee from Iraq sitting in Jordan could actually be sitting in your house in Lewes because the surroundings are very nondescript. They sit, but they are sophisticated people with computers and laptops, and the stories that I'm writing down...'—and that's why I was saying that Geert is a journalist as well as a photographer —'the things they tell me aren't reflected in the photographs I can take of them...' and, well, you should tell of the solution that you then came to in *Baghdad Calling*. You hit on the mobile phone pictures?

GvK Yeah. It was frustrating in a way because the stories that people were telling me were so extreme and the pictures I could take so mundane. I had only one question: 'Why? Why are you here? Why did you leave, what happened, why?' And then they explained to me what was happening, and, again, I would ask, 'Why is this happening?' It was a very simple question, and I've asked it of at least 60, maybe 80, different families from different religions, ethnic backgrounds, and they all came up with the same stories. It was about kidnap, murder, threats, torture, beheadings and ... my God. These stories went on and on and on. And the conclusion was very simple—Iraq was being ghettoised and ethnically cleansed. There were areas where people used to live together and now they couldn't anymore. All the Christians were chased out, all the Shia were chased out of Sunni areas, all the Sunni out of Shia areas, and so on. And then indeed I had pictures of people just sitting at home. And one night, I think it was about two in the morning, I was talking to these eight young doctors renting an apartment in Oman, and they were all eager to go back to Iraq to work there, and help the people, but they couldn't do anything because they had been threatened, some kidnapped, and they'd had colleagues killed. They had seen the most horrible things. And they told me one story, and maybe it's good to explain this story, and then I'll come to the mobile phones. It was about one of their best friends, who they said of: 'He was the strongest, he was the smartest, he was the most handsome guy, he was the most beloved one, he was a very good doctor. The

Mujahideen was in a fight with the American army, and one of the bullets went through four walls, and it ricocheted into his stomach and made a wound so big that we couldn't do anything. We took him in a car and we brought him to the Baghdad hospital where we had just arrived, and we said "We need this doctor", because they had a very, very good surgeon there. But they said "The surgeon was just kidnapped an hour ago."' They put their friend in their car and they put all their savings together, and they took the guy to Jordan, where he had an operation, and where in the end he died... Well, these guys were very emotional, and suddenly one of them took his mobile phone out and said, 'Look, this is our friend just before he died.' I looked at the image and was amazed. This is the first image I had seen that actually reflects the story. Of course, I first took a picture of the doctor holding the mobile phone image, and I came back to Zainab, a refugee who is an important source for the stories, and I said, 'Do you have any images of these stories?' And she said, 'Oh yes, Mr Geert. I have plenty!', and she just opened her laptop, and she had pictures from all of her friends and relatives, scattered all over Iraq. She had mobile phone images.

And this sending and receiving of images was going on among Iraqi refugees and those living in Iraq for months and months, and was astonishing to find. So in Iraq people take pictures to let the refugees know what is happening with their family, with their neighbourhood. And some of them can be very happy pictures (to say 'We are alright') and also very, very sad pictures—testimonies of wars. And I thought, well, this is so important, this is something nobody in the West knows about. I am trying to amplify this voice of these refugees, but it is more important to amplify the voice of what is happening inside Iraq. This story, that goes way beyond statistics and the number of casualties—*this* is the way to do it, to get their attention and to show what it is to be in this war.

BL And to show what they were fleeing from?

GvK Fleeing from, yes. Strangely, one night I received an image of a morgue, and then the second picture I got was a portrait of a baby. And I was thinking 'Oh my God, of course people ... even if there's war, people still make love.' You know?

BL So Geert resolved to make a combination of his own portraits of the refugees alongside their stories which were painstakingly recorded, and then put them alongside a set of mobile phone pictures. And the book is actually very cleverly designed by Mevis & Van Deursen in Amsterdam. The mobile phone pictures are of a different size than Geert's pictures and text. Some of the mobile phone pictures are, of course, badly pixelated and some of them have captions, some not. And when Geert's own photographs are reproduced in the book, they are of course less pixelated, and also bear his name. The distinction is left to the reader to sort out, and it is not always immediately apparent. You are intrigued, and you have to go from the back to the front, which is totally intentional because this unwrapping of these stories is in a way a little reflection of what Geert went through in trying to find these people and uncover their stories.

GvK Yeah, and what these people have gone through. The book feels uncomfortable, and war is (at the very least) uncomfortable, war is complicated. And I think the book is not that complicated but yet there are various elements in there, and I think that this is the most interesting part about photojournalism—once you have your collection of images and stories, you can put them to together in an exhibition or in a book, and sometimes you might call them art or you might call them just a book, but if it's done very cleverly, if you add great design, then you can look at it over and over again. And then the story twists, and it gives you new solutions or new riddles, and hopefully it will raise more and more questions.

BL And also, having been involved in the making of the book, what I really like is the fact that sometimes, when people didn't want their photographs to be shown, whenever you thought their story had to be told, the stories are in there without photographs. There's no hierarchy about what's important and what's not important in that sense. Ryszard Kapuściński says in his book *Travels with Herodotus* that a journalist makes no distinction about what is important or not, because life is too unpredictable to do that.[6]

GvK My books are about narratives. The story, that's the most important issue. The usual form of the photo-book seems to me to be like a magazine. So for me what matters most is the story.

BL And just very quickly—I feel we should say something about... because it sounds so simple: 'So, you just got the mobile phone pictures.' Of course, there's an incredible process that you had to go through with so many people helping.

GvK We first went to a Nokia shop. I thought 'I need to download all these images from cellphones', and everybody in the shop started to laugh because every Nokia has its own downloading cable. And just for Nokia they figured out you need 75 different cables.

BL So you couldn't?

GvK And when I went there everybody had an Ericsson! So there wasn't a way to do it. But quickly I found out that they all receive their images by email.

BL OK, so you set up a website. Or they set up a website?

GvK I had two people in Jordan, two refugees. Iraqis themselves who helped me collect them, and then my wife Connie was doing it from her side in Holland, and then I had two people, including Edie Peters, who set up a website.

So we started a website, and asked people, 'Who had received pictures from Iraq?' But then once you started to get all these images, the editing process was extremely fraught and complex: how did you go about editing it, and how did you judge what is true, what is real, and what is faked? Also, who was to give

6 Ryszard Kapuściński, *Travels with Herodotus*, Allen Lane, London 2007.

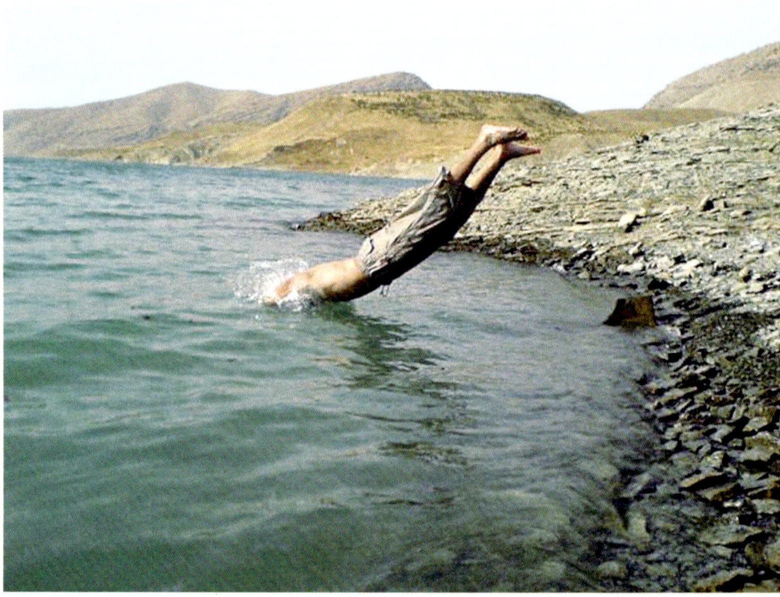

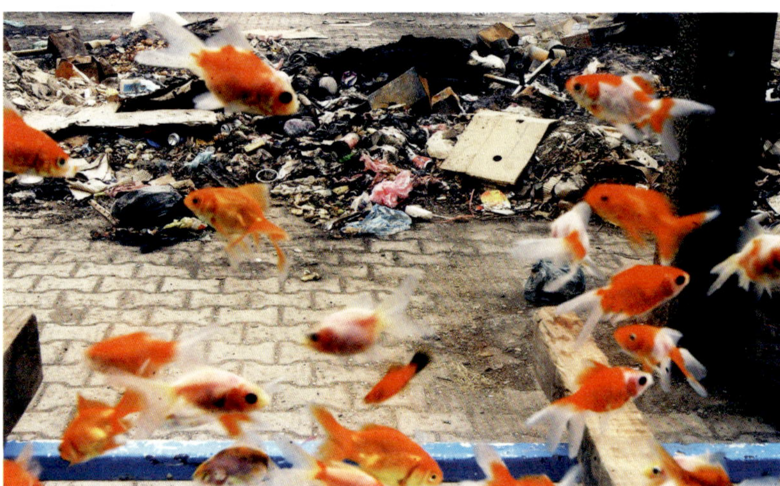

Top Geert van Kesteren/Collection Baghdad
Bottom Animal market, Baghdad, 30 May 2003

permission for an image to be used, and what might be the threat to the person who is in the image?

BL Some very sensational pictures were rejected because we thought it likely that they were faked. This book has now been published by Geert himself, but when we were visiting some very reputable publishers, who will remain nameless, they didn't dare to print these pictures because of the copyright issues. They said, 'At the end of the day it's the publishing house who are responsible for the clearance of copyright, not the author, and there is no way you can clear the copyright.' Well, Geert didn't have written permission from all these different sources.

GvK I got a lot of them.

BL You had a lot, but not enough to make many publishers happy.

GvK No, because if a refugee received a picture from his brother, and the brother received the picture from his fiancée, then you're already lost so far as chasing down the photographer concerned. I mean, that was the main problem.

What is very interesting is that we received so many images which I directly recognised as those of my colleagues in AP or Reuters, so many Iraqi people downloaded from the internet photographs about the war that they thought were important. They put it on their mobile phones, showed their friends and said 'look'... The mobile phone became so important in that war. It was a newspaper to them. Abu Ghraib has been photographed on mobile phones, Saddam's hanging has been filmed on it and, as I write in my book also, kidnappers are using them.[7] If you kidnap somebody, you take his phone and you find his father and you call him. People even receive a phone call and hear: 'Hi, I kidnapped your father, can you upgrade the credit on this mobile phone so we can negotiate?' Another woman picked up the phone and thought it was her sister and heard, 'Hello, this is the undertaker. We found this mobile phone on the body of a dead woman.' So people who flee the country—they end up in Syria, they end up in Jordan, they end up in Turkey, and they can't go anywhere. My own government gave last year 100 Iraqi asylum seekers a home in Holland. One hundred! So people do anything to leave the area; many people fled illegally into Europe. You need a mobile phone; that's all you need, to go from one place to another. If you arrive at a place, you call your brother back in Baghdad, and he goes to the trafficking office, and then he pays an extra $100 because you reached that place. And if you finally reach Sweden, he will pay the last remainder of $200, or something like that.

BL I've heard these stories before, and it still sort of really affects me, this idea of 'Can you increase the credit on your phone?' It's interesting, of course, this notion that the mobile phone is used as a sort of scrapbook. I mean, I'm not completely surprised that pictures of AP end up like that, on mobile phones. It reminds me

7 The Abu Ghraib photographs were actually shot on low-quality digital cameras.

a bit of how Donovan Wylie has a collection of scrapbooks from people who went through the troubles in Northern Ireland, and they have recipes next to photographs of funerals of the bombings, and it's that same feel of the combination of the very mundane and the unspeakable...

GvK Yeah, a curator of a Dutch photo museum also told me that he has a collection from the Second World War, photographs from Dutch civilians under occupation which were very similar to the Iraqi pictures. Most of the time you hardly see war, he says. You see a baby in a cart, things like that.

BL We've been speaking for a while. Would it be a good idea to open the discussion a bit to the audience?

Question 1 Do you need permission, release forms and so on, from the people in your photographs when you publish them?

GvK Of course, we asked permission from anybody who sent us an image. If we didn't have written permission from them, we never used an image. That was point one. But, as I just explained, sometimes you can't be a 100 per cent sure that the person who sent you the image also took the image. That's mostly where the problem lies. So anybody who sent us images said, 'Yes, I agree that this image will be used for the project *Baghdad Calling*. Only for the project *Baghdad Calling*.' There's another issue, raised for instance by the image of a Muslim family celebrating Christmas. I asked this family about six or seven times, 'Are you *sure* it's OK to publish because you can be recognised in the photograph?', and they said, 'Absolutely, it would be a total insult if you did not show our faces.' Security was important. We did not want anybody to be hurt just for being in a book. On two or three other occasions I've hidden the face on request, or when there are two guys drinking beer somewhere, I purposely made their faces fade because I know what consequences there can be. So there was the copyright issue, that was one thing, and then the other one is the safety of the people in Iraq, for themselves. And we had to be so, so careful, as careful as we could be. There are three photographs in the whole collection of executions on the street. I had images similar to those which I didn't use, although it's important to show these killings going on. Why those three? Because those were given to me by a source in Tikrit that I had known for a very long time, so I could be 100 per cent sure that what I see in the image reflects the truth. It's complicated because I also received an image of an American soldier sitting backwards on a donkey. It was obviously manipulated, it was hilarious, but manipulated, and we didn't use that because we thought the issue of why people left the country and what was going on was way too serious for that. Also, a lot of cartoons came in.

Question 2 To go back to the question at the beginning, when you said you were in Iraq for overall about ten months, you were embedded for two periods of time. When you weren't embedded were you acting as an independent?

GvK Yes. I just came there by car and I left by car, not with the American army,

so I only had six weeks embedded. And I lived in the Al Hamra hotel where all unembedded journalists were living together.

BL There are no unembedded journalists there now, are there? Or very few?

GvK Actually, it's important to know, and something we didn't mention, that in the five years now, almost six years, of war in Iraq, over 200 journalists have been killed. Thirty years of war in Vietnam and there were only 60 journalists killed. And yesterday or the day before I spoke with Ashley Gilbertson, who recently visited Iraq, and if you listen to the troubles he had to get access anywhere, paying *baksheesh* [bribes] to get a permit to go into an area, finally the militia in the area picks you up—and you want to show how poor the hospital looks, and they say, 'No, no, no ... it is too poor', and they show you only the bakery. So independent journalism in Iraq has not been happening—I think—for the past four years (and of course it didn't in the Saddam years either). And this is a reason why these phone-camera photographs are so important. We can't go anywhere, we'd get killed. And if you do go somewhere, it's controlled, you're embedded with the army, you're protected by bodyguards. At least there are a lot of Iraqi photographers now—maybe that's a little bit of the good part of the war—who were not such good photographers at the start of the war but are *great* photographers now. Those working for Reuters and AP are fantastic photographers. They do have some access, but even for them it's very difficult to go anywhere.

BL And dangerous as well.

GvK Extremely dangerous, so many have been killed or tortured or simply obstructed in their work...

Question 3 I was just wondering if you could say a little about showing *Why Mister, Why?* and *Baghdad Calling* together, and why that's been important and what those two exhibitions say to one another.

GvK Well, both projects are very linked with each other, although they are very different. In making this exhibition, we thought about the confrontation between them, it was so interesting. In *Why Mister, Why?* I'm very 'there' as a photographer, as when I work I tend to circle around a subject a lot so there are a lot of images about an action or about an important issue; and in *Baghdad Calling* my presence is very subdued, and in a lot of it, of course, I am completely absent. The circumstances shown in *Why Mister, Why?*, ten months after the war, led to the civil war that is still raging on, they led to the images you see in *Baghdad Calling*, and that's why we decided to bring them together as a whole.

Julian Stallabrass There's a way of looking at the developments in Iraq as having something broader to say about the increasing difficulties of making critical photojournalism. While some of these difficulties you have encountered are absolutely particular to Iraq and to all the terrible things that have happened there, what

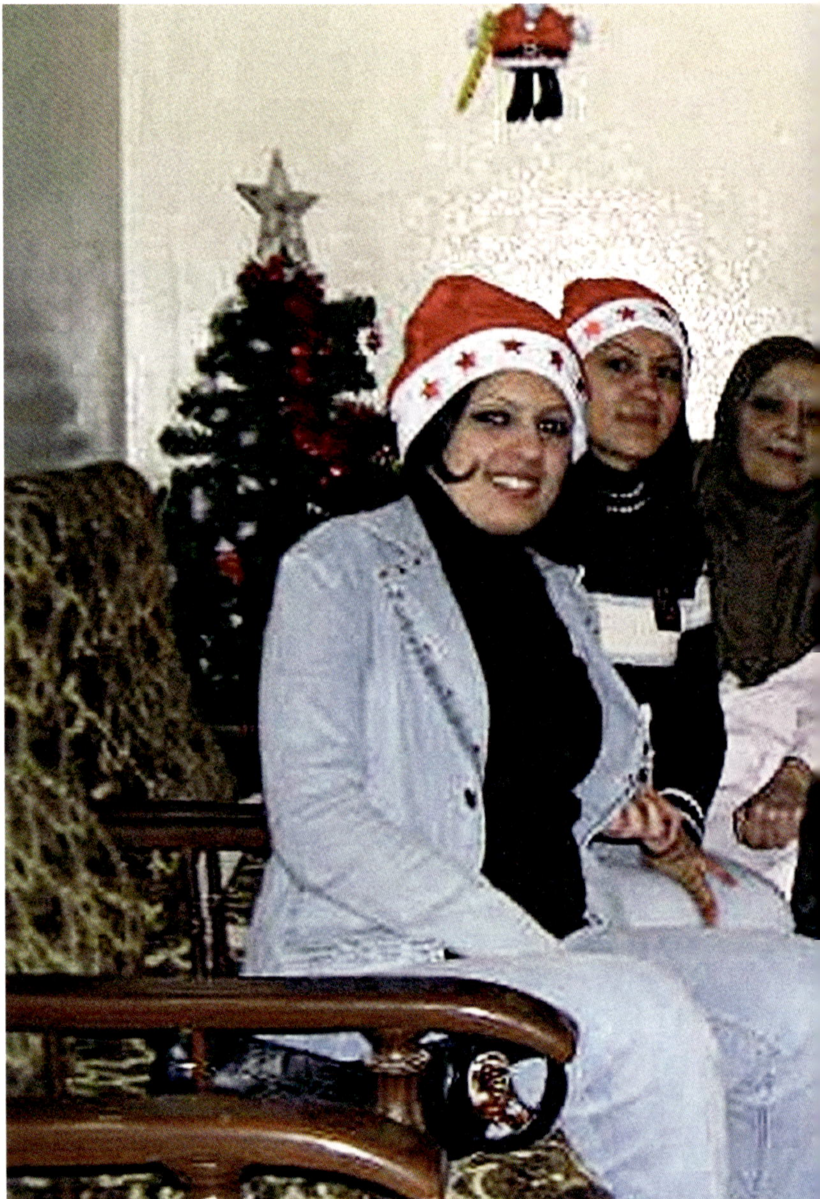

Geert van Kesteren/Collection Baghdad

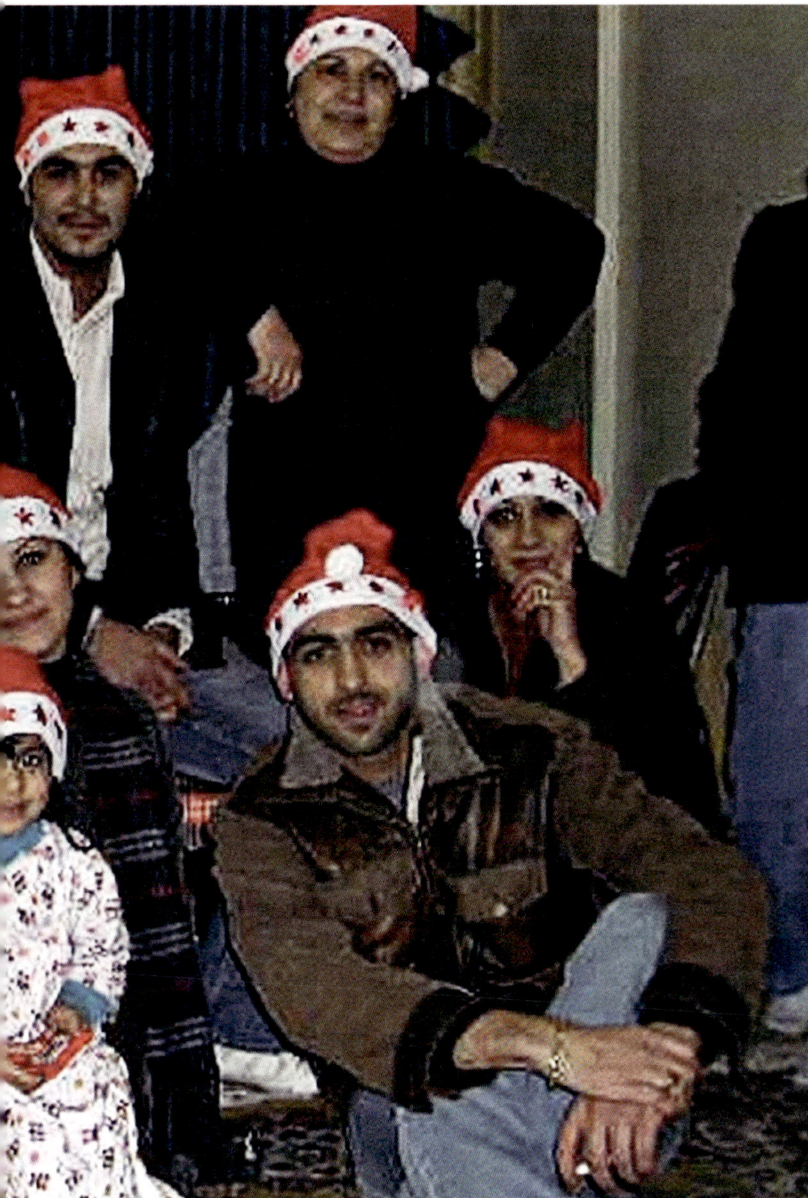

do you think about the way photojournalism is developing, what are its prospects, what are the difficulties for serious and reflective publication, either in the papers or in books?

GvK Yes, well I'm a born optimist, so let me first say I truly believe that journalism and art are pillars of democracy. They allow us to think and act freely, and in Iraq under the Saddam regime, a free press was impossible. It still isn't there. So can you imagine on what basis decisions have been taken in that country for decades now? And on the future of journalism, on the one hand, it's very difficult because magazines are printing fewer stories and paying less money; on the other hand, I think we have so many more opportunities—museums are opening up to photojournalism and we have possibilities on the internet. As for books, you couldn't imagine it, but my book became a collectors' item. It was never meant to be that—it's meant to be read. But this situation gives us photographers great possibilities. It gives us more possibilities to make books, to find our own way to express ourselves. It's a very optimistic story, though those photographers who are dependent on assignments are having a very hard time. Maybe Brigitte would like to add something to that.

BL It's well known that agencies all over the Western world are struggling because there are so few assignments. I've just finished a book about Eve Arnold and her working life, and if you just see the lists of assignments that someone like her would have in the sixties and seventies, and the access she had. Someone like Michael Rand would say to Eve, 'Go to China for six months and bring me back a story about Peking duck', you know. For the rest she could do whatever she wanted, the money was there, the visa was there. That golden age of assignment is gone, but I was speaking to one of my ex-colleagues at Magnum the other day, he's the head of the archive, and he said that this credit crunch disaster is already being reflected in the way that the magazines are laying out their next issues. So it's now already considered to be bad taste to have six pages of high-heeled shoes or how to entertain with clams and mussels. So it's really, really interesting that this whole lifestyle obsession may be on the decline.

GvK No, I remember the same thing because at *Stern* magazine there was this tendency for high-heel stories and then, after 9/11, they suddenly had so much photojournalism.

Question 4 *Baghdad Calling* can be seen in three different formats in this festival: there are the projected images at Lighthouse, there's obviously the book that's on display there as well, and then there's the enlargements that are outside in Jubilee Square. It's interesting with the projections, because in a way that's quite true to their original format, the camera-phone images—printing them is actually doing something to them that wouldn't have been done otherwise. I was just wondered what your experience was of those different formats of showing the work. Not necessarily that one's more successful than the other ones, but what's your experience of various audience responses, or your feelings about showing it in different formats?

GvK That's a nice question. I have this huge printer back in the studio, and I first printed one of these images really, really large, and you see huge pixels and blocks and chaos in that image when you're up close, but when you stand far away you see the image again. That added for me so much more to what it actually was. In the book itself we printed those images on newspaper paper. It was meant to express urgency. Once I published *Baghdad Calling,* I stopped collecting any of these images. The whole team had the feeling that we needed to give these back, this is from those people themselves. We took something out of it to show the world—OK, this is Iraq behind the curtain, and so this to us is also a kind of 'de-collection'. So if you try to present it as enlargements, each image will come alive, and if you look very carefully you will see in each image, you can read, a whole story. In one image a road is blocked, it looks like a very rich area in Baghdad and the situation looks ... not good. So that's the enlargement, and if you put a lot of these enlargements together, they suddenly become a whole narrative, a whole momentum of war, a story. When I project them in the Lighthouse it has the same effect of course, because it's enlargements of these photographs, but to bring it back in a very silent room, then you actually hear these refugees talk to you. I hope it becomes very human, that it becomes very accessible, because that's what I always try to do, to show you the chaos of war from the perspective of the individual and to bring to that chaos of war some order, so hopefully we, too, understand something of it all, or we can relate to it somehow.

BL Just so you know, these bodies of work are also going to be included in the big Barbican exhibition which has an exhibition of Robert Capa and also five contemporary artists dealing with themes of war.[8] Geert's work will be printed much bigger and displayed in grids.

GvK The spaces are different, but also because this is a biennial about images of war, in this context I think you can also be a little bit more, well, 'educational', and work with the other narratives on display, while in the museum, I think it's better that the audience get their own feeling, if they can, with their own knowledge of Iraq or their own feelings about the images. They take a look at it, and slowly it becomes something.

Question 5 Is there a project you're working on at the moment which you'd like to tell us about?

GvK For 16 years I've been covering wars, disasters, the AIDS pandemic in Africa, tsuanamis, earthquakes... You name it. And after 16 years I'm left with a question: how can we solve this? What can we do about it? And it's obvious that if we spend a trillion dollars on weaponry and only 50 billion on national aid, it won't help much. So within that knowledge and with all these questions in my head, I'll start my next project on that subject.

8 Barbican Art Gallery, *On the Subject of War*, 17 October 2008 to 25 January 2009.

Overleaf Ghaith Abdul-Ahad, An Iraqi boy celebrates after setting fire to a damaged US vehicle that was attacked earlier by insurgents. Baghdad, 4 April 2004

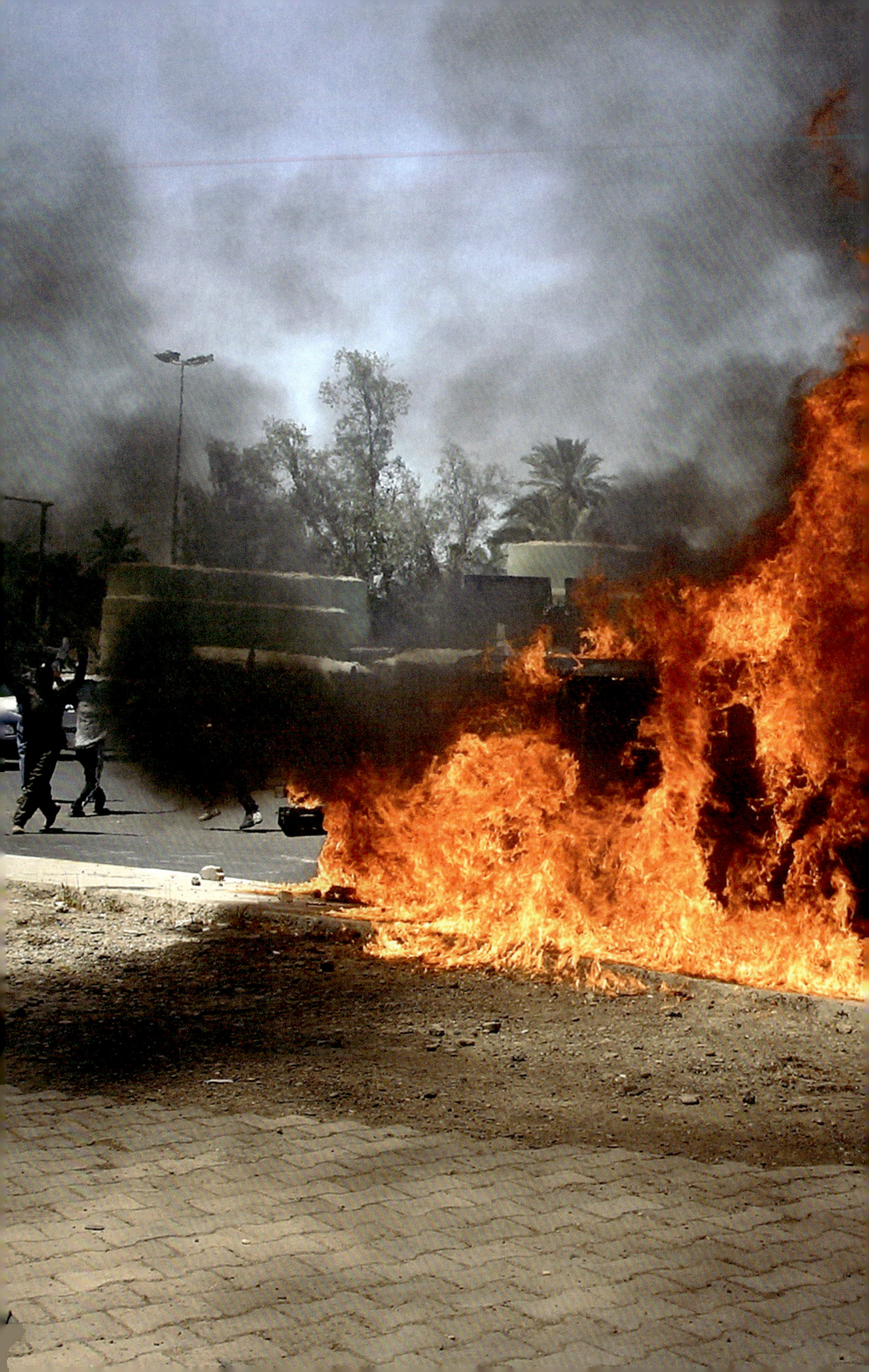

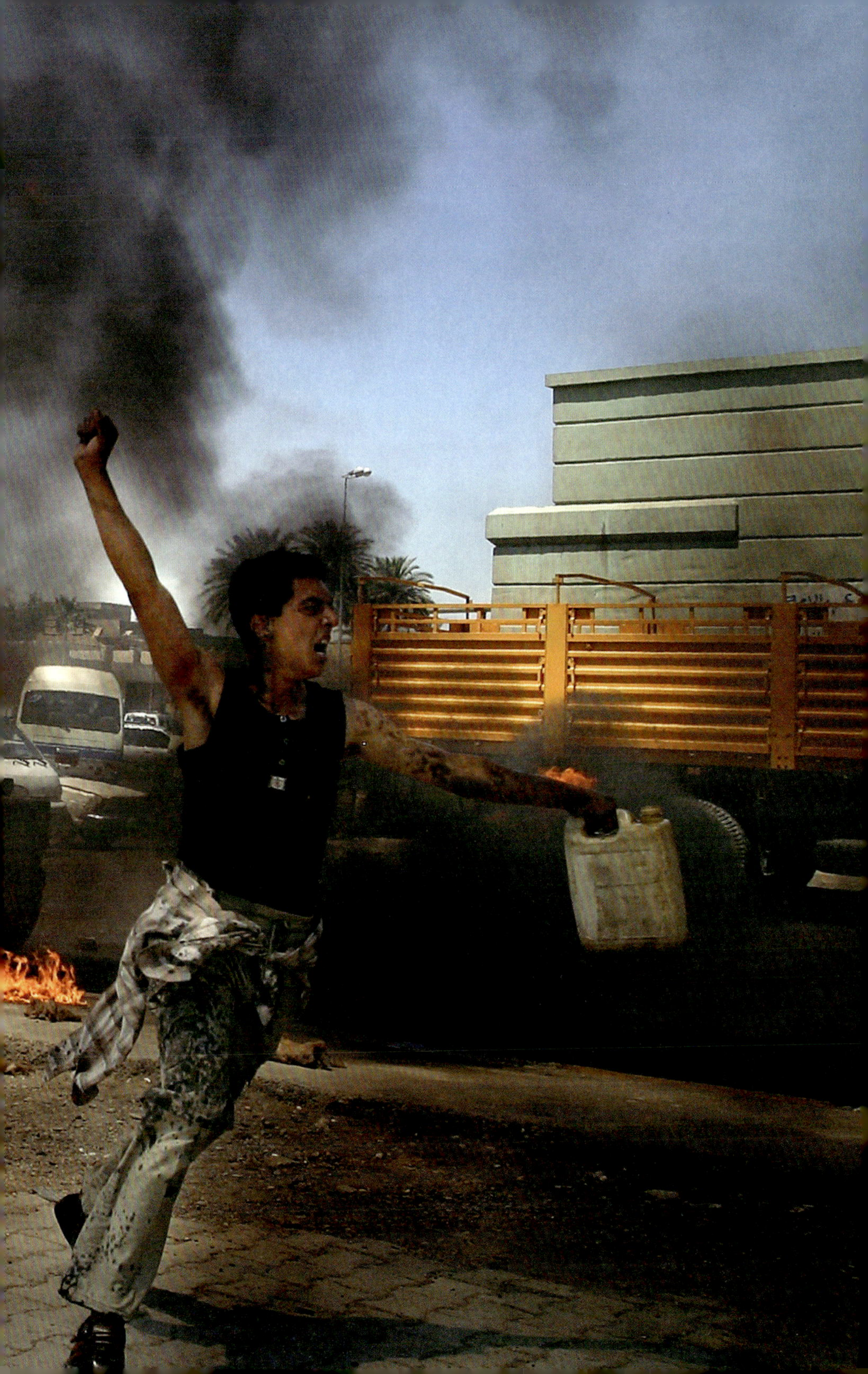

Image, War, Impactology
Stefaan Decostere

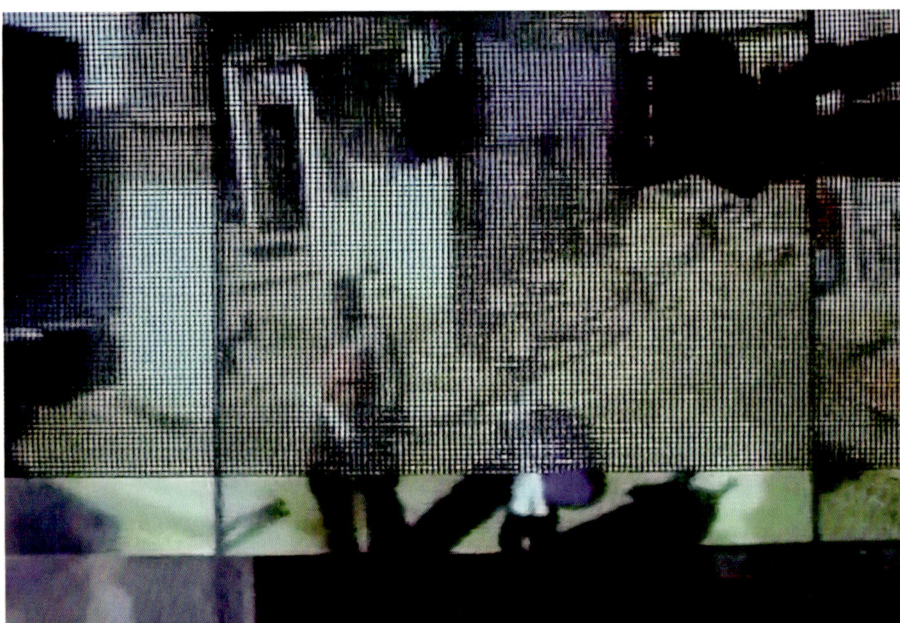

All photographs *Warem 2.0* installation, 2008

Chamber Of Echoes

Let's begin with some quotes about media impact, which begin to mark out the media environment which we inhabit:[1]

> *After all, we're at war. Endless war. And war is hell, more so than any of the people who got us into this rotten war seem to have expected. In our digital hall of mirrors, the pictures aren't going to go away. Yes, it seems that one picture is worth a thousand words. And even if our leaders choose not to look at them, there will be thousands more snapshots and videos. Unstoppable.*[2]

So wrote Susan Sontag in an essay following the mediatisation of Abu Ghraib images. And now Bernard Stiegler, the French media philosopher, argues that what media channels 'channel'

> *is the unconscious impulse. And in this case, it is a matter of provoking unconscious forces in the service of destruction: by short-circuiting the intergenerational game where it is precisely transgression that allows for construction—meaning the ability to care. And this is without doubt the first time that an attention control psycho-technique—which has become a psycho-technology—is no longer in the service of care. (With the exception of totalitarian social devices, contemporaries of the birth of cultural industries, which also sought to eliminate the psychic apparatus via psycho-technologies.)*[3]

For Stiegler, this 'psycho-technological' condition is driven by a system that is about to self-destruct. In an age of 'pervasive computing' and perception modelled by the media, the perception of 'reality' also seems to be in the throes of programmed visibility and mode-based viewing. The quality of the images

---

1 Thanks to Stoffel Debuysere, Geert Lovink and Julian Stallabrass for their comments on the essay; also to the *Warum 2.0* team and visitors. Apologies to all the persons quoted for imitating parts of their reasoning. 2 Susan Sontag, 'Regarding The Torture Of Others', *New York Times Magazine*, 23 May 2004.
3 Bernard Stiegler, *Prendre soin: de la jeunesse et des générations*, Editions Flammarion, Paris, 2008, p. 79. The original reads: 'c'est la pulsion qui sollicite l'inconscient. Mais ici, il s'agit de provoquer les forces de l'inconscient au service de la destruction du ça: en court-circuitant le jeu intergénérationnel où précisément la transgression permet la construction du ça—c'est-à-dire du soin. Et c'est sans doute la première fois qu'une psychotechnique de l'attention—devenue une psychotechnologie—n'est pas mise au service du soin. (A l'exception des organisations totalitaires de l'appareil social, contemporaines de la naissance des industries culturelles, qui visaient elles aussi à éliminer l'appareil psychique par les psychotechnologies).' Thanks to Sara Knelman for all the translations in this essay.

no longer seems relevant. The power of images is extracted from them by the repressive strategies with which they are employed.

When I interviewed him in autumn 2006 about *Warum 2.0*, a project I was developing on image, war and impact, Paul Virilio said:

> *Hear Octavio Paz, 'The impact of the moment is as uninhabitable as the future.' I want to say, when an artist is an impact-maker: this is futurism. Remember that Marinetti inspired fascism. Don't forget that the Blitzkrieg emerged from fascist Italian futurism. I'm half Italian, and it's not by chance that I am sensitive to this futurisation phenomenon. We are faced here with a futurism of the moment. The impact of the moment is as uninhabitable as the future. Therefore, the moment today is a masked futurism leading to fascism, new fascisms which have nothing to do with Panzers, the goose-step, Mussolini or Hitler, but fascisms linked to technical achievements ... And this is a great threat to democracy and collective thought.*[4]

After the standardising and synchronising of products and information, he warned, we are entering another phase of synchronisation—that of fleeting emotions:

> *We have passed from the standardisation of opinion and the democracy of opinion to the democracy of emotion, which is no longer a democracy. We have moved from the democracy of opinion—the representative democracy of meetings—to the presentative 'democracy' of emotions, to the point that this 'democracy of instantaneous emotions' or, as I call it, the 'communism of affects', since we are no longer talking about democracy, but of a totalitarianism as communism was.*[5]

A few days before the 2004 presidential election, Ron Suskind, a columnist who had long been investigating the White House and its communications, wrote in *The New York Times* about a conversation with a presidential adviser in 2002. The aide told him that guys like him were in the 'reality-based community', which he defined as people 'who believe that solutions emerge from a judicious study of discernible reality'. Suskind nodded and murmured something about enlightenment principles and empiricism. But the aide cut him off, saying:

---

4 Paul Virilio, interviewed by Stefaan Decostere at La Rochelle, 2007. **5** Ibid.

> *That's not the way the world really works anymore. We're an empire now, and when we act, we create our own reality. And while you're studying that reality—judiciously, as you will—we'll act again, creating other new realities, which you can study too, and that's how things will sort out. We're history's actors and you, all of you, will be left to just study what we do.*[6]

These remarks are not just cynical and Machiavellian. They sound like they come from the theatre rather than from an office in the White House. Not content with renewing the ancient problems once discussed in cabinet offices, pitting idealists against pragmatists, moralists against realists, pacifists against warmongers or defenders of international law against supporters of the use of force, they display a new concept of the relationship between politics and reality. The leaders of the world's superpower were not just moving away from *realpolitik*, but also from realism, to become creators of their own reality, the masters of appearance, demanding a *realpolitik* of fiction.

The technology they use is called 'storytelling', a 'new world order' technology of narration focused on marketing and (political) branding, formatting the perception of reality as fiction. And one of the techniques of storytelling is 'impact making'. Whereas 30 years ago, in her book *On Photography*, Susan Sontag called for a restrictive and conservationist 'ecology of images' (for censuring and perhaps censoring the visual stimuli with which our consumerist society assaults us), in her last book *Regarding the Pain of Others*, she predicted that there will never be that kind of ecology:

> *There isn't going to be an ecology of images. No Committee of Guardians is going to ration horror, to keep fresh its ability to shock. And the horrors themselves are not going to abate.*[7]

The changing situation did not turn us into insensible viewers, as Sontag had thought in her earlier book—and this she freely admitted in the later one.

In book after book, both Stiegler and Virilio come very close to fatalism. Yet, just before falling into the abyss of doom that looms before them (and us), they turn their whole approach inside out, and call for a 'university of disaster' (Virilio), and a 'technology of debate' (Stiegler). Virilio:

---

6 Ron Suskind, 'Faith, Certainty and the Presidency of George W. Bush', *New York Times*, 17 October 2004.
7 Susan Sontag, *On Photography*, Penguin Books, London 1979, p. 180; Sontag, *Regarding the Pain of Others*, Hamish Hamilton, London 2002, p. 97.

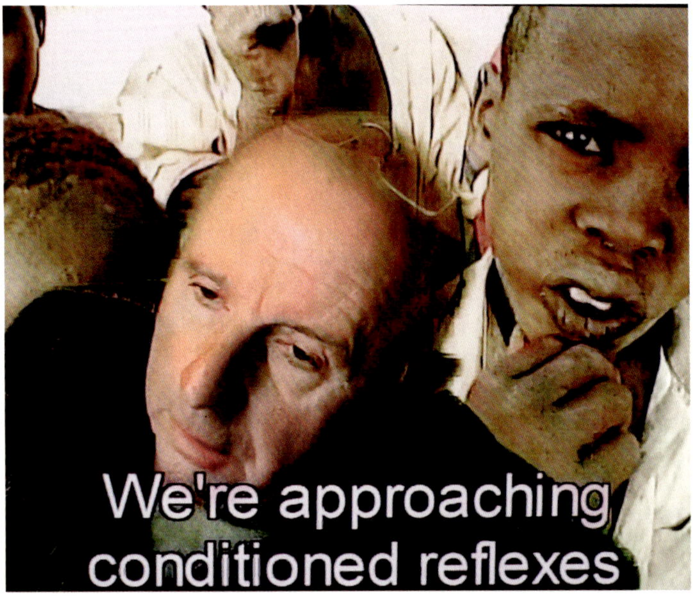
We're approaching
conditioned reflexes

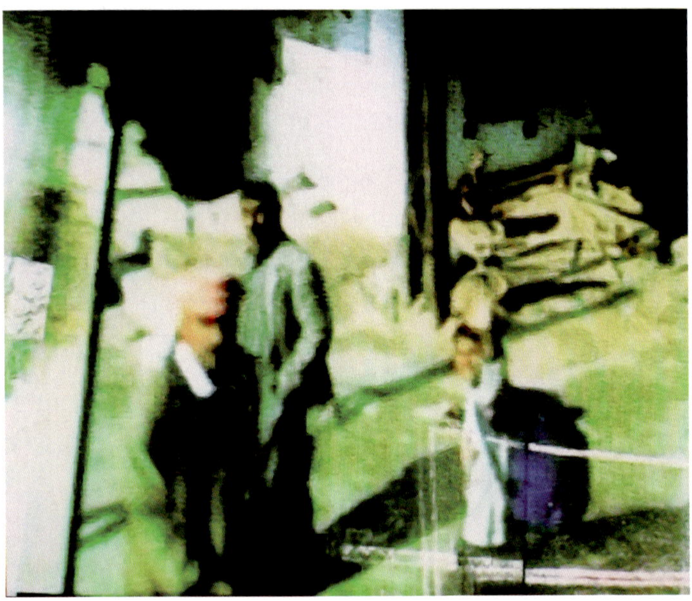

> *For me, the University of Disaster will oppose the integral accident, the accident of knowledge, the accident of a techno-science which has gone mad and become imperial, a religion. Somewhere we are confronted with the crash test of science, or rather techno-science. The University of Disaster must test this disaster, ecology being the important illustration of this. Ecology touches upon everything: there is an ecology of images, of thought. Ecology is the centre. And we are just at the beginning! Ecology as we see it is at the degree zero of writing.'*[8]

Stiegler:

> *Our problem is one of debating technologies, nanotechnologies, biotechnologies, neurotechnologies. But it's also on the subject of the technologies of debate themselves. It is absolutely fundamental that we lobby in order to ultimately develop a politics of technologies of debate.*[9]

Virilio again:

> *Today, faced with what's happening in science and knowledge in general, not only science but philosophy too, political philosophy, we need people who are not afraid of tragedy but who interpret, analyse, dissect, talk about things. It's the opposite of storytelling. It's something much more modest and in my opinion more useful today than grand spectacles.*[10]

Alternative ecology, updated critical enlightment, true testimonials: first, to become realised, these theorists say, they need to occupy a distance, far from impact, and far from the strategies of marketing. They need a space of their own. Virilio says that they need a 'contra-arsenal'. By implication, he claims that they need to stop ignoring their own technological situation. Stiegler calls this awareness 'pharmacological' (technologies are not good or bad; it all depends on their use). The techniques for caring, for being responsible, and in addition, the techniques of attention, of appropriation

---

8 Paul Virilio, interviewed by Stefaan Decostere at La Rochelle, 2007. **9** 'L'innovation à l'époque des technologies transformationnelles', lecture by Bernard Stiegler, 18 March 2008; once available at http://arsindustrialis.org but the site is now down. Original: 'Notre problème, c'est de débattre sur des technologies, des nanotechnologies, des biotechnologies, des neurotechnologies. Mais c'est aussi sur les technologies de débat lui-même. Il est absolument fondamentale que nous fassions du lobbying pour que enfin se développe une politique des technologies de débats.' **10** Decostere interview with Virilio, 2007.

and of transinviduation are the same as the ones that form, deform and transform the libidinal economies. The sciences of knowledge are in need of new techniques of perception.

Hall of Mirrors

How then do radical media-makers respond to this effect of impact? Lars Von Trier communicated his protest in the form of a short manifesto, called 'defocalising':

> *The subject we fiction makers are looking for is to be found in the same reality that inspires the fabricators of fiction. It's in the same reality that journalists think they are describing. But they never succeed in finding the subject, because their techniques blind them. In fact, they don't want to find it, because their techniques have become a goal in themselves.*[11]

He continues:

> *How to rediscover the subject? ... The ultimate challenge of the future is to see without looking: defocus! In a world where the media lie prostrate before the altar of clarity, and this empties life of all life, the DEFOCALISER will be the communicator of our time—no more, no less.*[12]

Christian Salmon, in his book on storytelling, writes of this technique for at once fabricating stories and formatting minds:

> *Through the use of stories launched by those in positions of power, we are witnessing the emergence of a new narrative order. But symbolic practices of resistance assert themselves seeking to stop the machinery that produces stories, by 'defocusing', by desynchronising these stories. Nothing short of an anti-narration.*[13]

---

11 Lars Von Trier, Manifesto on 'defocalising', *Rageleje*, March 2000. Available at http://www.films-sans-frontieres.fr/5obstructions/page.htm (retrieved 7 December 2012). Original: 'Le sujet que nous cherchons se trouve dans la même réalité que celle qui inspire les faiseurs de fiction. C'est la réalité que les journalistes pensent décrire. Mais ils ne parviennent pas à trouver ce sujet peu commun, car leurs techniques les aveuglent. En fait, ils ne veulent pas le trouver, car ces techniques sont devenues le but en soi.' **12** Ibid. Original: 'Comment redécouvrir le sujet? ... Le défi ultime du futur est de voir sans regarder: défocaliser! Dans un monde où les médias se prosternent devant l'autel de la netteté, et ce faisant vident la vie de toute vie, le DEFOCALISATEUR sera le communicateur de notre époque—ni plus, ni moins.'

How to generate media consciousness? How to wrestle free from a conservative entrapment (or feedback loop)? How to reject the dominance of media-generated meanings whereby our imagination is framed, and the territory is pre-bought, and free it from its naturalised association with narrative, storytelling and vision denigrated into consumerism? These are the questions that many artists ask themselves, and many try to find answers by using the very same techniques and media that they want to dismantle. Keith Sanborn is one of them:

> *Since it has existed, the net has displayed a dialectic of potlatch and recuperation, followed by détournement. ... Intelligence and generosity are exploited for fantastic profits, but the exploited can be hijacked as well. In place of one-way broadcast communication, the 'new' spectacle offers inter-passivity, pseudo-agency. Creating resistance requires bringing forward the background. 'Pay no attention to the little man behind the curtain, ... indeed, pay attention to the curtain. ... In the spectacle, everything promises to be at your disposal: stupefied super-models at least half-naked, powerless tyrants in the final humiliations of their executions. In the digital world, equivalence reigns—that is, the commodity form. Equivalence is presented as equality, democracy, value, power, freedom. It is, in actuality, the source of inequality, the rule of the few, the loss of judgment, powerlessness, unfreedom. It is, unnoticed, horrific in its banality. In place of the encyclopedia, it offers the search engine, for controlled access to pseudo-knowledge. But the digital world sometimes still folds over on itself, escaping the grasp of even its most aggressive handlers, from Youtube.com to the so-called 'People's Republic of China'.*[14]

In February 2008 I was given the opportunity to give it a try myself, with the installation *Warum 2.0*, in the charged area of our radically changed relation to the documentary image. Our material was video by the Belgian cameraman Daniel Demoustier, including news footage of war and human

---

13 Christian Salmon, *Storytelling: La Machine à fabriquer des histoires et à formater les esprits*, Editions La Découverte, Paris, 2007, p. 20. Original: 'À travers l'injonction aux récits lancée par toutes les instances du pouvoir, nous assistons bien à l'émergence d'un nouvel ordre narratif. Mais s'affirment aussi en résistance des pratiques symboliques visant à enrayer la machine à fabriquer des histoires, en 'défocalisant', en désynchronisant ses récits. Rien de moins qu'une contre-narration.'

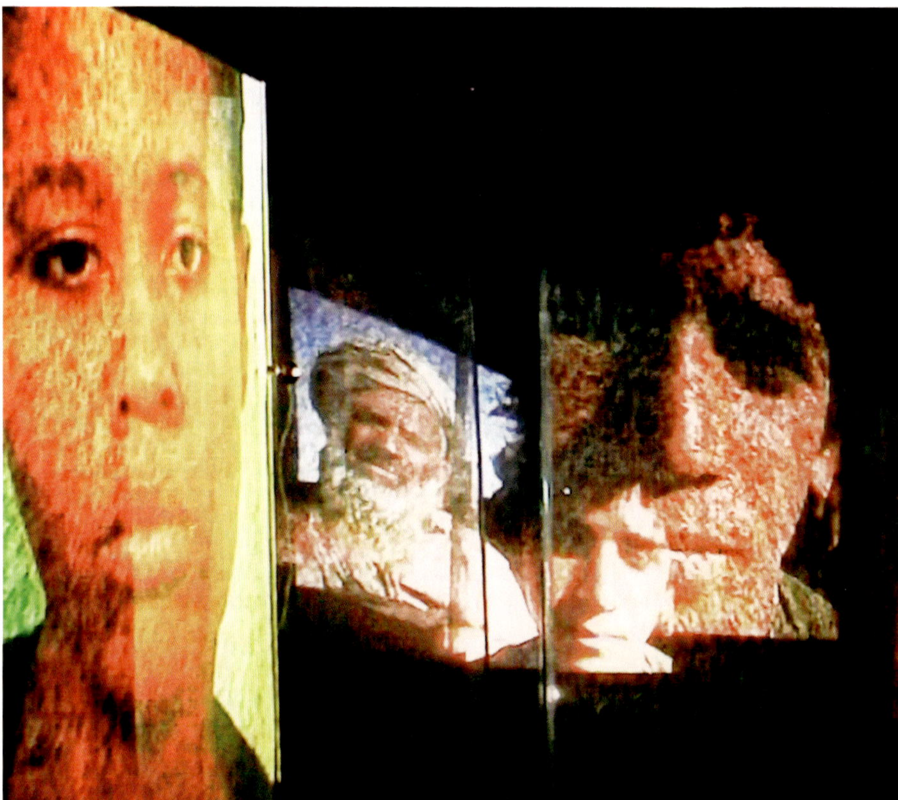

suffering from Haïti, the Middle East, Darfur, former Yugoslavia and Afghanistan. It had been shot by Demoustier for ITN and Doctors Without Borders. During the on-site construction and the opening week, I ran a blog where visitors could find statements of intent, comments, views and video clips, with excerpts from my interview with Virilio, which forms part of the installation.

The '2.0' was added to the questioning word of the title ('warum' meaning 'why' in German), and reflected on the treatment of the original themes in my 1985 video *Warum wir Männer die Technik so Lieben* on themes of men, war and technology. This also had the collaboration of Virilio, who at that time was interviewed by Chris Dercon. In 2008, the question was: what will version '2.0' bring about? Is the documentary video art form—and, by extension, the installation as an expanded media form—becoming a manifestation of so-called 'user-driven content'? Or does it carry with it hilarious forms of semantic kitsch? If not, will entropy be the final outcome?

For more than 20 years I was active as a maker of documentaries for BRT (Belgian Radio & Television). That was abruptly put to an end in 1997 when the director-general was replaced by a corporate manager. The network was given a true spiritual leader. He successfully turned the TV station into a company and made it absolutely market-driven. In all strategic positions, managers were put in place who believed in the future, and all personnel were given the opportunity to enter paradise regained. As for me, I was relocated from the art department (which was soon after dismantled) to the news service (where reality was made to burst into entertainment). This was the new horizon.

I was putting four news broadcasts to air each day, and had to adapt to an ergonomic work floor that resembled a military command-and-control centre. As a bonus, I was allowed to follow a series of workshops on storytelling. There I saw my former colleagues sweating it out, learning the latest formatting techniques of documentary-making, and fast internalising the techniques for creating impact and keeping their viewers clustered around the screen, whatever the content.

In the end, those who execute this 'training' are not concerned with us (visitors, users and makers who want to express works and opinions of our own). They are mostly operating from a specific strategy and a desire for power: populist circumstantial interventionism; a cult of scientific–

---

14 'Video Vortex: Keith Sanborn programme': http://www.diagonalthoughts.com/?p=70 (retrieved 7 December 2012); Keith Sanborn, from 'YouTube.World, or: Jeder Mann sein eigenes Avatar', in Geert Lovink and Sabine Niederer, eds, *Video Vortex Reader: Responses to YouTube*, Institute of Network Cultures, Amsterdam 2008, pp. 195–6.

military messianism; a cult of the arsenal; a lust for unheard-of strategic possibilities for social, environmental and psychological management; an extermination of personal expression on a daily basis, bypassing arenas, open public forums and even institutions of justice.

I was in shock. I went part-time in 1999 and founded Cargo, at first as a refuge platform for survival, and then slowly developing it into a network of kindred spirits interested in criticism, (new) media development and independent artistic creation. It included Geert Lovink, Arthur Kroker, Rosi Braidotti and Matthew Fuller. With them, I initiated research projects, organised workshops and held open-door sessions. For ten years, however, Cargo hesitated to go public, as the paradigmatic shift in cultural production was hardly limited to television. Indeed, the corporate religion was found everywhere, not in the least in the homes and heads of the working and consuming public itself.

In 2006, Cargo decided to come out. How else could it have done so, if not with a platform that was capable of taking a distance from the phenomenon of impact, and yet employ those same techniques of impact to turn them around and see their effects? Obviously Cargo had to come up with something more than a piece of work. It had to be an environment capable of showing the great transformation of the media environment. It was given the title *Warum 2.0*, and was finally built and tested in February 2008 during the Artefact Festival in Stuk (Leuven, Belgium).

Warum 2.0 is an installation arena, an installation of installations, where nothing is limited to what is, but is constantly doubled into something else, not according to the logic of 'this or that' (to be or not to be), or of 'if/then' (one thing results from another), but of 'this is as if it is' (the refusal of what is). It is a tragic space, in which no event can stand for reality; with which nobody can engage for longer than the time it takes to escape; in which words, sounds, things and images happen in a constant state of suspense.

In this technological environment, Virilio was invited to give some of his warnings against 'impact', against its makers, against their techniques of 'storytelling', and against the renewed possibility of 'synchronising affects' on a massive, even global, scale.

What follows is a list of events that helped me through the development phase of *Warum 2.0* before and through its first installation. I was very anxious to see what kind of event would happen there, in a situation far from impact, or at least just far enough away to create a certain distance, to give hope, to allow visitors to realise how technology had already changed them, and ultimately to test new kinds of freedom.

My Road to Impact

Event 1 Brussels, October 2007, the Video Vortex international symposium, part 1, organised by the Institute of Network Cultures, in collaboration with Argos, Centre for Art & Media. One of the speakers was Keith Sanborn.
I heard Sanborn describe an installation project he had produced not long before in Antwerp, where he showed a collection of very extreme video clips, all equally loud and simultaneously visible on multiple screens of all sizes. Sanborn had definitely succeeded in creating impact there, and this was my first introduction to the idea. No one, he said, could stand that environment longer than five minutes. But then he said something very strange: he wanted to understand the impact of being surrounded by these images, and beyond that, that he wanted in this way to discover new ways of relating to the images.

At first, these remarks made me think only about the idea of impact, and its relevance to video making, television and, more specifically, to internet video (the theme of the Video Vortex symposium). But then I started to think more about our reactions to impact. Whenever impact happens, I thought, one either runs away from it, taking shelter, or responds with counter-impact—that is, with more impact. When one is confronted with impact—a bomb, an explosion, a news-bite, a shout (from an artist, a guru, a politician), an info bomb—the thing one definitely cannot do is to start thinking about it, to reflect on it, to try to understand it, let alone to start searching for new ways of understanding and expression. Impact excludes and annihilates creation. It only calls for reaction or even intensification and repetition of the same.

Event 2 Amsterdam, January 2008, the follow-up Video Vortex international symposium, part 2, organised by the Institute of Network Cultures, in collaboration the Netherlands Media Arts Institute.
At this symposium, I was invited to give a short presentation, which I called ‘impactology’.

The whole notion was still very new to me, though in the time between the first and second Video Vortex symposia, I had interviewed Virilio. I needed more time to develop the idea, and definitely wanted to add some ‘lightness’ to Virilio’s doom-laden thinking. Having noticed during the first instalment of Video Vortex how critics, academics and artists employ techniques of impact to enforce their presentations with performance skills and visuals, I went for the element of surprise and the sublime, and introduced ‘impactology’, gloriously as a brand new science.

The aim of 'impactology', I said, is to study 'impact', to take impact as a concept, to turn it into a new science, and to analyse impact, chart and define it, and to study its practical consequences. With 'impactology', the aim would be to invest impact as a mode and tool of analysis, rather than just as an object of it. I proposed 'impactology' as a science of the techniques of impact, such as 'storytelling': a machine for fabricating stories and revising histories, for formatting spirits and ways of synchronised thinking and reacting. In this field of study, even YouTube could be seen and understood as a recent technique of impact.

Event 3 1985: Elem Klimov's film *Come and See*

In 1985 another artist created a great impact: Elem Klimov, with his film *Come and See*, a film on war, and specifically on Nazi Einsatzkommandos burning down hundreds of villages in Belarus and systematically slaughtering their inhabitants. Looking back for extreme examples of artists acting as impact-makers, I arrived at Klimov. In seeking impact, Klimov made his fiction extraordinarily powerful. The director remembers that some viewers had to be taken away in ambulances.[15] Klimov had decided to repeat the original horror of the fact on screen, and to employ all his cinematographic skills towards this one goal of 'killing' his audience. If the effects on the audience were extreme, so were the effects on Klimov himself: he never made another film. So then, I thought, this is a limit case: Klimov, the film, the main character, the audience—all of them and us have to be sacrificed. In this logic of impact, in this logic of war, everything and everyone is destined to be trapped and destroyed.

Event 4 From January 14 till the end of February 2008: building the *Warum* 2.0 installation arena and the first public presentation, during the Artefact Festival in Stuk (Leuven, Belgium).

There it is, then, *Warum* 2.0, a complex array of projection screens installed on four centrifugal curves spreading out in a dark space of 200 square meters, around a transparent, suspended 360° panorama. Many visitors walk through it. They take up viewing positions and try to relate to the projected images, discovering the many transparencies and superpositions. The installation employs and displays the interface of an automatic scanning system that translates their movements into parameters, instantly changing the positions

15 See the video interview with Klimov at http://www.youtube.com/watch?v=FnyO1m9HOIw (retrieved 7 December 2012).

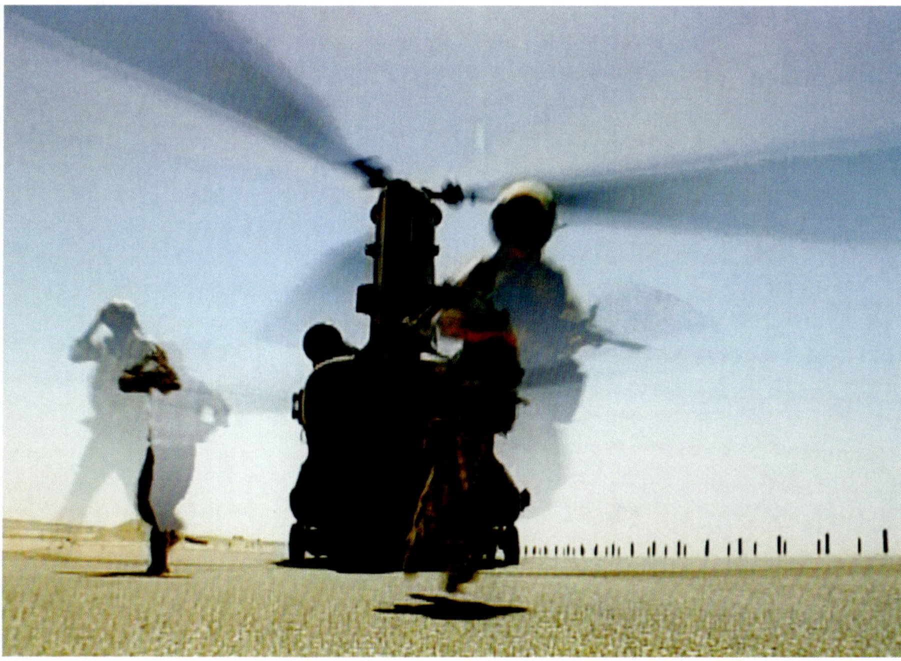

of the projected pictures. There is a dynamic surround-sound system of shooting, bombing and crying. At one point, the voice of Paul Virilio can be heard; at another, the shrieks and shouts of assaulting marines on some desert battle exercise. Visitors handle the joystick of a networked surveillance camera and grab views and pictures of their friends, unaware or waving back and smiling into the camera lens attached high up on the ceiling. Three cut-outs in a huge human Tetris wall-sculpture invite visitors to take in and mimic positions of falling victims or shooting soldiers while activating sensors, interacting and playing with the footage of more training soldiers in combat. Other visitors teleport their hands into a live double of *Warum 2.0* on Second Life, while a robot hand steers an avatar around and about falling pictures of war victims, which are also on display in the physical arena. Other visitors use laptops to add YouTube videos of their choice to the overall projection. From every side, faces of war victims stare at the public. They were all shot by Demoustier in Darfur, Afghanistan, Lebanon, Kosovo and Haïti.

You may well say that this sounds like impact too. It is impossible to give a fully convincing proof here, but it was not the case. All the sounds, pictures, tools and machines were exactly those with which impact is usually created. But here there was none, except by accident, now and then, when a visitor felt like testing the sensors in some frenzied way, running or jumping to see if the scanning system would hold. Visitors were testing out the apparatus and its potential. They were discovering and learning more about the techniques of impact, instead of being manipulated by them. They appreciated the opportunity, and said so, again and again, to the five hosts standing by, ready to explain, answer questions, and engage in discussions.

Through a complex network of 'roads' and 'entry points', visitors could enhance their experience of images of war and victims of war, not by reacting to them directly but by responding to them through a growing awareness of the tools and techniques with which impact was being achieved. *Warum 2.0* was staged as a tragic space, as technological and tragic as war itself, and the visitors were invited to be part of it, as a chorus: interpreting, testing, dissecting and commenting—responding to a pattern of organisation, not to raw sensation.

As I have mentioned, *Warum 2.0* had its origins in a videotape I made nearly 25 years ago, with Virilio acting as a 'lector of reality', setting up links between technology, war and cinema. As for war and technology, between then and now, in essence nothing has changed. One could say, there is just more war, more technology and there are more victims. But what really changed, because of technology, is the way we relate to war, to pictures of war and victims, and to the documentary image in general. New media technology had changed all that. Precisely for this reason, *Warum* became *Warum 2.0* because it reflects on and challenges the notion of 2.0.[16] Over the years, it had become clear to me that 2.0 is a fraud, at least if one understands it as a situation of 'user-made content', instead of what it is: 'user-driven impact'.

Event 5 1984. '1984' is not only Orwell, it is also the year Virilio published his book *Negative Horizon*.
Before I interviewed Virilio for *Warum 2.0*, I re-read *Negative Horizon*.[17] It was as if I was reading a new book. Obviously because I had changed, but also because the times had changed. Now, it read like a prophecy fulfilled. In the book I even found passages which were like literal descriptions of the main element of the physical installation arena *Warum 2.0*. At one point, Virilio describes the 'dromosphere' (the sphere of speed) as a 'centrifuge', a stadium for one person, in which one is witness of the anamorphosis of speeded-up reality, an environment driven by technology in which one experiences—as daily while driving a car—the grotesque deformations of what we once called 'reality'.

Again and again, in many books, Virilio demonstrates the extent to which technology has changed our perception of reality, and, by extension, of ourselves. In *The Vision Machine*, he warns against the effects of vision without seeing, the automation of perception, the disappearance of the point of view of the living, replaced by the vision machine.[18] In a way, his argument is similar to the distinction Douglas Hofstadter makes in his book *I Am a Strange Loop* between God's point of view (of the all-knowing scientist, a specialist in particle physics) and the much more low-level, but at the same time much more reliable, view ordinary humans have, when it comes to understanding what knowledge, self-knowledge and consciousness are about.[19]

Cybernetic feedback looping is a major technique of impact, in which people become unconscious components of an automatic circuit. Short-circuiting it could well be an effective way of breaking through this 'hall of mirrors'. Or, as Hofstadter suggests: put paradox into the loop, making it 'strange', having it cross levels of understanding by bringing back into

---

16 'Web 2.0' was the term famously used by Tim O'Reilly in 2004 to describe what have become known as 'social media'. See Tim O'Reilly, 'What is Web 2.0?': http://oreilly.com/web2/archive/what-is-web-20.html (retrieved 7 December 2012). **17** Paul Virilio, *Negative Horizon: An Essay in Dromoscopy*, trans. Michael Degener, Continuum, New York 2005; first published as *L'Horizon Negatif*, Editions Galilée, Paris 1984. **18** Paul Virilio, *The Vision Machine*, trans. Julie Rose, British Film Institute Publishing, London 1994, pp. 59–60. **19** Douglas Hofstadter, *I Am a Strange Loop*, Basic Books, New York 2007.

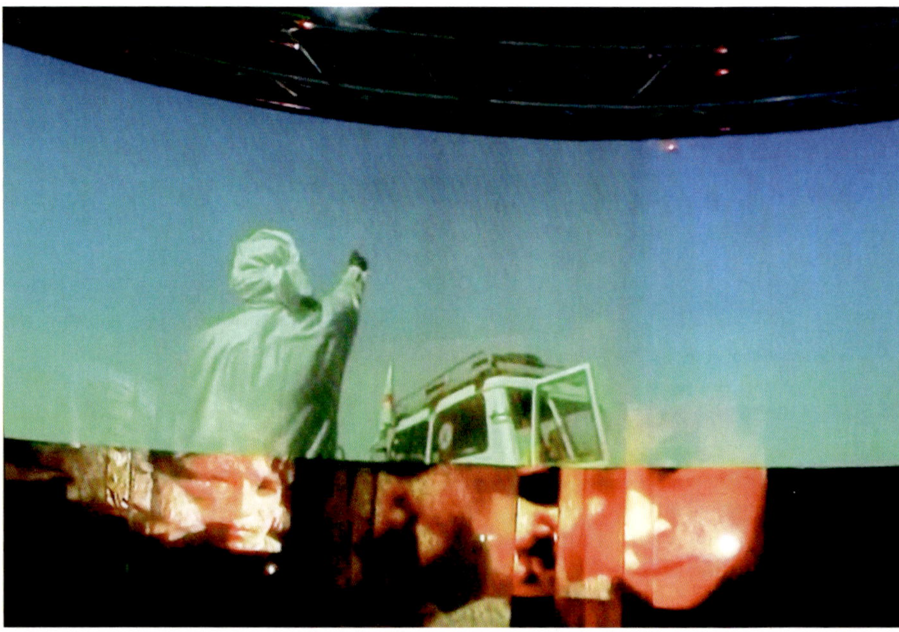

it the 'I', the 'being human', always self-centered, always self-perceiving, rather than just (neurobiochemically, genetically determined) perceiving outside events.

Warum 2.0 made it clear that techniques of circularity, self-reference and 'strange' feedback looping could be employed to create a spatial and critical distance from impact: a distance in which visitors could experience (media) events and images in a human, 'self-centred' way, making them meaningful, part of themselves, of their condition, of their own memories of pain, desire, anxiety, love and hope.

What a tragedy it would be if we could not tell stories any longer in our own way; if we could no longer have and express feelings when seeing images of people suffering; if we lost faith in our strong ludic power to bring lightness into doom, to resist and to play?

Event 6 In 1983 Vilém Flusser published his book *Towards a Philosophy of Photography.*

Talking about photography and visual media in general, Flusser offers a model of investigation based on four basic concepts: the image, the apparatus, the program and information.[20] And what is important, I think, is that he defines 'information', not as data but as 'information that informs about a quality': the degree in which the resulting photographs express the critical 'handling' of this trinity of image/machine/program.

What about transporting Flusser's reasoning into impactology? The apparatus, the tool, the gadget would be seen as instruments of impact-making with media. The tools with which pictures are now taken digitally are part of an apparatus that has a power over photographers, that programmes their gestures. The photographers no longer take views of the world but merely realise the potential of the program of their apparatus. For them, the world is reduced to input, to information as data, to a pretext. The more they handle their apparatus in an automatic, uncritical way, the more effectively they fulfil their role in magically programming the living and the real in favour of the apparatus itself. Feedback only takes place in the apparatus (in its black box), and, by extension, in the loop between the user and the apparatus.

In the same way, *Warum 2.0*, being an apparatus itself, a super-gadget of interconnected gadgets, would do the same, unless its many black boxes

---

20 Vilém Flusser, *Towards a Philosophy of Photography*, Reaktion Books, London 2000, p. 76. The book was first published as *Für eine Philosophie der Photographie*, Andreas Müller-Pohle, Göttingen 1983.

are broken up and handled critically. Ways had to be found of short-circuiting the programs, of holding them in internal feedback loops, of exposing their interfaces, of giving the visitors the opportunity to watch programs watching themselves. As Virilio said at the end of our interview: 'we are done with the idea of the spectacle'.

Spaces Out of Media

1969 was a very special year. Then, for the first time ever, humans jumped and bounced on the surface of the Moon. But more than that, it was the first time 'looping' manifested itself as an epiphenomenon, as millions of humans watched the event in real time on their newly bought TV sets. By means of televisual mediation, a unique technological event was witnessed from a distance, and this became an event in itself—one that was, in scale and magnitude, at least as important as the 'real' one in space. During that moment, it didn't matter what really was real. 'Looping' had taken it all in.

Forty years have passed, and many a loop has surprised us since. Remember 9/11 and the Asian tsunami. Again and again we find ourselves, by the millions, within the media and their feedback loop. The very first video engineers, and after them the video art pioneers, have always been fascinated by visual looping. There is indeed something very revealing about visual loops, especially so when we are part of it, when we are at the same time outside (as observers) and inside (present in the ongoing visualisation) of displays of media that watch themselves.

In *Warum 2.0*, the space that allowed escape from media impact was there for those who were in the loop. But for outside observers, looking at it from a distance (if not from the Moon), it had something of the feeling of an obscene (sexual) act. It had turned the observers into voyeurs. This may sound negative but it proves that the experiment was working, as it touched the core of what media are all about. It is the circularity, the looped character, of the technological system and situation that brings patterns into existence and makes them persist. Once these patterns make their way to the screen, they manifest themselves in space, as epiphenomenon.

∞

The key lies in not dancing the same dance but in substituting out-of-controllness by concrete 'exercises' that start trivially but that can grow in subtlety and in humour. Just as one statement can speak on two levels at once; just as a second meaning can lie lurking inside a first meaning; just as someone outside a movie can feel the affects provoked by someone inside the movie, so can 'spaces out of media' be experienced as physical spaces. Adding media, content and context to *Warum 2.0* enhanced the impact of the structure on the visitors, but this alone would not have lifted it out of the ordinary feedback loop. Such is (unfortunately) the case with most interactive installations and 'programmable architecture'. In order for it to 'light up' from within, next to adding media, content and context, it had to be integrated into a more complex and many-faceted alignment. It needed to be an arena of a more diversified and, if possible, hybrid alignment of situations in which the final potential, destination and function would be indeterminate: 'dancing' and 'jumping', looping round and round, between layers of activity, attention and (visual/physical) presence.

Obviously, for media to become more than a cybernetic application, they need an 'architecture' (in the sense of an 'event', as conceived by Alain Badiou).[21] And together, media and architecture, to evolve beyond representation and statement into a living ecology, need to have the capacity 'to shift our attention to far higher levels of brain activity in order to find symbols, concepts, meanings, desires, and ultimately, our selves'.[22]

It was a pleasure to see visitors ultimately seeing a display neither as a dead-end representation nor as a technological 'wonder' nor as a 'take-it-or-leave-it' statement on art. This inverted the standard experience of media so that visitors were discovering that even media have the potential to function as working models, which can be used and reinvested for further use and appropriation. Ultimately, they could be empowered as witnesses to become part of and inhabit media-spaces as evolving worlds. Visitors to *Warum 2.0* showed me, the media maker, how self-referential meanings in a formal pattern, such as an installation, can have a causal potency just as real as that of the pattern's usually frozen, low levels of inference.

---

21 Badiou has written about the event in many works. For an accessible collection of his works, including writings on the event, see Alain Badiou, *Infinite Thought: Truth and the Return of Philosophy*, trans. Oliver Feltham and Justin Clemens, Continuum, London n.d. **22** Hofstadter, *I Am a Strange Loop*, p. 196.

0.10000000I

> *A dog does not imagine or understand that certain large arrays of colored dots can be so structured that they are no longer just huge sets of colored dots but become pictures of people, houses, dogs, and many other things. The higher level takes perceptual precedence over the lower level, and in the process becomes the 'moral real' of the two. The lower level gets forgotten, lost in the shuffle. Such an upward level-shift is a profound perceptual change.*[23]

Then how is it, when it comes to understand media work, some of us tend to stick to a lower level of understanding?

Hofstadter comments:

> *When it comes to understand our own nature as humans the tables are quite turned, for a very similar rigid prejudice in favour of high-level (and only high-level) perception turns out to pervade and even to define 'the human condition'.*[24]

The *Warum 2.0* public experiment was born out of a refusal to deny this alternative point of view. It meant to give rise to strange loops and inspiring traps.

As Oliver Sacks showed in his book *Musicophilia*, what the body misses or loses, the brain produces as hallucinations.[25] The integrative activity of the human brain entertains dynamic systems that generate perceptions, images and hallucinations that are automatic, uncontrollable and non-pathological. Strong phantom sensations deliver precise data, even long after a limb is missing. Today, they even feed the willed phantom movements of the bionic industry. What returns with the spectre is no longer the visionary future haunted by the past but a present that no longer has to be in order to exist. In this vast field of hallucination, doubles of originally disabled selves are invited to look around and check if there is something 'for them' to explore and exploit.

---

23 Ibid., p. 202. 24 Ibid. 25 Oliver Sacks, *Musicophilia: Tales of Music and the Brain*, Alfred A. Knopf, New York 2007.

Warum 2.0 took the form of a hallucination as epiphenomenon. Repetition and suspension, that is, of what could have been live, alive, testimony, archive and memory. This space no longer had anything to do with confusion, neither of fiction and reality nor of the real and the artificial. It managed and produced a very strange phenomenon: second-order observing.

What value does ‘impactology’ have, if not to ‘criticise, criticise, criticise’? It activates a cross-examination of the present and ourselves. Does it also give some answers about what we are doing (with media), and why, while we are doing it, we ignore what we are doing? If you ask my opinion, whatever we do will never be far from impact. To understand this condition, I start from that position, uneasily clicking away the spam on my screen. Spam, indeed: another technique of impact. In moments like that, I see myself sneering at my own grotesqueness.

This brings to mind another dimension in the domain of ‘reacting’ to impact, namely the modus of the grotesque, which shows up in situations where everything seems upside down, in the ambivalent abnormal. To observers, extreme forms of reaction can look grotesque in two ways: for some they will appear as expressions of fear, but for others as expressions of a creative explosion.

Interview with **Trevor Paglen**

Julian Stallabrass

Negative Dialectics in the Google Era

Since 2006, in a series of performances, publications, exhibitions and installations, Trevor Paglen has explored the world of hidden military projects and infrastructure. One of his best-known series is entitled *Limit Telephotography*, in which Paglen took lenses designed for astronomical photography and turned them to the very long-range photography of secret military bases in the US. Paglen is one of many artists who have evolved new and various ways of engaging with the military and the secret state in the years following the declaration of the 'war on terror'. He has made works that raise fundamental questions about what can be known and seen, while simultaneously writing investigative exposes of the shadow state. This interview explores some of the relations and tensions between the two. It was conducted by email in 2011.

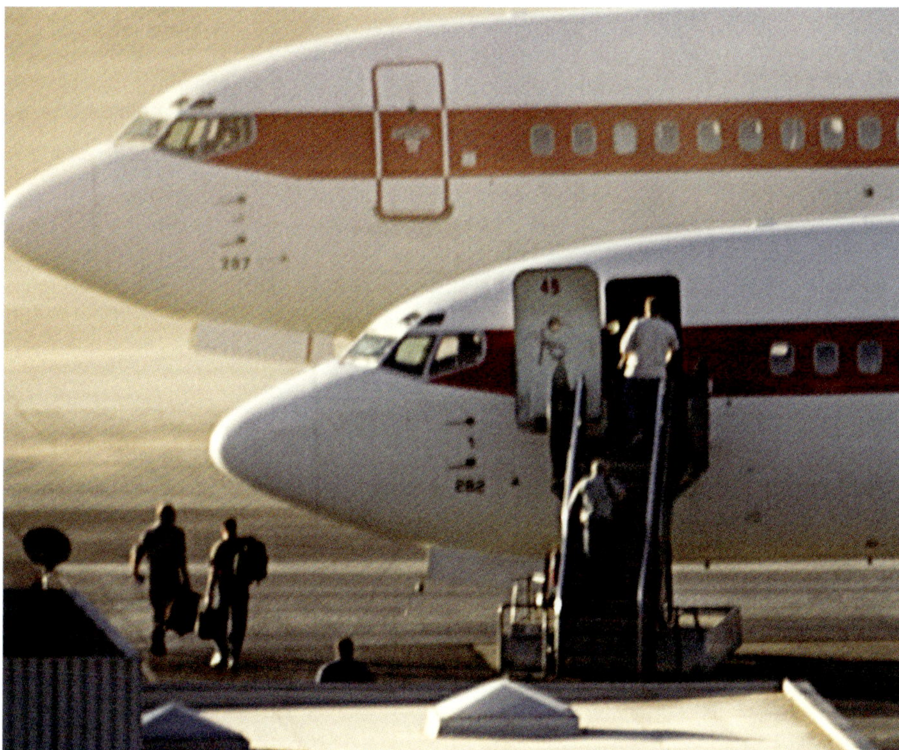

Morning Commute (Gold Coast Terminal), Las Vegas, NV, Distance ~ 1 mile. 6:26 a.m, 2006:
Each weekday morning, a fleet of unmarked Boeing 737s using the call-sign 'Janet' shuttle defence industry workers to a series of classified (or 'black') military installations deep in the Nevada desert. The Janet fleet is based at a dedicated terminal at Las Vegas' McCarren airport called 'Gold Coast'

Julian Stallabrass Artists making photographs now have to send their work out into a world that is replete with networked cameras, in which publishing a picture online can be done with a few presses of a touchscreen. Tourists at any reasonably well-known spot can be sure that they will find dozens or hundreds of decent photographic records of the place online, so taking their own pictures has become a performative token act. How do artists working in the medium place themselves in and/or against this remarkable proliferation of public images?

Trevor Paglen This is a great question, and it's something I spend a lot of time thinking about. There have been a number of discussions about the 'future of photography' and that sort of thing among fine-art people, and I think that whole conversation has to do with the question you're posing here. It seems to me that photography is at a bit of a crossroads. I think that there's still a place for 'fine-art-gallery' work because when you make a nice print and put it on a wall, you're creating a space for people to pay a certain kind of attention to the image or work. Viewing a photograph in an institution is a much slower process than looking at a Flickr page or a Facebook attachment. I think that the space for paying slow attention is becoming more relevant and significant as our forms of everyday communications, imaging and viewing increasingly speed up. As a corollary to this, I've been thinking about photographic materials in a much more 'sculptural' way recently—thinking about how different imaging and print processes can help form the critical 'text' of a photograph. What I mean by this is taking the materiality of photography seriously—thinking about different processes, the lifetimes of various media, as well as different photo processes as they relate to socio-historical processes. I've been working recently with everything from albumen prints to the satellite video-feeds of American Predator drones. The point, for me, is developing forms of post-representationalist photography and imaging, wherein both the materiality and what I sometimes think of as 'relations of photography' that form a given work are intrinsic to what the work is. In other words, photography that doesn't just point to something but actually is that something.

The other part of my answer has everything to do with what you called the 'performative' act of photography. I'm sure we both agree that the 21st century so far has been characterised in part by a huge expansion of photographic machines, imaging systems, and the means of networking them. Here I mean things like digital point-and-shoot cameras and Flickr accounts; local police vehicles outfitted with cameras designed to take a picture of every single licence plate that passes by and 'run' the plate in a police database; predator drones over Pakistan flown via video from pilots in Nevada, with intelligence analysts in Virginia and commanders in Florida, all part of the same real-time 'network'. There are an incredible number of examples. I think these new 'geographies' of seeing-machines are something photographers haven't dealt with

that much, but I think that there's an incredible amount to critically engage with. Of course, what it means to 'do' photography in relation to this larger geography of machine-seeing might look quite different from shooting sheet film with a view camera. In sum, I think there are a lot of opportunities for photographers to take the 'relational' aspects of what they do far more seriously. This is what I was alluding to earlier when I mentioned this idea of 'sculptural' or 'relational' photography.

JS So there's a self-conscious tension in your answer between valuing the slowness that comes with the display of the fine art print in the gallery and practices that embrace the flow of imagery through networked imaging systems. The latter reminds me of the controversy surrounding an 'honourable mention' given to Michael Wolf in this year's World Photo Press awards for rephotographing what he called 'unfortunate events'—accidents, people collapsing, fires—that happened to be caught on Google Street View cameras. I think the controversy was generated because such acts of appropriation have far less of a history in photojournalism than they do in fine art.

But I wonder about the basic contention that digital images are necessarily consumed rapidly, especially since you now sometimes see HD screen displays showing photographs in galleries. Given the screen technology and the resolution with which digital images are now displayed, there seems no reason why they should not be the subject of sustained attention (and do we know for certain that they are not?). It is true that Facebook (and perhaps Flickr) encourages shorter attention spans, as do all social media sites that are focused on the flow of images and events. Do we need the physical photographic print and the gallery space to slow viewers down? And if so, why does that work?

This is related to an interesting discussion at a recent conference on conflict and photography at University College Dublin at which David Campbell asked why there had been so few deep, textured, complex online works tying together words and images in sophisticated data structures, of the type that had been held out as models in the age of hypertext.[1] It occurred to me that one reason might be that engagement with digital and social media is largely about capturing attention simultaneously with an ongoing current of material (Twitter is the obvious example of this), in a manner that does not seem compatible with the very laborious construction of multiply branching data structures that the hypertext model once promised. So my question is: can you square that circle?

TP Well, to be honest I haven't thought about the question of viewing as much as you have. It definitely seems to me that the 'space' of the museum or gallery or what-have-you has more to do with the kind of attention we pay to art works than the medium itself. I don't think we necessarily need the 'print' if we want to ask people to slow down, but I think we do need some sort of space (gallery,

1 'Medium and Message: Conflict Photography in the Digital Era', University College Dublin Clinton Institute, May 2011.

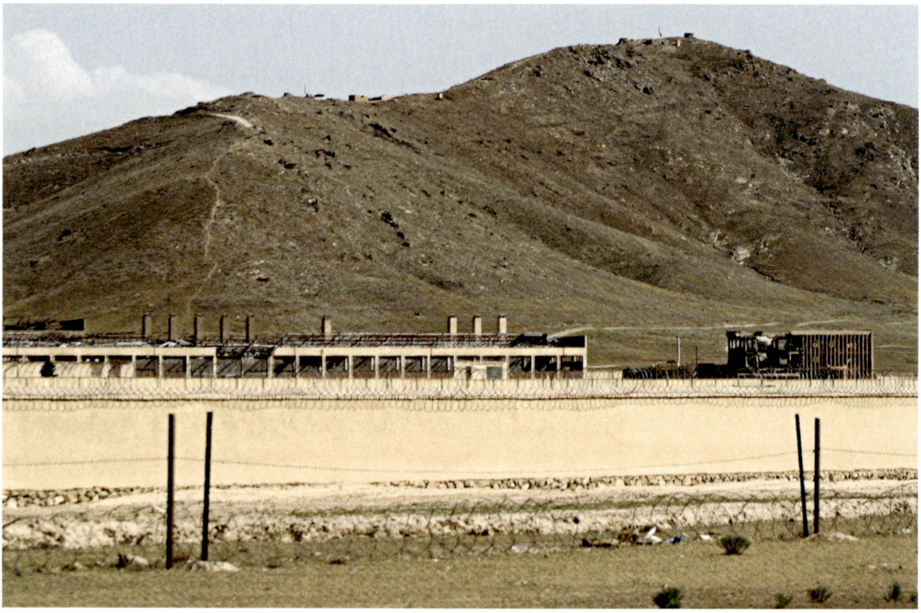

The Salt Pit, Northeast of Kabul, Afghanistan, 2006

museum, etc.) that asks us to pay closer attention to what we're looking at than we might otherwise do (online, for example).

But the overall question of the cultural politics of 'viewing' art is something I just haven't spent that much time working out. I have a sense of what works for my own art, but don't really have a meta-theory of it. As opposed to the conditions of 'consuming' art, I'm much more interested in the cultural politics of producing art. I have long understood art works as congealed social, political and cultural relations. I'm much more interested in exploring that aspect of cultural production than I am in the question of viewing. If I have anything to contribute to how we understand cultural production, it probably comes more from a 'geographic' perspective rather than a more traditional cultural studies perspective. In a lot of my works, I try to set up various relations of seeing from which the artwork emerges. If I go out in the desert and spend a week photographing covert military operations, for example, it's quite likely that I'll ultimately end up with something quite formal or abstract looking. But the means by which I got to that particular abstraction are crucial to the work—implying a politics of seeing, relations of seeing, and so forth. I think that there are tremendous and largely unexplored critical possibilities in this approach.

JS That's something that intrigues me about your work, the apparent disjunction between process and visual result. When you photograph secret military installations or black sites from very long distances, using extreme telephoto lenses, in one sense you seem to be spying for citizens against unaccountable power; yet, softened and distorted by heat haze, the results evoke painting or pictorialist art photography in quite a range of 'styles', from Edward Hopper to colour field painting. How do the apparent art-historical references and the process of producing the work come together, and do such art-historical references work towards bringing out the politics and relations of seeing that you talk about?

TP You're bringing up two really important aspects of my work. On one hand, we have what we might call the politics of production. By this I mean what sorts of relational practices are behind the work and go into its making. On the other hand, we have the politics of viewing or spectatorship—here we find more of the questions about spectatorship, art history, and so forth. Taking both sides of this seriously is fundamental to what I do. If we're talking about the politics of production, there are a lot of things going on. On one hand, I might be camping out on a mountaintop taking photos of a secret military base, or determining the location of CIA 'black sites' so I can go photograph them. Maybe researching front-companies used in covert operations, or working with amateur astronomers to track classified spacecraft in Earth orbit. These are all relational practices and they all have various sorts of politics to them. Photographing a secret military base means insisting on the right to do it, and enacting that right. Thus, we have a sort of political performance. Finding CIA black sites means, well, finding

secret black sites. Working with amateur astronomers has a whole politics of collaboration as well as what I call 'minoritarian empiricism', which has to do with experimenting with the radical possibilities of classical empiricism. All this happens long before I even think about making a piece of 'art' and put it in front of other people to see.

When we get into the question of what the image actually looks like, I use a lot of art-historical references as a way to suggest how contemporary forms of seeing (or not seeing) rhyme with other historical circumstances artists have responded to. I look at a lot of abstract painting as a response to its historical moment. In someone like Turner, we find a vision of what the 19th-century 'annihilation of space with time' looked like; in Dada or in some of the smarter abstract expressionists, we can find a response to some of the 20th century's greatest horrors and an artistic response suggesting the utter failure of representation in relation to the Bomb or the Holocaust, for example. There was something radical and profound—at those historical moments—in the kinds of abstractions some of those artists came up with. We've moved way beyond that, however, and some contemporary artists who've retreated into a sort of pseudo-Greenbergian abstraction I think are being really disingenuous.

All in all, I think we're at a historical moment where we're rightly very suspicious of representationalism (and by this I mean the belief in an ontological separation between representations and the things representations purport to represent; although a lot of 20th-century critical theorists have taken issue with it, this view is very much a part of our collective 'common sense'—it's particularly bad among photographers; there are all sorts of corollaries to this—the notion of a representation of something else, for example, which can often lead to equating Google Earth and Google image search with political transparency, for example). Abstraction can be a response to that, even a critical response (the refusal to 'speak' sensibly seems completely legitimate to me), but I think that abstraction for its own sake (I sometimes think of this as New York 'Chelsea abstraction', which once had a real stake in the past but comes across as kitschy now) just isn't interesting. The refusal to speak can be a radical gesture, but it can also be—and usually is—a form of reactionary fetishism. The difference between the two has something to do with the politics of production I mentioned earlier.

JS I have a couple of questions that come out of your very interesting reply. So the radical aspect of your work lies precisely in the disjunction between the gallery print (say, of a spy satellite trail in a starry night sky, which yields information only to the small minority with specialist knowledge) and the social and technical process that goes into making it. I find it interesting that the models you mention for the way the work looks, and for getting at a critique of or a refusal of representation, are avant-gardist. Each also deals with the consequences of waves of technological change that had profound consequences for the experience of the everyday—whether it was steam power, mechanised warfare

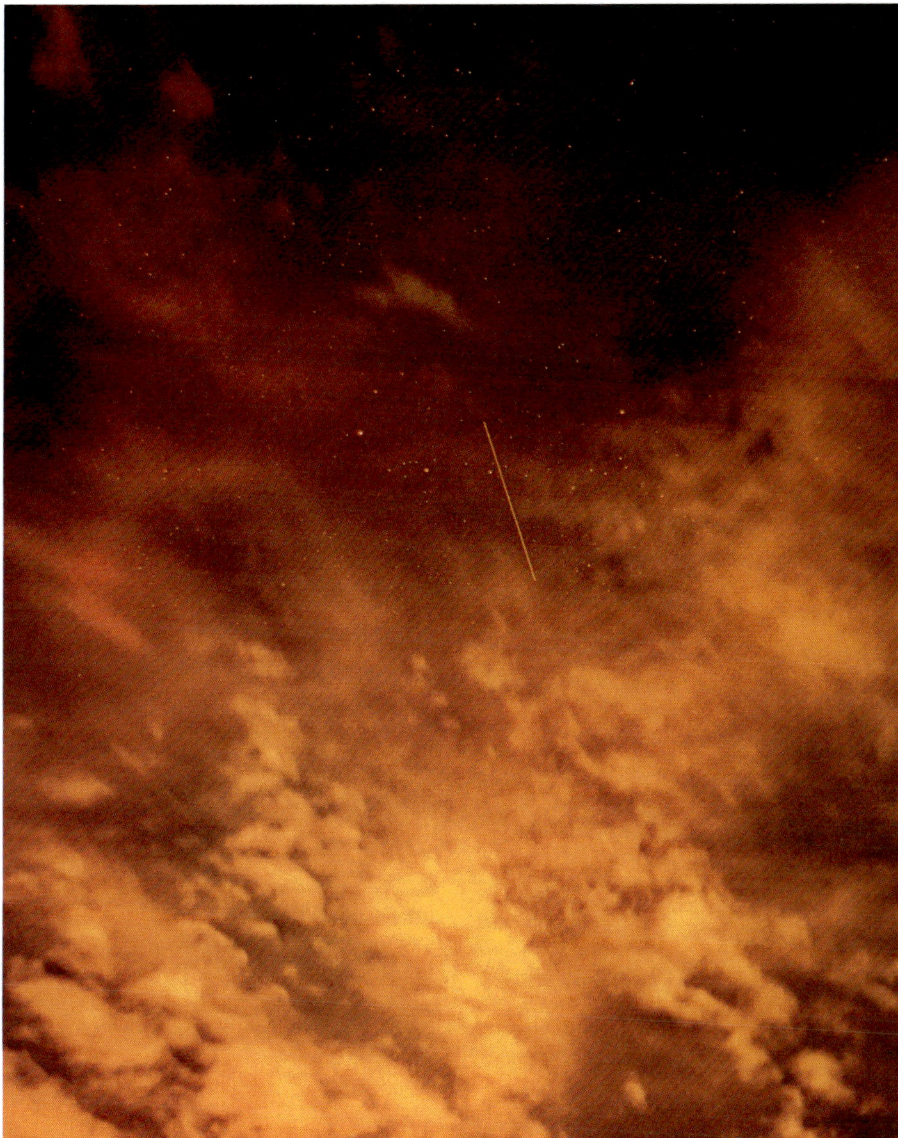

KEYHOLE 12-3/IMPROVED CRYSTAL Optical Reconnaissance Satellite Near Scorpio (USA 129), 2007

and its transformation of commercial road and air travel, or technologically advanced genocide and the Bomb. All arguably established a relation to the technological sublime—an awe in the face of vastly complex systems and their uncontrollable consequences (though in Dada this was taken parodically). Obviously, the postmodern period often thought of itself as a time of exhaustion and perhaps decadence, in which the passive consumption of reproductive technologies (above all, television) appeared to dominate over the romance and fears attached to innovative productive ones. Is your reference back to these older forms a way of saying that we no longer live in such times?

My second question is this. Conventionally, critics have looked at documentary photography and film and bemoaned its inadequacy to describe its subject. One consequence of the ubiquity of photo and video recording would seem to be that sometimes we get documents that are as adequate as one could reasonably want: the Wikileaks video of murders by an Apache helicopter of Iraqi civilians would be a case in point, since they give context, dialogue and direct evidence of the slaughter, all of which allows the viewer to see not just the fact of the killings but the operation of the military mechanism which brought them about, and the enjoyment of the crew in the exercise of their deadly power.[2] What relation does your suspicion of representation have to that kind of 'documentary' image?

TP The short answer to your first question is 'yes'. I think most people agree that any sort of classic avant-gardism is over, but I think there's an underlying impulse in the avant-garde that I find especially relevant today. What I'm interested in isn't really even the critical impulse so much as the productive impulse animating much avant-gardist practice. But again, I'm interesting in looking at that paradigm of cultural production from a contemporary post-postmodern perspective.

Throughout my life, I've found much of canonical postmodern art to be very cynical, an artistic echo of Thatcher's 'there is no alternative'. On the other hand, I'm profoundly influenced by artists like Gregg Bordowitz, Gran Fury, Group Material, Paper Tiger and other 'postmodern' cultural producers whose work didn't abandon itself to a complacent version of unlimited semiosis but sought instead to develop forms of radical humanism from postmodernism's critical insights. All in all, I'm not interested in a return to modernism, but I find some of modernism's underlying impulses to be particularly relevant today, a historical moment where it's hard to imagine, let alone find examples of, how society might be different. In terms of art-making, I sympathise with a revised form of negative dialectics as a response to an image-saturated society.

On your second question, I definitely agree with you that the Wikileaks gunship footage is as good as we could reasonably want. But if there were a wrongful death lawsuit with that video as the prime piece of evidence, I wonder whether it would hold up in a courtroom. I'm thinking

---

2 The video may be found in many places online, including http://www.time.com/time/nation/article/0,8599,1978017,00.html (accessed 13 June 2011).

here of the Rodney King footage—when you repeatedly scrutinise any kind of documentarian media, you can capitalise on the fact that representations don't transparently represent reality-as-it-is. This also applies to the Abu Ghraib photos, which Donald Rumsfeld could plausibly dismiss as the work of a 'few bad apples'. We all know this. And yet some forms of documentary constitute, as you say, the best kind of images we could ask for, but there's no magic image or documentation that exists outside or beyond the limits of representation. Documentary media can still become social facts, regardless of how faithfully it reproduces reality. I take all of this as a starting point. In terms of my own aesthetic vocabulary, I tend towards images that manifest this dialectic. Images that (1) make a truth claim ('here's X secret satellite moving through X constellation', for example); (2) immediately and obviously contradict that truth claim ('you believing that this white streak against a starry backdrop is actually a secret satellite instead of a scratch on the film negative is a matter of belief'); (3) suggest a form of practice that could give rise to such an image ('if it's true that this is a secret satellite, then there's a whole lot more going on behind this image'); (4) suggest all of the above as an allegory for something about 21st-century images, knowledge, practice, aesthetics and politics. Not all of the work I produce fits all of this—it's just a loose way I use to think about what it is I'm doing.

JS That's a fascinating answer, and picks up on many of the issues that came to mind as I look at your work. I notice that you write in your Aperture monograph of a dialectical opposition between images' claim to represent and the undermining of that claim, and it's good that you specify that further here.[3] It's easy to see that Adorno's concentration on the specificity of the object, and the instrumental and contradictory social forces that bring about its misdescription, have an affinity with your work. Beyond that, I wonder: is there something about the military (and the most secretive aspects of the military) that has a further affinity with negative dialectics? Is this part of the point of your listing of hundreds of code names of secret projects?

This may be a point less in the spirit of Adorno for whom the immersion in the specificity of the object through immanent critique engages the dialectic, but these days artistic focus on the full detail of the object often leads in the direction of the sublime. We see this in a lot of large-scale museum photography, in which the viewer is overwhelmed by a mass of data which they lack the conceptual tools to make sense of: the 'data sublime', we may call it. Your work plays with this feeling brought to another level, because of course much of the point is that we are denied the information to make sense of it. You evoke both the mathematical and the dynamic sublime in your satellite imagery, particularly in images of the night sky and of trails over pristine landscapes that evoke 19th-century landscape photographs of the American West. The sublime is often used for conservative purposes: to frame or manage

3 Trevor Paglen, *Invisible: Covert Operations and Classified Landscapes*, Aperture, New York 2010, p. 151.

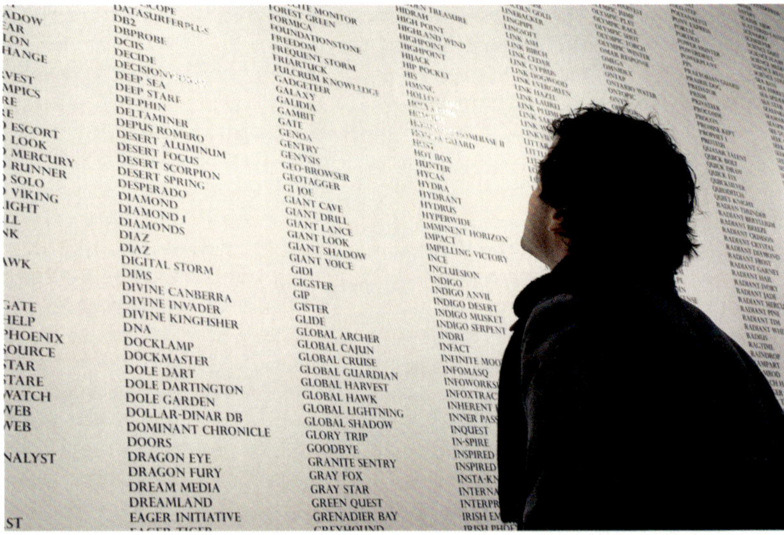

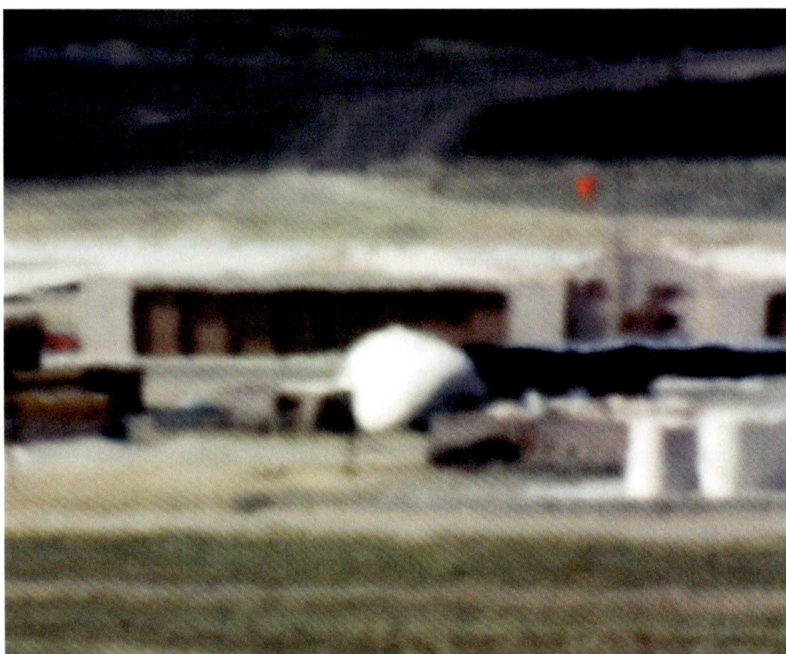

Top Code Names: Classified Military Programs Active Between 2001 and 2007. Lettering, dimensions variable (installation detail)
Bottom Large Hangars and Fuel Storage, Tonopah Test Range, NV, Distance ~ 18 miles, 10:44 a.m., 2005

a common social fear (of the masses, quite often, but also more recently of data overload) and offer it up for consumption. How do the sublime and negative dialectics come together in your work?

In another register, your work has a definite performative and subversive side: the reproduction of secret code names is presumably illegal; some of your *Limit Telephotography* series offers not just evocative images of the operations of secret bases but data—for example, the tail numbers on aircraft. The same could be said of the remarkable mission patches and challenge coins, referring to secret units and operations, which you have collected and photographed. Rebecca Solnit points out that invisibility is a type of shield, while democracy is founded upon visibility:[4] your work does something to peer under the rock, and surely there are conservatives in the US who would accuse you of treason. Do the sublime and negative dialectics protect you from arrest? How do you decide how much information to offer the viewer, and how much to hold them in awed suspense before the spectacle of military apparatus?

Lastly, Adorno held out a faint hope that negative dialectics contained a transformative and utopian vision of society no longer divided by conflict and domination. Is there an element of your work that contains such a seed?

TP I think there are definite ways that negative dialectics resonates with military and intelligence activities. I've looked at a lot of things that are secret but which have profound effects on culture and politics. Most of the time, I don't exactly know what I'm looking at, photographing or researching. So I quickly end up in situations where the question is, 'How do I point to, engage with, and represent something that I don't quite understand?' The answer often has to do with trying to represent that epistemological/political gap or in-between space, or that moment of incomprehension. The *Code Names* piece (a list of classified military operations and organisations) is, in my opinion, an example of that. I hope that a lot of my work is. Incidentally, this isn't just particular to the military. Some projects I'm working on now have very little to do with the military, but are still centrally concerned with this question. The political/epistemological 'gap' I'm talking about here relates to Jean Luc Nancy's definition of the sublime, which I can't quote off the top of my head, but has to do with the 'sensibility of the fading of the sensible'.

As for how the sublime and negative dialectics come together, well, I think I'm sorry to have to say here that I'm not quite sure. I'm not sure I'm the person who can really theorise this—I'm extremely influenced by both concepts, but at the risk of sounding like a stereotypical artist, it's really something I 'feel' more than something I can articulate in a cogent philosophical manner.

Do the sublime and negative dialectics shield me from arrest!? Hahaha ... not at all! I'm quite careful about how I go about doing work.

4 Ibid., p.10.

When dealing with authority, I'm polite but firm. But I've gotten plenty of death threats along with angry military and intelligence officers. That's just the nature of the work, I suppose. In terms of deciding how much to offer the viewer, it's a strange thing. I really think that the materials I research and explore actually tell me how they want to be represented. I know that's an odd thing to say, but it's really been my experience. When I was doing my PhD in geography, I went into my advisor's office one day—a really wonderful and incredibly smart man named Allan Pred, who really liked that I was also an artist—I was complaining about the fact that I hadn't taken any classes on methodology and didn't have a clue as to what I was doing in that regard. He told me that cookie-cutter methodologies were nonsense and that I should just keep doing my research until my materials told me how to study them. At the time, I probably thought he was a crazy old man, but I think he was absolutely right. Having said that, I've written a couple of books about some of the same things that my art work is about, and they're pretty standard non-fiction in terms of style and argumentation.[5] Art can show the world in a particular way—that's what's powerful about it—and the same is true for prose. But they're incommensurable forms, so with my visual work, I try to focus on what visuality does well.

The utopian aspect is the not-so-secret secret of negative dialectics, as I understand it. I think it points in the direction of unfulfilled forms of freedom and justice, but only indirectly and obscurely. I think this is related to what we were talking about when the subject of avant-gardism came up in our conversation. I really do want to believe in a more just world. I often think of Fanon, who insisted on a 'new humanism' without ever really articulating what that might look like. I'm not sure even what it might mean to articulate that as a meta-theory. Perhaps that's the whole point of it, which leaves us again in the space of negative dialectics, no? For me, this is what art can do—orient our seeing and suggest practices in ways that suggest (even negatively) more liberatory forms of being—but it's really hard to say what those forms might be.

---

5 Trevor Paglen and A.C. Thompson, *Torture Taxi: On the Trail of the CIA's Rendition Flights*, Melville House Publishing, New York 2006; Trevor Paglen, *Blank Spots on the Map: The Dark Geography of the Pentagon's Secret World*, Dutton, New York 2009.

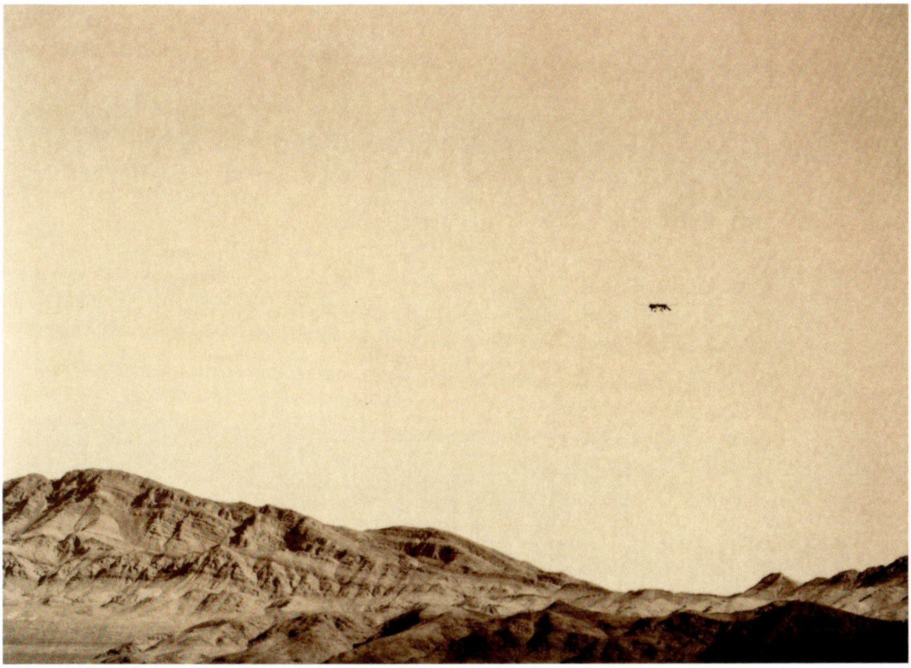

Time Study (Predators; Indian Springs, NV) (detail), 2010
Overleaf Spc Lee Davis, Soldiers from Bravo Company 1-505 Parachute Infantry Regiment, 82nd Airborne Division, raid a suspected terrorist's home on 25 October 2003, Fallujah, Iraq

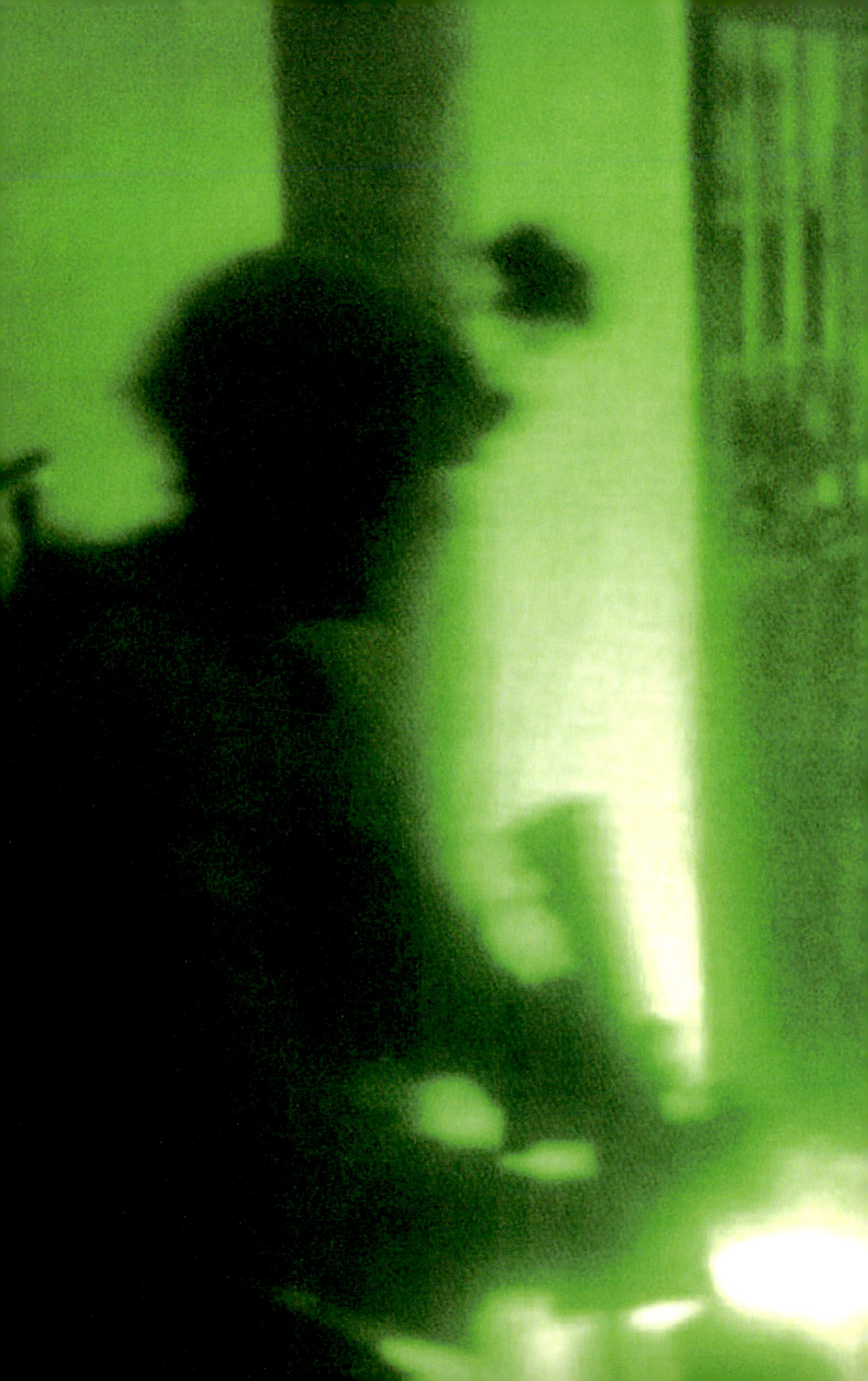

Adam Broomberg and **Oliver Chanarin** are artists living and working in London. Together they have published nine monographs and have had numerous international exhibitions including at the Gwangju Biennale, the Stedelijk Museum, the International Center of Photography, KW Institute for Contemporary Art, The Photographers Gallery and the Mathaf Arab Museum of Modern Art. Broomberg and Chanarin teach at the Zurich University of the Arts and are Visiting Fellows at the University of the Arts London. Their work is represented in major public and private collections including Tate Modern, the Stedelijk Museum, Victoria and Albert Museum, Musée de l'Élysée and the International Center of Photography.

Stefaan Decostere has made more than 30 documentaries for the arts department of Belgian television. They were also broadcast abroad and received prizes at festivals. Some were further elaborated on online platforms and in media installations. Many artists and theorists were involved in their making. Since the late 1990s, Decostere has also worked as a publisher, as a curator and, above all, as a coach and initiator of workshops on 'artistic research and creation development' for the organisation he runs (Cargo) and for several other art institutions. For the last four years, he has been mentor on the Master of Film of the Filmacademie Amsterdam.

Coco Fusco is a New York-based interdisciplinary artist and writer. She is a recipient of a 2013 Fulbright Fellowship, a 2012 USA Arts Fellowship and a 2003 Herb Alpert Award in the Arts. Fusco's performances and videos have been included in two Whitney Biennials as well as other biennials in Shanghai, Kwangju, Johannesburg and Sydney, and exhibitions at the Museum of Modern Art, The Tate Liverpool, the Museum Boijmans Van Beuningen and the Contemporary Arts Museum in Houston. She is the author of *English is Broken Here: Notes on Cultural Fusion in the Americas* (1995), *The Bodies that Were Not Ours and Other Writings* (2001) and *A Field Guide for Female Interrogators* (2008).

Ashley Gilbertson photographed the Iraq War for *The New York Times*, and wrote a book, *Whiskey Tango Foxtrot* (2007), that reflected on his experiences and put together a visual argument about the conduct of the war. He won the Robert Capa Gold Medal for his photojournalism in 2005. Since then, Gilbertson has been examining veterans' issues including post-traumatic stress and suicide for *Time* magazine, *The Virginia Quarterly Review* and *The Times*. In 2007, he began working on *Bedrooms of the Fallen*, a collection of photographs depicting the intact bedrooms of service members who died in Iraq and Afghanistan. That series was published by *The New York Times Magazine*, and went on to win the documentary photography National Magazine Award.

Philip Jones Griffiths was one of the best-known British photojournalists of his generation. He covered the Algerian War in 1962, and moved to Central Africa. From there he moved to Asia, photographing in Vietnam from 1966 to 1971. His book on the war, *Vietnam Inc.*, crystallised public opinion and gave form to Western misgivings about American involvement in Vietnam. A member of Magnum since 1966, in 1980 Griffiths moved to New York to assume the presidency of Magnum, a post he held for a record five years. He is also the author of *Dark Odyssey* (1996), *Agent Orange* (2003), on the effects of the defoliant in Vietnam, and *Recollections* (2008), a selection of his work from the UK. He died in 2008.

Sarah James lectures in Art History at University College London. Sarah has published numerous articles, chapters and catalogue essays on photography and contemporary art. She also writes on contemporary art as a critic, contributing regularly to the magazines *Frieze*, *Photoworks*, *Art Review* and *Art Monthly*. She was an Alexander von Humboldt Postdoctoral Fellow at the Humboldt Universität zu Berlin (2008–2009), and a Lecturer at the University of Oxford (2009–2010). Her book *Common Ground: German Photographic Cultures Across the Iron Curtain*, was published in 2013.

Brigitte Lardinois is Deputy Director of the Photography and the Archive Research Centre at the University of the Arts in London. She worked at Magnum Photos to set up their Cultural Department in London, and was involved in many Magnum group exhibitions, notably *Magnum Ireland* (2005), as well as solo shows for Henri Cartier-Bresson, Martin Parr, Josef Koudelka, Eve Arnold and Elliott Erwitt. She edited *Magnum Magnum* (2009), the 60th Anniversary book of the agency which was published in eight languages. She also curated Eve Arnold's 2012 memorial exhibition *All About Eve*.

Rita Leistner is a politically and socially engaged lens-based artist. Her work has been exhibited widely and published in many magazines. She is co-author of several books, including *Unembedded: Four Independent Photojournalists on the War in Iraq* (2005), and *The Edward Curtis Project: A Modern Picture Story* (2010), co-created with Métis/Dene playwright Marie Clements. Her upcoming book *Looking for Marshall McLuhan in Afghanistan* will be published in late 2013. She has just completed her first documentary film *Miklat: The Bomb Shelter Project*, the second part of her trilogy *Portraitscapes of War—Lebanon, Israel, Palestine*. Leistner teaches the history of photojournalism and documentary photography at the University of Toronto.

Geert van Kesteren is a Dutch photojournalist, known for his innovative methods of display and dissemination. He is the author of *Mwendanjangula! AIDS in Zambia* (2000), and *Why Mister, Why? Iraq 2003–2004* (2004), one of the most successful photographic books reporting on the war. The book garnered many prizes and awards. He is also the author of *Baghdad Calling: Reports from Turkey, Syria and Iraq* (2008). In 2009, he received the Infinity Award in Photojournalism from the International Center of Photography in New York for *Baghdad Calling*. He is working on a film, exhibition and book project with Noa Ben-Shalon called *After the Ceasefires* that raises the question why the people of Israel and Palestine no longer allow themselves to dream about living in peace.

Trevor Paglen is an artist, writer and experimental geographer working out of the Department of Geography at the University of California, Berkeley. His projects involve close examinations of state secrecy, the California prison system, and the CIA's practice of 'extraordinary rendition'. Paglen's visual work has been shown in galleries and museums including MASSMOCA (2006), the Warhol Museum (2007), Diverse Works (2005) and at numerous other arts venues, universities, conferences and public spaces. Paglen is the author of *Torture Taxi: On the Trail of the CIA's Rendition Flights* (co-authored with A.C. Thompson, 2006) and *I Could Tell You But Then You Would Have to be Destroyed by Me* (2007) on the visual culture of 'black' military programmes, and *Blank Spots on the Map: The Dark Geography of the Pentagon's Secret World* (2011).

Julian Stallabrass is a writer, curator, photographer and lecturer. He is Professor in Art History at the Courtauld Institute of Art, and is the author of *Art Incorporated* (2004), *Internet Art: The Online Clash Between Culture and Commerce* (2003), *Paris Pictured* (2002), *High Art Lite: British Art in the 1990s* (1999) and *Gargantua: Manufactured Mass Culture* (1996). He is the editor of *Documentary* for the MIT/ Whitechapel Documents of Contemporary Art series (2013).

The gestation of this book has been long and complex, and there are three (often overlapping) categories of people and organisations to whom a great debt of thanks is owed: those who worked on the Brighton Photo Biennial of 2008; those who worked on the book itself; and those who have enriched its content through conversation about shared interests.

Thanks are due first to the 2008 Biennial staff and board: on the staff, Juliette Buss, Helen Cadwallader, Bruno Ceschel and Chloe Hoare; on the board, Rebecca Drew, David Chandler, David Edwards, Philippe Garner, Matt Locke, Antony Mayfield, David Alan Mellor, Emma Morris, Karen Norquay, Mark Power and Mark Waugh.

Brighton Photo Biennial 2008 was supported by many individuals and organisations, and of those whose work contributed to the book, thanks are due to: Ghaith Abdul-Ahad; Kael Alford; Broomberg and Chanarin; Julian Germain; Ashley Gilbertson; Thomas Hirschhorn; Bilal Hussein; the late Philip Jones Griffiths and the Philip Jones Griffiths Foundation; Geert van Kesteren; David Leeson; Harriet Logan; Benjamin Lowy; Susan Meisalas; Simon Norfolk; Wissam al- Okaili; Tim Page; Paul Seawright; Hilary Roberts at the Imperial War Museum; Brigitte Lardinois at London College of Communications; the late Gigi Giannuzzi and Hannah Watson at Trolley Books; Sophie Wright and Fiona Rogers at Magnum; Timothy Prus, Barbara Adams and Ed Jones at the Archive of Modern Conflict.

Special thanks are due to those who gave their time as interns and who made great contributions to the running of the Biennial. Corinne Silva provided invaluable curatorial assistance over many months; Heejin No also helped with curatorial matters. The following interns helped with research: Anne Blood, Gabriela Cala-Lesina, Daisy Jones, Nikoo Paydar, Ashley Stiple, Abigail Shapiro, Katy Wan and Madeleine Wilson. Volunteers working with the Biennial team were Phil Bedford, Fiona Burgess, Verity Combe, Victoria Jenkins, Sina Krause, Clare Levitt, Jamie Orlando Smith and Harry Watts.

In making this book happen, thanks are due to all the staff at Photoworks, particularly Celia Davies and Benedict Burbridge, Deborah Bullen and Helen Wade; and to all at SMITH design. Many thanks also to all the authors and interviewees, who were generous with their time and in granting permission to illustrate their work. The Courtauld Institute Research Committee granted funds which helped subsidise its production and raised the extent and quality of the imagery we were able to reproduce.

In addition, Julian Stallabrass owes many thanks to the Leverhulme Trust and to the Paul Mellon Centre, who granted him fellowships to work on the book. His understanding of the complex issues of war and its imagery has developed in large part through conversations with colleagues, students, artists and friends, particularly Adam Broomberg, Malcolm Bull, Benedict Burbridge, Oliver Chanarin, Edmund Clark, Steve Edwards, Regina José Galindo, Gigi Giannuzzi, Ashley Gilbertson, Philip Jones Griffiths, Sara Knelman, Sarah James, Paul Lowe, Renzo Martens, Antigoni Memou, Alexandra Moschovi, Mignon Nixon, Emilia Terracciano, Hannah Watson and Sarah Wilson.

Parts of this book have previously appeared elsewhere:

'In Conversation: Julian Stallabrass and Ashley Gilbertson', *Journal of Visual Culture*, vol. 8, no. 3, December 2009, pp. 349–57.

'War, Photojournalism and Art Photography: An Interview with Adam Broomberg and Oliver Chanarin', *The Myth of Europa*, May 2009, pp. 13–15.

'A Conversation with Trevor Paglen', *October*, no. 138, Fall 2011, pp. 3–14.

Pages 2, 29, 57, 60–1, 65, 70, 73, 79, 80–1 © Philip Jones Griffiths Foundation/Magnum Photos

Pages 3, 140–1 © Thomas Hirschhorn

Pages 4, 34, 102, 106–7 © of Ashley Gilbertson.

Pages 5, 114, 117 (top), 120 © Simon Norfolk

Pages 6, 82, 88, 91, 92–3, 96 © Rita Leistner

Pages 7, 142, 144, 147, 153 © Coco Fusco

Pages 8, 161, 164–5, 168, 172, 176–77, 180–1 © Geert van Kesteren

Pages 9, 182, 186, 190, 195, 198 © Stefaan Decostere

Pages 10, 205, 208, 211, 214, 217 © Trevor Paglen

Page 12 © Bilal Hussein

Page 18 © Museo de la Palabra y la imagen, El Salvador

Pages 20–1, 31 © Mitchell Library, State Library of New South Wales

Pages 22, 40 (top), 218–19 © US Army

Page 25 © International Council of Graphic Design Associations Archive, University of Brighton Design Archives

Pages 36–7 © Courtesy of Benjamin Lowy

Page 39 © Courtesy Wissam Al-Okaili/AFP

Page 40 (bottom) © Courtesy US Marine Corps

Pages 112–13 © Courtesy Kael Alford/Panos Pictures

Page 117 (bottom) © Courtesy Gabriele Basilico and Studio Guenzani, Milano

Page 126 © Courtesy Paul Seawright

Pages 131, 139, 149 © Courtesy Adam Broomberg and Oliver Chanarin

Pages 180–81 © Courtesy of Ghaith Abdul-Ahad/ Getty Images

First published in an edition of 1000 in 2013 by

Photoworks
58–67 Grand Parade, Brighton, BN2 9QA
T: +44 (0)1273 643908
E: info@photoworks.org.uk

www.photoworks.org.uk

Photoworks curates, commissions and publishes new writing on photography, produces exhibitions, books and events including the Brighton Photo Biennial.

Edited by Julian Stallabrass
Design by SMITH
Alice Austin, Maria Juelisch, Allon Kaye,
Kuba Rudzinski, Justine Schuster
www.smith-design.com
Printed in Italy by EBS

Photoworks ISBN 978-1-903796-49-8

A Photoworks Production

photoworks

Supported using public funding by
ARTS COUNCIL ENGLAND